Unblind Tibbin is a master West-African Djeliba/Griot/Storyteller by calling for equal rights, social justice, sustainable lifestyles, and being an africentric advocate in Toronto. He is fully trilingual and cares deeply about environmental sustainability, the youth, and Afrikan greatness restoration. He has worked in many capacities with many organizations, always supporting youth and their blossoming genius. Embodying a sustainable lifestyle, he is vegan.

Unblind is a Sierra Leonean-Canadian who was born in Freetown, Sierra Leone, and grew up in Switzerland and Toronto, Canada. He has an Undergraduate bilingual honors degree in International Studies and a Masters degree in Economics.

To Neber Tcher, our Shepsu/Egungun/enlightened ancestors, Grandma Jane, Aunty Hannah, Boris Stevens, Sam Paul, Ade Paul-Short, Jide Paul-Short, Dennis Johnson, Siaka Probyn Stevens, Hannah Paul-Short #1, Junior Paul-Short, Alex Hindolo Stevens, Alfred Fawundu, Desmond Fowler, Amina Kamara and all those who have come and returned to the ancestral realm may they go to the light and their wisdom guide our lives in peace, love and truth.

Unblind Tibbin M.A

Afrikan Ancestral Manuscript

Your Time is NOW!!!

Austin Macauley Publishers™
London • Cambridge • New York • Sharjah

Illustrated By: Aaron Hosannah El

The story, the experiences, and the words are the author's alone.

Ordering Information
Quantity sales: Special discounts are available on quantity purchases by corporations, associations, and others. For details, contact the publisher at the address below.

Publisher's Cataloging-in-Publication data
Tibbin M.A, Unblind
Afrikan Ancestral Manuscript

ISBN 9781685628604 (Paperback)
ISBN 9781685628611 (ePub e-book)

Library of Congress Control Number: 2024900763

www.austinmacauley.com/us

First Published 2024
Austin Macauley Publishers LLC
40 Wall Street 33rd Floor, Suite 3302
New York, NY 10005
USA

mail-usa@austinmacauley.com
+1 (646) 5125767

I would like to thank these past and present entities: Sen Ntiu Baa School, The Achievers Program, Poetree of Life Collective, Athenee de la Sapience, CUSO Nigeria, Mom Her Excellency Yvette Stevens, my sisters (Rebecca, Yvette and Yvonne), Amani Lewen, The Lion's Circle, Richard "Ausar" Stewart, Shekhem Kai Ner Maa, One Love Foundation, Africa U, Claire Fowler, The Afrikan community in Toronto and all those who support an accurate depiction of our Afrikan ancestors.

Table of Contents

How to Use This Book

In order to commune with the ancestors in this book and to enable the best with the connection with our great inspirations in this book there is a simple but effective means that can be applied.

Each time you need to commune with an ancestor in order to uplift and enlighten your journey in life and receive their assistance it will be necessary to open the book inspired by your spirit in a "so called" random manner to a coincidental page and find which ancestor's bio is on that page. This ancestor will have a message for you that you will need to carry on that day in order to align yourself with your divine destiny. This might seem like a random practice however it is necessary to understand that nothing happens by mistake. We each have a psychic power that enables us to tap into the akashic records, when we use our psychic energy to bypass thought and select a page based on our divinity directing us. Each one of us has access to the higher faculties of the Paut Neteru (Tree of Life) and sphere 2 of the tree of life is Tehuti or the divine will.

After having selected the ancestor in this manner you can read the short bio and if need be collect more information on that Hero or Shero and from there carry a good thought for them by adding them to your libation or if you do prayer instead you can pray for their soul and ask for them be in the light. After this you can meditate and reflect on their life's work and achievements possibly for 5 to 10 minutes and then during the day you're faced with challenges/opportunities you can reflect on how some of the key virtues the ancestor manifested during their life can be applied to assist you to create a win/win and bring harmony to your opportunity.

It is important to understand the African proverb “There is no death, there is just transition from one realm to the next.”. Our ancestors live again and have a greater significance and more peace because we enable them to live by learning and knowing about them and seeking to enable cross-generational alchemy. I will you great success. We are our ancestors, and our ancestors are us, remember we are who we have been waiting for. It’s time to actualize. Also keep in mind that we are never alone when accompanied by our great ancestors and paying homage and respect to their sacrifices is necessary in order for us to take humanity to are more divine plain of existence. ASHE

Introduction

The Afrikan Ancestral Calendar's journey continues. We are now traveling from the calendar into a full manuscript of the same great global Afrikan's of the past and present that were portrayed in the calendar format.

Each bio is a story of a person who lived life like all of us and had their share of struggles, victories and shortcomings. Through their lives, we can gain arch-types that help us negotiate our lives better and fulfill our highest goals and objectives.

For us to forget our ancestors would be for us to lose a myriad of invaluable lessons that have the potential to enhance and unleash our highest potentials. Our people have been, are, and will be great, but it is important to have intergenerational mediums that can connect the past to the present and emancipate our future.

With 2023 and the post *plandemic* upon us, it is incumbent upon us to seize the time and create a better destiny for our children. One that is aligned with the greatness of our traditions of yesteryear.

The Afrikan Ancestral Manuscript is a next step in the journey to reassemble the puzzle of 'Our story'. The powers that be have done their best to cloud our vision of our ancestors with falsehoods and demeaning, untrue depictions. In this manuscript, our ancestors are given the respect they are due, and their lights are allowed to shine in order for all our lights to be magnified. "In Joy."

II
Ow

The Story of All Stories

In a nothingness that cannot be described existed consciousness. Consciousness existed without existing. All that it was able to be conscious of in this nadir was of itself as the nothingness that could not be described: Amen.

Consciousness decided that in order for it to have a more amusing experience of itself, it needed to create some things, a plethora of things in which it would manifest itself partly and fully, therefore it willed forward energy that it called Ra. Ra then enunciated the word and the word brought life. Within the word-life were twins called Tefnut and Shu.

The word implanted within Tefnut, a strong receptive essence, and in order to make things interesting, it implanted within Shu a strong active essence.

Within both of them, a minor essence of the other existed in a power-enhancing microcosm.

The coexistence of Tefnut and Shu was codified into a sacred and divine law around which all remained in harmony: Maat. MaaKheru was the state in which this law was in full application.

Tefnut then intermingled with Shu in a MaaKheru state and from their intermingling was birthed Geb (Father Earth) and Nut (Mother Universe). Both Nut and Geb were filled with living creatures that were reflections of each other. The creatures existed in a state of chaos until Nut and Geb would come together.

Nut and Geb were attracted to each other by MaaKheru, and the aspect of Geb which encompassed Tefnut bridged them together through the aspect of Nut which encompassed Shu. Both of these when combined became known as Ptah. Ptah connected Geb to Nut with MaaKheru, and from their union originated the Neteru.

The whole process of change and self-creation which started at the start of time was Khepera. Khepera went on to bring the Neteru to Geb's surface. In order of manifestation, first came Ausar, The Unifier. Then came Heru, The Elder. Then came Auset, The Nurturer, followed by Nephyte, The Gestater and finally emerged Set, The Emoter.

The creatures that existed in Geb all partly of fully manifested Amen. Those creatures that fully manifested Amen were not aware of their true identity and therefore, defined themselves as fallible humanity. They governed themselves by emotions, ideas and beliefs instead of Maat's divine law (MaaKheru). In the world, there existed a tyranny of ideas and opinions. The humans fought each other and found no peace.

This was the case until Ausar came to the land of Kamit (the land of the blacks) and proposed to the people that they let him have the honor of being their leader. He told them that through following the ways of Maat, that all of Kamit would benefit and that the land would be greater than it ever was.

Hearing this and seeing Ausar behave as a God-Man, the people intuitively agreed. Hence, Ausar became the ruler that unified Kamit with truth and righteousness. His wife and queen was The Nurturer, Auset.

The people of Kamit greatly benefited from Ausar's reign. They had peace, justice and order, and operated out of love for each other. It was a win-win situation for all. They loved every cell in Ausar's body because of his correct and fair leadership.

After ten years of good governance, Ausar decided that he needed to travel around the world to bring civilization (MaaKheru) to the rest of Geb's inhabitants. The people in Kamit were saddened and Auset wept for seven days, but everyone due to their upliftment saw the benefit of sharing MaaKheru with others less fortunate. They gave Ausar their blessings for him to travel far and wide.

Ausar thanked his people for their innerstanding and set sail on the bark of a million years to share the ways of the wise with those who's divinity still did not rise.

Before leaving, Ausar had decided to give regency of Kamit to its most devoted citizen, his wife, Auset, and hence regency of Kamit was left in her learned hands. When Ausar departed, under Auset's leadership Kamit kept on trodding the right path. Auset demonstrated complete devotion to Ausar's way of truth and sacrificed her emotions to maintain balance in the land.

Set, the brother of Ausar, who was married to Nephyte, strongly emoted at the departure of Ausar and was very jealous that Auset, instead of him, had been given regency over Kamit. His jealousy grew daily in Ausar's absence.

Auset was a great leader because she had been the greatest follower of MaaKheru and now led by example. Her way of being left the people awestruck and they could do nothing but try their best to emulate her righteousness.

After ten years of spreading MaaKheru around Geb's surface, Ausar finally decided to return to Kamit. For his return, a great feast was scheduled by Auset. Set volunteered to be one of the major organizers of the celebration along with Ausar's general, Sebek. Set convinced Sebek, the Opener and Closer of the Way, to conspire for villainy. Auset, on the other hand, rejoiced at the idea of her husband's return and trusted Set fully with his organization of the feast.

The main achievement which Set flaunted around and talked about celebrating with Ausar upon his return was the creation by him and seventy-two other architects of a sarcophagus which was the exact fit for Ausar, and which would help to eternalize the King's greatness upon his return to the ancestral realm.

Ausar returned in triumph to his homeland and everyone in Kamit celebrated vigorously the return of their beloved king. Everywhere he went, petals of roses were thrown on the ground for him to trod on. He was now shown even more respect for his selflessness in the spreading of MaaKheru.

The night of the feast arrived and the celebration was unrivaled. People came from far and wide to welcome Ausar home. After delivering a moving speech to the crowd, Ausar was requested by Set to go into a secret chamber with Set and his colleagues. The gathered congregation were fed heavy dishes and given large doses of alcohol in order to inebriate them.

In the secret chamber, Ausar's sarcophagus was revealed to him. Since this was a surprise, Ausar was very pleased and thanked Set for his caring work. Set asked Ausar to test the fit of the sarcophagus in order to make sure that he and the other architects had not made any mistakes. Along with his seventy-two co-conspirators, Set opened the sarcophagus and invited Ausar to lie within.

Ausar seeing no villainy in their request, lay in the sarcophagus. As soon as he did this, Set and his co-conspirators fell upon the sarcophagus and sealed it shut. Ausar immediately understood the villainy of Set, put himself into a deep meditative state and visualized being rescued.

The casket was thrown by Set, Sebek and their co-conspirators into the river Hapi, and Set emoted himself unto the throne of Upper and Lower Kamit. Through psychic energy and white magic, Set made the people believe that his coup d'état was legitimate and that Ausar had vanished, never to return. Sebek, Set's general, corroborated Set's story and Nephyte, his wife, visualized it as being true for all the people of Kamit.

Heru the Blind followed the rest. Only one of the royals and one person in Kamit felt in her heart that this was a lie and it was Auset. Being totally devoted to her husband, Ausar, she pledged to MaaKheru that she would not rest until she found her husband and restored MaaKheru to Kamit. Kamit was now once again ruled by the tyranny of ideas, opinions, emotions and beliefs which were Set's dominion.

Auset packed her bags and followed her premonition which told her to follow the river Hapi until she could feel the essence of Ausar, whom she had a psychic connection with that always pointed out to her where he was. Auset set out on the journey of her life and followed the river Hapi until she came to the kingdom of Ibidos. She demanded an audience with the king and when she arrived at his temple, she knew right away that Ausar was in the center pillar.

Auset talked to the king of Ibidos and explained to him her situation. She pleaded of him to allow her to remove the pillar and save her husband from bondage. The king reflected and once he realized that Ausar was the great civilizer who had brought MaaKheru to his people, he was quick to comply.

Auset had the pillar removed and within it, as she predicted, was the sarcophagus of Ausar. She opened it to find Ausar in deep meditation, hibernating and dead to the things of the world.

Auset knew she must hide Ausar from Set as he recovered, and therefore, took him deep into the mountainous caves of the Mountains of the Moon, their place of origin.

While Auset hid Ausar, Set the Emoter used his animal essence to emote that Ausar had been saved and then used Sebek, his fox-like general, to track him down. They waited till Auset left the cave for her daily emersion into the river Hapi and once again captured Ausar. Being very enraged and not wanting Ausar to be saved again, Set had Ausar cut into fourteen pieces and set each piece adrift on the river Hapi again.

When Auset discovered the fate of her husband, flood waters ran down her eyes with grief. She was inconsolable and decided that she would once again sacrifice her time and other pleasures in order to recover all of Ausar's pieces and reassemble her great husband. She met with Nephyte in secret and when Nephyte found out the extent of the villainy of Set, she decided she must help Auset in her journey to reassemble Ausar.

They worked together and traveled to the ends of the river Hapi. Everywhere that they recovered one of Ausar's pieces, a temple had been built to vindicate a school of thought that sought to uplift humans to their Godhood. Together, the women recovered thirteen of Ausar's fourteen pieces. The only piece they did not recover was his phallus that had been eaten by the Nile (Hapi) catfish.

Using magic, they reassembled Ausar's thirteen pieces and replaced his phallus with an obelisk. After this, Auset used magic and trance in order to impregnate herself with Ausar's seed, once this task was complete, she tranced some more to borrow the seed to Nephyte who gestated it.

When the child came to the world, he was named after his Uncle Heru, but unlike his uncle, he was not blind but had eagle vision. Auset hid the boy and home-schooled him in the ways of MaaKheru. However, he was deeply angry at his Uncle Set for having killed his father and swore in his heart that when he was big enough, he would get his revenge.

Heru was nourished on a healthy vegan diet by his mother, Auset, and grew big and strong. He also excelled in intellect and always asserted his independence. He eventually left his mother's house and went out into the world, where he gathered a strong army in order to overthrow Set and avenge his father's murder.

Heru trained his army well in Qi Gong and the deadliest martial arts, and at the opportune time, he declared war on his Uncle Set, his general, Sebek, and their emotional army.

The war seemed to spiral in a torrent of unending battles with neither party gaining a clear advantage over the other. Heru made no headway in his struggle since he fought Set also with an army of his own emotions.

At the apex of the war, Heru believed he had Set cornered and attacked, but Set unleashed his spear of rage and bludgeoned one of Heru's eyes. Blinded by the pain, Heru ran for the hills.

Now knowing that this deadlock would never end, Heru sought counsel from his father's wise advisor, Tehuti, who he had shun thus far. With his bludgeoned eye, Heru ran into Tehuti's dwelling place, breathing a sense of urgency. He met a calm and collected Tehuti who had just come out of meditation.

He motioned to Heru to come into the light, and before Heru could explain his misadventure to him, Tehuti told Heru all what he had endured.

Tehuti's only question to Heru was whether he was now ready to listen to the sage. If so, he told Heru that he would restore his damaged eye and replace it with an all seeing eye, and then he would send Heru to Mount Behutet to perform a further sacrifice of his emotional guides.

Heru knew Tehuti was really wise and in doing what he told him, he would be victorious, so he ignored his emotions and followed the word of the sage. He went to Mount Behutet and as instructed, he cut himself away from his emotional guides. When he returned, Tehuti offered him the all seeing eye as a replacement for his physically damaged eye.

This eye always saw the whole picture and therefore, functioned exclusively to restore MaaKheru. Having implanted the new eye into Heru, Tehuti told him he was free to go and told him not to worry because with MaaKheru, triumph was guaranteed.

On their next battle, Heru entered the field of battle with Sekert and MaaKheru. His soldiers were health, devotion, communication, visualization, action, justice, love, power, wisdom and unity. Set's emotional stale-warts were no match to Heru this time, and Sebek, Set's general, seeing Heru's line-up, decided to change sides. Set could do nothing but waive the white flag and he was immediately taken to the highest court of the land presided on by Tehuti and Maat.

Tehuti, his sister, Maat, and the other members of the court decided that Heru was the only legitimate ruler of Kamit as he was the son of the great mother Auset. Set was deemed to be in contempt for murdering Ausar. Nevertheless, he was not sentenced for beheading. Instead, he was sentenced to defend Kamit against intruders who sought to destroy MaaKheru. In this role, he felt dignified and was happy that he had been given the chance to restore and rehabilitate himself.

Heru took the throne of Upper and Lower Kamit and was installed in a ceremony full of flare with his mother, Auset, proudly gazing on. The ceremony was of such grandeur that it remained enshrined in the consciousness of the people of Kamit for eternity. During Heru's installment, his father's astro-body was enlightened in the ancestral plane and he was crowned with the white crown of unity to rule over the heavens.

Heru had restored MaaKheru to Kamit, thanks in great part to the devotion of his mother, Auset, who he recognized as his inspiration. If Kamit were ever to fall out of the hands of Maat in the future, everyone knew that it would take the devotion of a great mother like Auset to put the fourteen pieces of Ausar's truth back together for MaaKheru to triumph eternally once again.

Stori cam, stori goh, y lef pan yu oh

January

John Henrik Clarke

John Henrik Clarke was born in Union Springs, Alabama on New Year's Day, 1915. His family came from a long line of sharecroppers. Clarke noticed that although many Bible stories "unfolded in Africa…I saw no African people in the printed and illustrated Sunday school lessons," he wrote in 1985. "I began to suspect at this early age that someone had distorted the image of my people. My long search for the true history of African people the world over began." That search took him to libraries, museums, attics, archives and collections in Asia, the Caribbean, Europe, Latin America and Africa.

What he found was that the history of black people was worldwide and that "the first light of human consciousness and the world's first civilizations were in Africa"; that the so called Dark Ages were dark only for Europe, and that some African nations at the time were larger than any in Europe; that as Africa sends its children to Europe to study because that is where the best universities are, early Greece once sent its children, and that enslavement, although devastating, was neither the beginning nor the end of black people's impact on the world.

Clarke gathered his findings into books on such figures as the early 20th century mass movement leader Marcus Garvey, into articles with titles like *Africa in the Conquest of Spain* and *Harlem as Mecca and New Jerusalem*, and many books including American Heritage's two volume *History of Africa.*

While he was teaching at Hunter College in New York and at Cornell University in the 1980s, Clarke's lesson plans became well known for their thoroughness. They are so filled with references and details that the Schomburg Library in Harlem asked for copies. Clarke made plans to provide them, he said, "so that fifty years from now, when people have a hard time locating my grave, they won't have a hard time locating my lessons."

In 1985, the year of his retirement, the newest branch of the Cornell University Library—a 60 seat, 9,000 volume facility—was named the "John Henrik Clarke Africana Library."

He transitioned to the ancestral realm on 16 July 1998, having left a great legacy of pride for blacks worldwide.

C. L. R James

C. L. R James was born on 4 January 1901 in Tunapuna, Trinidad. He went on to become one of the greatest historians of his time.

James was certified as a teacher at Queen's Royal College in Port of Spain, Trinidad (1918). In 1932, he moved to England, where he published *The Life of Captain Cipriani* (1932; revised as *The Case for West-Indian Self-Government*, 1933) with the personal and financial support of the Caribbean cricketer and politician, Learie (later Lord) Constantine. During the 1930s, James was a cricket correspondent for The Guardian (Manchester) and became increasingly involved in Marxist politics and the Afrikan and Caribbean independence movements.

His most notable work was *The Black Jacobins* (1938), a Marxist study of the Haitian slave revolution of the 1790s, which won him widespread acclaim. In this book, he talked about the brave struggle of the Haitian people to gain independence from the French and emancipation from enslavement, and then later on to form their own free nation.

James left England to live in the United States (1939–53), but he was expelled for political reasons. He was interned at Ellis Island in New York City, where he wrote an analysis of Herman Melville's Moby Dick called *Mariners, Renegades, and Castaways* (1953). Thereafter, he moved between London and Trinidad, where he was secretary of the West Indies Federal Labor Party (1958–60).

In ***Beyond a Boundary*** (1963), James discussed the importance of cricket to the British character and to the development of the Caribbean. His other books included the novel ***Minty Alley*** (1936), ***World Revolution*** (1937), ***Notes on Dialectics*** (1971), *Nkrumah and the Ghana Revolution* (1977), and *Cricket* (1986), a collection of articles spanning the period 1935 to 1985.

He transitioned to the ancestral realm on 31 May 1989 in London, England having worked tirelessly to give to his people the true story of their past greatness.

Nanny of the Maroons

Nanny was a leader of the Maroons at the beginning of the 18th century. She was known by both the Maroons and the British settlers as an outstanding military leader who became, in her lifetime and after, a symbol of unity and strength for her people during times of crisis.

She was particularly important to them in the fierce fight with the British, during the First Maroon War from 1720 to 1739. Although, she has been immortalized in songs and legends, certain facts about Nanny (or 'Granny Nanny', as she was affectionately known) have also been documented.

She was a person who had exceptional leadership qualities. She was a small, wiry woman with piercing eyes. Her influence over the Maroons was so strong, that she can be called supernatural and this was said to be connected to her spiritual powers. She was particularly skilled in organizing the guerrilla warfare carried out by the Eastern Maroons to keep away the British troops who attempted to penetrate the mountains to overpower them.

Her cleverness in planning guerrilla warfare confused the British and their accounts of the fights reflect the surprise and fear which the Maroon traps caused among them.

Besides inspiring her people to ward off the troops, Nanny was also a type of chieftainess or wise woman of the village, who passed down legends and encouraged the continuation of customs, music and songs, that had come with the people from Africa, and which instilled in them confidence and pride.

Her spirit of freedom was so great that in 1739, when Quao signed the second treaty (the first was signed by Cudjoe for the Leeward Maroons a few months earlier) with the British, it is reported that Nanny was very angry and in disagreement with the principle of peace with the British, which she knew meant another form of subjugation.

Nanny is documented as the leader of the Maroons during the First Maroon War which was the most outstanding of them all. She lead her people with courage and inspired them to struggle to maintain that spirit of freedom, and life of independence, which was their rightful inheritance.

Constance Cummings-John

Mrs. Cummings-John's strong commitment to the ideals of justice and fairness was shown through her active participation in the political struggle for national freedom.

As a woman, her struggle was two-fold: untying the knot of colonialism, and gaining acceptance in a western-influenced Sierra Leone Colony, where women were not usually expected to engage in political activities.

Born into a prominent Krio family on 7 January 1918, it was perhaps inevitable that she should be interested in politics, since her family was very engaged in community affairs and local business. The young Constance received her early education in Freetown: Annie Walsh Memorial School, Methodist Girls' High School and Freetown Secondary School for Girls. She then went to England at the age of seventeen and entered Whitelands College in Putney, where she trained as a teacher.

In London, she also found time to participate in the activities of two pan-African organizations, the West African Students' Union (WASU) and the League of Colored Peoples (LCP). Both were pressure groups fighting the Afrikan cause.

In 1936, she went to the United States to do a six-month course at Cornell University. It was a shocking experience. The racial insults heaped on her and the lack of understanding from Afro-Americans affected her political consciousness profoundly. Depressed but undaunted, she resolved to return home and 'throw the white man out'. In 1937, she married Ethanan Cummings-John, a lawyer, and the same year they returned to Sierra Leone.

In Freetown, she was appointed as principal of the A. M. E. Girls' Vocational School. She found the school in a dilapidated state, and immediately embarked on a fund-raising campaign to make improvements. Through this venture, she pioneered the construction of a new domestic science building with modern equipment.

When I. T. A. Wallace-Johnson returned to Sierra Leone in April 1938, she immediately joined forces with him in the establishment of a 'chapter' of the West African Youth League (WAYL). The move was a resounding success, for in the Municipal Council elections in November 1938, the WAYL candidates swept the polls. Mrs. Cummings-John received the highest number of votes of any candidate.

As councilor, Mrs. Cummings-John was mainly concerned with the improvement of city services, particularly sanitation, library facilities and conditions in city markets. In recognition of the importance of women in community affairs, she established a network of leading market women; in 1951, with their support, she established the Sierra Leone Women's Movement, which played a leading role in the struggle for self-government.

After independence, Mrs. Constance Cummings-John became the first woman mayor of the Freetown Municipality. The transitioned to the ancestral realm in 2000 at the ripe old age of eighty-two.

Sekou Toure

Sekou Toure was born on 9 January 1922 in Faranah, French Guinea (now Guinea)—he transitioned to the ancestral realm on 26 March 1984 in Cleveland, Ohio, U.S.; first president of the Republic of Guinea (1958–84) and a leading African politician.

Although, his parents were poor and uneducated, Toure was the grandson of Samory, a military leader who resisted French rule at the end of the 19th century, long after many other Africans had surrendered. Reared as a Muslim, Toure attended a French technical school at Conakry, from which he was expelled after one year for leading a food riot (1936).

In 1940, Toure was hired as a clerk by a business firm, the Niger Frangais, and the following year, he took an administrative assignment in the postal service. There he developed a strong interest in the labor movement and organized the first successful strike, lasting seventy-six days, in French West Africa.

In 1945, he became secretary-general of the Post and Telecommunications Workers' Union and helped to found the Federation of Workers' Unions of Guinea, linked to the World Federation of Trade Unions, of which he later became vice president. Toure became active in politics in the mid-1940s and in 1946, he helped Felix Houphouet-Boigny of Cote d'Ivoire form the African Democratic Rally.

Toure proved to be a powerful orator and was elected to the French National Assembly in 1951 as a representative from Guinea, but he was not allowed to take his seat. Reelected in 1954, he was again barred. After being elected mayor of Conakry by a large majority in 1955, he was finally permitted to take his place in the National Assembly the following year. By the end of 1957, Toure had become vice president of the Executive Council of Guinea.

When French President Charles de Gaulle in 1958 offered French territories a referendum on whether to join a new federal community or to become independent, Toure and the Democratic Party of Guinea-African Democratic Rally led a successful campaign for independence. Guinea's voting population overwhelmingly rejected de Gaulle's offer and instead chose complete independence; Guinea was the only French colony in Africa that did not accept the proposal.

On 2 October 1958, Guinea became the first independent French speaking state in Africa, and shortly afterward Toure was elected its president. The French reacted by recalling all their professional people and civil servants and by removing all transportable equipment. Threatened by an economic breakdown, Toure accepted support from the communist bloc and at the same time, sought help from Western nations.

In African affairs, Toure was an ardent supporter of Ghana's president Kwame Nkrumah and his program for African political unity, but a union of the two nations proclaimed in 1958 never became effective. When Nkrumah was deposed in 1966, Toure granted him asylum. After an unsuccessful invasion from neighboring Portuguese Guinea (now Guinea-Bissau) in 1971, he undertook a political purge and imposed severe restrictions on opposition forces in his country. He was reelected without opposition in subsequent elections and ruled powerfully.

Despite his harsh domestic policies, Toure was viewed in international politics as a moderate Islamic leader. In 1982, he led the delegation sent by the Islamic Conference Organization to mediate in the Iran-Iraq War; he also was a member in the Organization for African Unity (OAU). He transitioned to the ancestral realm while undergoing cardiac treatment in the U.S. in 1984. His legacy of pride and resistance remained engraved in the world's consciousness.

Kimpa Vita

Kimpa Vita was a popular female prophet in the kingdom of the Kongo, a precursor of the prophetic figures of the independent churches, and the creator of a movement that used Christian symbols but revitalized traditional Kongo cultural roots.

The latter half of the 17th century was one of cultural disintegration and political disarray in the Kongo (which included parts of present-day Congo, Zaire, and Angola). Portuguese forces had defeated the Kongo, the Christianity of AFONSO I had fallen into syncretism, a mix of Christian and African traditional religions, and three ruling families contended for power. Into this political and cultural vacuum, a number of messianic prophets arose to proclaim their socio-religious visions.

The most important of these was Kimpa Vita, a young girl who believed herself possessed by the spirit of St. Anthony of Padua, a popular Catholic saint and miracle worker. She began preaching in the Kongolese city of San Salvador, which she said God wished restored as the capital. Her call to unity drew strong support among the peasants, who flocked to the city, which Kimpa identified as the biblical Bethlehem. She told her followers that Jesus, Mary and other Christian saints were really Kongolese.

Kimpa planned with the general of Pedro IV, one of the contenders for the throne, but she was captured. Both Kimpa and her baby—conceived by her 'guardian angel'—were burned at the stake for heresy, at the instigation of Capuchin missionaries.

The Antonian movement, which Kimpa began, outlasted her. The Kongo king, Pedro IV, used it to unify and renew his kingdom. Her ideas remained among the peasants, appearing in various messianic cults until, two centuries later, it took new form in the preaching of Simon Kimbangu. Her faith and devotion remain even centuries after her transition to the ancestral realm.

Thomas Peters

Thomas Peters was a courageous Afro-American whose efforts made possible the founding of Freetown.

He was born enslaved in the North American colonies and worked in his master's flour mill in North Carolina. During the American Revolution, Peters ran away and joined the British Army, becoming a sergeant in the Black Pioneers. When the British lost the war, they evacuated Peters and hundreds of other Black Loyalists to Nova Scotia, but after seven years in Canada, the former slaves had still received no land and were living only on a meager government ration and suffering from the cold.

Peters, though poor and uneducated, found the courage to travel to England in search of help for his people. He was in serious danger from the moment he left Canada, as he was still legally a slave in the newly-independent United States, and could have been taken there and sold back into slavery by an unscrupulous sea captain. But Thomas Peters managed to reach London, and he convinced the Sierra Leone Company to send ships to help his people establish a colony in Africa.

He then returned to Nova Scotia and, by sheer force of charisma, persuaded over eleven hundred former slaves to join him in the voyage to Sierra Leone. Thomas Peters and his 'Nova Scotians' founded Freetown in 1792, near the site of the Province of Freedom, which had been destroyed several years earlier.

But problems soon developed when the white men of the Sierra Leone Company insisted on running the colony as they saw fit. Thomas Peters confronted the English commander, demanding that his people run their own affairs through an elected committee, but he was unsuccessful in his attempt to establish self-rule. He transitioned to the ancestral realm shortly afterwards, a victim of malaria in the colony's first rainy season.

Thomas Peters was totally committed to freedom, and fought for it until the very last day of his life. More than anyone else, he exemplifies the spiritof hope and determination that gave birth to the city of Freetown.

Mohammed Ali

In his most famous words, "Fly like a butterfly, sting like a bee," Muhammad Ali became the greatest boxer in world history. With no other fighter before him as heavily promoted, he had the attitude, charisma, and rhymes to create hot anticipation even before he stepped into the ring.

Born Cassius Clay Jr on 17 January 1942, Ali started with his first coach who led him all the way to the Rome Olympics. While there, Muhammad won a gold medal in the light, heavyweight division—an event that solidified his path to the professional boxing ring in the United States. He would later throw his gold medal into a river because he could not stand representing a country full of racism. It was this act and his public presence that intrigued Malcolm X to invite Ali into the Nation of Islam.

Before changing his name to remove the yoke of enslavement from himself, Ali was ranked in the top ten fighters in the country. As Ali climbed the rank in the boxing circuit, he also received more coverage than any of the other boxers. Some claim it was Muhammad Ali alone who revitalized a sport many sports enthusiasts stopped watching. With such attention and a public profile, he was offered a 50-50 split of his fights—the highest ever offered in boxing history.

In his first battle for the heavyweight championship of the world, Ali fought Sonny Liston in Miami. Claiming he was destined to win the fight, Muhammad came into the ring as sharp, strong, and pumped as ever. Although, Liston was the more powerful contender, he couldn't keep up with Ali who maintained his endurance, and eventually outsmarted Liston to become the World Champion at only twenty-two years of age.

As the Vietnam war led to the draft in the United States, Muhammad Ali, being of a member of the Islamic faith, was a conscientious objector. With his quick and witty tongue, Ali revealed, "I ain't got no quarrel with those Vietcong…no Vietcong ever called me nigger." Due to his anti-war status and refusal to enter the draft, Ali was stripped of his boxing title and was sentenced to five years in prison—a decision that was later reverted in the appeals process.

During this time, Ali fought abroad and gave talks at different public institutions against racism and fought hard to teach others about equal rights. Only in 1970 was Ali allowed to fight in the United States, an act granted by a senator of Georgia, as the state had no boxing commission. The Fight of the Century, as it was later dubbed, saw Ali versus Frazier at their best. The fight went until the last round when Ali was knocked to the ground.

This was Ali's first loss as a professional fighter. In his next, highly advertised fight, Ali fought George Foreman in The Rumble in the Jungle, which was created by none other than Don King. Ali knew Foreman didn't have the same endurance he did so he let Foreman pulverize him against the ropes in the early rounds, which wore Foreman out. By the eighth round, Ali came back to knock-out Foreman with one striking blow.

Currently, Muhammad Ali is retired and has two battles which he faces daily; his own long-lasting fight against Parkinson's disease, and helping those less fortunate in the world, especially in Afrika. Ali published an oral autobiography of his life in the early 1990s. And, in the acclaimed movie *Ali* in 2001, Will Smith portrayed the fighter's life, his fights, and his personal and religious battles on the big screen.

Along with many other awards given to him for his humanitarian deeds, Ali received the Presidential Medal of Freedom at the White House in 2005.

Daniel Hale Williams

Dr. Daniel Hale Williams was an Afrikan-American physician who made history by performing the first successful open heart surgery operation.

Daniel Hale Williams was born on 18 January 1856 in Hollidaysburg, Pennsylvania, the fifth of eight children. His father was a barber who died when Daniel was only nine. His mother was unable to provide for all the children on her own, so she moved the family to Baltimore, Maryland to stay with relatives.

An apprenticeship with a shoemaker was found for Daniel; he remained there as a shoemaker's apprentice for three years while he was still a young child. As a teenager, he learned to cut hair and became a barber, living and working with a family who owned a barber shop in Janesville, Wisconsin.

In Janesville, Daniel began to attend high school. He graduated from Hare's Classical Academy in 1877. While working as a barber, he met Dr. Henry Palmer, a leading surgeon, who became the Surgeon General of Wisconsin. Dr. Palmer took Daniel on as a medical apprentice; he had two other apprentices at the time.

Dr. Palmer helped the three apprentices apply for admission to a top medical school, the Chicago Medical School, which was affiliated with Northwestern University. All three were accepted and began their studies in 1880. Dr. Daniel Hale Williams graduated with his medical degree in 1883.

Dr. Williams began to practice surgery and medicine at the South Side Dispensary. At the same time, he held a position at Northwest University, as an instructor of anatomy. He worked for a time as a medical doctor for the City Railway Company and for the Protestant Orphan Asylum. Dr. Williams's practice began to grow, as did his reputation as a skilled surgeon.

In 1883, he was one of only four Afrikan-American doctors in the Chicago area, yet he gained so much respect within the medical community that six years later, in 1889, he was appointed to the Illinois Board of Health.

Dr. Williams observed that Afrikan-American patients were routinely subject to second-class medical care. Also, opportunities for most black physicians were extremely limited, and it was difficult for Afrikan-Americans to gain admission to medical and nursing schools because of institutionalized racism. Dr. Williams met a young woman, Emma Reynolds, who had been refused admission by every nursing school in the area.

This prompted him to launch a new venture, the first Afrikan-American owned hospital in the United States. It started as a twelve-bed facility, named Provident Hospital. At Provident Hospital, Dr. Williams also opened the first nursing school for Afrikan-Americans, where Emma Reynolds and six others made up the first graduating class.

Dr. Williams employed Afrikan-American and white doctors at Provident Hospital, emphasizing the need to provide the best available care to everyone. He required that the doctors at Provident keep abreast of the latest advances in medicine.

Two years later, in 1893, a young man named James Cornish was rushed to Provident Hospital with a stab wound to the chest. Doctors at this time did not have X-ray machines, and the doctors at Provident were unsure what to do for Mr. Cornish. His condition began to deteriorate; his pulse was getting weaker and he started to go into shock, which are signs of internal bleeding.

In the operating room, Dr. Williams made the decision to open up Cornish's chest and see what could be done before he bled to death internally. The surgical team found a pierced blood vessel and a tear to the pericardium tissue around the heart. Dr. Williams sutured both of these injuries to stop the bleeding. James Cornish survived the operation.

Newspaper headlines reported: "Sewed Up His Heart! Remarkable Surgical Operation on a Colored Man!" Cornish recovered and lived another twenty years. It was the first successful open heart surgery ever performed.

Dr. Williams's medical career prospered and he became surgeon-in-chief at Freedmen's Hospital in Washington, D.C. He organized the hospital into specialized departments such as Medical, Surgical, Gynecological, Obstetrical, Dermatological, etc.

He helped organize the National Medical Association, which at the time was the only medical organization open to Afrikan-Americans. In 1898, he married Alice Johnson, a school teacher, and moved back to Chicago where he acted as chief of surgery at Provident, which had grown to be a much larger institution. He continued on to hold top positions in teaching and as head surgeon at another Chicago hospital.

Dr. Williams was often invited to speak to doctor's associations around the country on the subject of health care for African-Americans. He encouraged African-American leaders to open hospitals in other cities where African-American people would receive first rate care. He received numerous honors and was the first black physician named as a Fellow in the American College of Surgeons.

In 1926, he retired after suffering a stroke. Dr. Williams transitioned to the ancestral realm in Idlewild, Michigan, in 1931, after a life of history making accomplishments.

Bessie Coleman

Bessie Coleman was born 26 January 1892, in Atlanta, Texas, one of thirteen children. Her mother was black and her father was of American Indian and of black descent. Her father left when she was seven and her mother did her best to raise the family alone. The children helped by picking cotton; and the girls, as soon as they were old enough, helped with the washing their mother took in to make ends meet.

Bessie had a drive to better herself and became an avid reader. By using the traveling library that came through two or three times a year, Bessie managed to finish high school (not a small achievement in those days). Although, her mother let her keep her earnings from washing and ironing, Bessie could only afford to attend college for one semester. She was determined to get ahead, and show the way to others, handicapped by what were the evils of racism, poverty, and ignorance.

Shortly after World War I, she made a firm decision to learn to fly. She read everything she could on the subject. She tried applying to one flying school after another, but was quickly turned down. In those times (1919 and 1920), her race was an obvious reason and her sex was another for being denied.

She did not stop there. With the help of an editor and publisher of the *Chicago Weekly Defender*, Bessie learned French and contacted an aviation school in France. With her savings from her manicurist's job and working in a chili parlor, Bessie made two trips to Europe. There she learned about the hazards of flight and in 1921, earned her license (two years before Amelia Earhart) from the Federation Aeronautique Internationale. She was the only licensed black pilot in the world.

After taking aerobatic training, she returned to the U.S. where for five years she toured the country, barnstorming, organizing exhibition flights and speaking in churches and schools about the potential both of flight and of her race. Bessie was one of hundreds of high-spirited stunt flyers. They flew World War I 'Jennies' (U.S. Army Curtiss JN-4) and DeHavilands. When a woman parachutist failed to show to perform a stunt, Bessie made the jump. She always did what she thought had to be done.

Proclaimed 'Queen Bess' by the Chicago Defender, her daring airborne feats thrilled thousands. She also dreamed of opening a flying school so she did stunt-flying and barn-storming to further raise money. While on the barn-storming circuit in 1926 at Paxon Field, Jacksonville, FL, Bessie's Jenny went into a nose dive and Bessie was thrown from the plane to her death during a test flight.

Shortly after her death, Bessie Coleman Aero Groups were organized by William J. Powell and on Labor Day, 1931, those flying clubs sponsored the first all-black air show in America. Bessie's dream of a school for black aviators finally became a reality in 1932.

Frederick Douglass

Frederick Douglass was born in an enslaved cabin, in February 1818, near the town of Easton, on the Eastern Shore of Maryland. Separated from his mother when only a few weeks old, he was raised by his grandparents. At about the age of six, his grandmother took him to the plantation of his master and left him there. Not being told by her that she was going to leave him, Douglass never recovered from the betrayal of the abandonment.

When he was about eight, he was sent to Baltimore to live as a houseboy with Hugh and Sophia Auld, relatives of his master. It was shortly after his arrival that his new mistress taught him the alphabet. When her husband forbade her to continue her instruction, because it was unlawful to teach slaves how to read, Frederick took it upon himself to learn. He made the neighborhood boys his teachers, by giving away his food in exchange for lessons in reading and writing.

At about the age of twelve or thirteen, Douglass purchased a copy of *The Columbian Orator*, a popular schoolbook of the time, which helped him to gain an understanding and appreciation of the power of the spoken and the written word, as two of the most effective means by which to bring about permanent, positive change.

Returning to the Eastern Shore, at approximately the age of fifteen, Douglass became a field hand, and experienced most of the horrifying conditions that plagued slaves during the 270 years of legalized slavery in America. But it was during this time that he had an encounter with the slave-breaker Edward Covey. Their fight ended in a draw, but the victory was Douglass', as his challenge to the slave-breaker restored his sense of self-worth.

After an aborted escape attempt when he was about eighteen, he was sent back to Baltimore to live with the Auld family, and in early September 1838, at the age of twenty, Douglass succeeded in escaping from slavery by impersonating a sailor.

He went first to New Bedford, Massachusetts, where he and his new wife, Anna Murray, began to raise a family. Whenever he could, he attended abolitionist meetings, and, in October 1841, after attending an anti-slavery convention on Nantucket Island, Douglass became a lecturer for the Massachusetts Anti-Slavery Society and a colleague of William Lloyd Garrison. This work led him into public speaking and writing.

He published his own newspaper, *The North Star*, participated in the first women's rights convention at Seneca Falls, in 1848, and wrote three autobiographies. He was internationally recognized as an uncompromising abolitionist, indefatigable worker for justice and equal opportunity, and an unyielding defender of women's rights. He became a trusted advisor to Abraham Lincoln, United States Marshal for the District of Columbia, Recorder of Deeds for Washington, D.C., and Minister-General to the Republic of Haiti.

Douglass said, "What is possible for me is possible for you." Frederick Douglass created for himself and others a life of honor, respect and success that he could never have dreamed of when still a boy on Colonel Lloyd's plantation on the Eastern Shore of Maryland. He transitioned to the ancestral realm on 20 February 1895.

William P. Hubbard

William Peyton Hubbard (1842–1935), City of Toronto Alderman from 1894 to 1914, was a popular and influential politician, of particular historical note as the city's first politician of Afrikan descent Born in Toronto, Hubbard was the son of enslaved Americans who escaped to Canada via the Underground Railroad. He became a baker by trade, and one well-known for his strong political opinions. Armed with a sharp wit and powerful oratory skills, he eventually found his way into politics.

He was first elected in 1894 in a quiet, tree-lined ward of grand homes that happened to be the wealthiest and whitest ward in the city (encompassing an area between University Avenue and Bathurst Street).

Hubbard was known for his strong sense of public duty, and made a name for himself fighting against the privatization of Toronto's water and hydroelectric supplies. He was elected to the powerful Toronto Board of Control in 1904, and topped the polls in the city-wide election to the Board in 1906. He was re-elected in 1907 but defeated in 1908. He served as Acting Mayor on more than one occasion.

Losing an election in 1915, Hubbard retired to the Riverdale area of the city building a home that he would spend his remaining days in until he transitioned to the ancestral realm at the age of ninety-three. Coincidentally, the alderman dubbed the Grand Old Man by Toronto press in his political days, serving well into his 70s, was the quite literally the oldest man in the city for a short period before his death.

February

Langston Hughes

He was born on 1 February 1902, in Joplin, Missouri. He is usually considered the dean of Afrikan-American poets. His parents divorced when he was a child, and his father moved to Mexico. He was raised by his grandmother until he was thirteen, when he moved to Lincoln, Illinois, to live with his mother and her husband, eventually settling in Cleveland, Ohio. It was in Lincoln that Hughes began writing poetry.

Following graduation from high school, Hughes spent a year in Mexico and a year at Columbia University. During these years, he held odd jobs as an assistant cook, launderer, and a busboy, and traveled to Africa and Europe working as a seaman. In November 1924, he moved to Washington, D.C. Hughes first book of poetry, *The Weary Blues*, was published by Alfred A. Knopf in 1926.

He finished his college education at Lincoln University in Pennsylvania three years later. In 1930, his first novel, *Not Without Laughter*, won the

Harmon gold medal for literature. He was one of the foundational inspirations behind the Harlem Renaissance. Paul Lawrence Dunbar, Carl Sandburg, and Walt Whitman were Hughes primary literary influences.

He is known for his insightful, colorful portrayals of black life in America from the 20s through the 60s. He wrote novels, short stories and plays, as well as poetry, and is also known for his engagement with the world of jazz and the influence it had on his writing, as in montage of a dream deferred.

His life and work were influential in the shaping of what came to be known as the Harlem Renaissance of the 1920s. Unlike Claude McKay, Jean Toomer, and Countee Cullen, Hughes identified fiercely his personal experience with that of the common experiences of the American Negro. He wanted to tell their stories that reflected their dignity, humor, suffering, and language.

Langston transitioned to the ancestral realm of complications from prostate cancer on 22 May 1967, in New York. In his memory, his residence at 20 East 127th Street in Harlem, New York City, has been given landmark status by the New York City Preservation Commission, and east 127th Street was renamed 'Langston Hughes Place'.

Rosa Parks

Most historians date the beginning of the modern civil rights movement in the United States to 1 December 1955. That was the day when an unknown seamstress in Montgomery, Alabama, refused to give up her bus seat to a white passenger. This brave woman, Rosa Parks, was arrested and fined for violating a city ordinance, but her lonely act of defiance began a movement that ended legal segregation in America, and made her an inspiration to freedom-loving people everywhere.

Rosa Parks was born Rosa Louise McCauley in Tuskegee, Alabama, to James McCauley, a carpenter, and Leona McCauley, a teacher on 4 February 1914. At the age of two, she moved to her grandparents' farm in Pine Level, Alabama, with her mother and younger brother, Sylvester. At the age of eleven, she enrolled in the Montgomery Industrial School for Girls, a private school founded by liberal-minded women from the northern United States.

The school's philosophy of self-worth was consistent with Leona McCauley's advice to "take advantage of the opportunities, no matter how few they were."

Opportunities were few indeed. "Back then," Mrs. Parks recalled in an interview, "we didn't have any civil rights. It was just a matter of survival, of existing from one day to the next. I remember going to sleep as a girl hearing the Klan ride at night and hearing a lynching and being afraid the house would burn down." In the same interview, she cited her lifelong acquaintance with fear as the reason for her relative fearlessness in deciding to appeal her conviction during the bus boycott.

"I didn't have any special fear," she said. "It was more of a relief to know that I wasn't alone."

After attending Alabama State Teachers College, the young Rosa settled in Montgomery, with her husband, Raymond Parks. The couple joined the local chapter of the NAACP and worked quietly for many years to improve the lot of African-Americans in the segregated south.

"I worked on numerous cases with the NAACP," Mrs. Parks recalled, "but we did not get the publicity. There were cases of flogging, peonage, murder, and rape. We didn't seem to have too many successes. It was more a matter of trying to challenge the powers that be, and to let it be known that we did not wish to continue being second-class citizens."

The bus incident led to the formation of the Montgomery Improvement Association, led by the young pastor of the Dexter Avenue Baptist Church, Dr. Martin Luther King, Jr. The association called for a boycott of the city-owned bus company. The boycott lasted 382 days and brought Mrs. Parks, Dr. King, and their cause to the attention of the world. A Supreme Court decision struck down the Montgomery ordinance under which Mrs. Parks had been fined, and outlawed racial segregation on public transportation.

In 1957, Mrs. Parks and her husband moved to Detroit, Michigan, where Mrs. Parks served on the staff of U.S. representative, John Conyers. The Southern Christian Leadership Council established an annual Rosa Parks Freedom Award in her honor.

After the death of her husband in 1977, Mrs. Parks founded the Rosa and Raymond Parks Institute for Self-Development. The institute sponsors an annual summer program for teenagers called Pathways to Freedom. The young people tour the country in buses, under adult supervision, learning the history of their country and of the civil rights movement.

President Clinton presented Rosa Parks with the Presidential Medal of Freedom in 1996. She received a Congressional Gold Medal in 1999.

When asked if she was happy living in retirement, Rosa Parks replied, "I do the very best I can to look upon life with optimism and hope and looking forward to a better day, but I don't think there is any such thing as complete happiness. It pains me that there is still a lot of Klan activity and racism. I think when you say you're happy, you have everything that you need and everything that you want, and nothing more to wish for. I haven't reached that stage yet."

Mrs. Parks spent her last years living quietly in Detroit, where she transitioned to the ancestral realm in 2005 at the age of ninety-two. After her transition, her casket was placed in the rotunda of the United States Capitol for two days, so the nation could pay its respects to the woman whose courage had changed the lives of so many. She is the only woman and second Afrikan-American in American history to lie in state at the Capitol, an honor usually reserved for presidents of the United States.

Queen Ahmose

Queen Ahmose was the Ancient Egyptian royal queen of pharaoh, Thutmose I, and the mother of queen and later, pharaoh, Hatshepsut. Ahmose was the Great Royal Wife of Thutmose I, a military general, whose rise to become pharaoh was likely assured because of her marriage to him. Her sons were Princes Amenmose and Wadjmose.

Both of them and Ahmose's elder daughter, Neferubity, are thought to have died before their father's death. Queen Ahmose was the royal granddaughter of Queen Ahmose-Nefertari and the daughter of Amenhotep I of Egypt. She also had a daughter, Mutnofret, who soon had many sons with her husband, Thutmose.

Amenhotep I came to power while he was still young himself, and his mother, Ahmose-Nefertari, was regent for him until he reached maturity. This is evidenced because both his mother and he are credited with opening a worker village at the site of Deir el-Medina. This would never have been recorded as such if she had not been regent. Later, Amenhotep took for his Great Royal Wife, his sister, Ahmose-Meritamon.

The second royal daughter of Ahmose, Hatshepsut, was thought to be very close to her parents, being placed into important administrative positions in the government, including the chief advisory role to her father. She survived her father and became the influential royal queen of Thutmose II, and then later, to rule in her own right as one of Egypt's greatest pharaohs.

Bob Marley

Robert Nesta Marley was born on 6 February 1945 in the parish of St. Anns in Nine Miles, Jamaica, to Norval Sinclair Marley and Cedella 'Ciddy' Malcom. Norval was a British Marine officer and Ciddy was a native Jamaican. Soon after his birth, Bob's father left and had little contact with him, although he did financially support his son.

When Bob was five, his father took him to Kingston, Jamaica. It wasn't until a year later that Bob saw his mother again. Soon after, he moved with his mother to Trenchtown, a section of Kingston notorious for its rough ghettoes.

In 1961, at the age of sixteen, Bob released his first song, *Judge Not*, which did not do well. This did not discourage Bob. He continued to pursue a career in music, and in 1965, he formed a group called 'The Wailers' with Bunny Livingstone (later known as Bunny Wailer) and Peter McIntosh (later known as simply Peter Tosh.)

Bob acted as front man for the group and wrote most of the group's material. The trio released *Simmer Down, Rule Them Rudie* and *It Hurts To Be Alone*, all of which were hits in Jamaica. In 1966, Bob Marley married Rita Anderson, his long-term girlfriend. The next day, he went to the United States and stayed long enough to gain financing for his next record.

The next year, Bob and Rita's first child, Cedella, was born. Soon after, the Marleys set up their own recording label, Wail 'N Soul 'M Records, and produced a single, *Bend Down Low/Mellow Mood*. That same year, the record label was ended.

Their next child, David (Ziggy) was born in 1968. The Wailers continued to release singles without producing an album. The band formed another label, Tuff Gong, and finally reached a degree of success. By that time, the Wailers were famous in the Caribbean, but were unknown in the rest of the world.

Finally in 1971, the Wailers got a break. Island Records forwarded them 8,000 pounds for the production of a full album. The Wailers were the first reggae band to receive so much money and to have access to the best recording studios. They produced two albums, 'Catch a Fire' and 'Burnin'', the latter which included *Get Up Stand Up* and *I Shot the Sheriff.*

The Wailers began to extensively tour the United States and the United Kingdom, and when Eric Clapton covered *I Shot the Sheriff,* the Wailers soared to instant fame. Soon after their success in the U.S., the band changed their name to Bob Marley and the Wailers, and then released their next album, 'Natty Dread'.

The album included the hit single *No Woman No Cry*, perhaps their most popular song. Soon after, Bunny and Peter left to pursue solo careers and were replaced by new members. By 1976, reggae fever had swept the United States. Rolling Stone magazine named Bob Marley and the Wailers the 'Band of the Year' and 'Rastaman Vibration' rose to the top of the charts.

On 3 December 1976, an assassination attempt was made on Bob Marley, his wife and the managers of the Wailers to keep him from playing at the Smile Jamaica concert in Kingston. His concert was scheduled for 5 December after a presidential candidate's election rally, a presidential candidate who happened to be at odds with the U.S.

Some people believe that the assassination attempt was executed by the U.S. government, for fear that Marley's performance would sway the vote.

Despite receiving two gun-shot wounds, Bob Marley performed anyway and then left for the UK.

Bob Marley and the Wailers went on to produce their next album, 'Exodus', in 1977. The release of this album propelled Bob to an international superstar. Later, in May of the same year, Bob found out that he had cancer in his toe. Doctors recommended that he have the toe removed, but Bob refused since this was against his Rastafarian beliefs.

In July, the rest of the Exodus tour was canceled.

In 1978, the band released another album, 'Kaya'. The group's songs went from protest anthems to love songs. In April, Marley returned to Jamaica to perform in the One Love Peace Concert, and later that year, he received a Peace Medal of the Third World from the United Nations. Bob Marley also traveled to Africa for the first time, making stops in Kenya, Ethiopia and Zimbabwe.

The band went on touring throughout the U.S. and Europe and produced a few more albums, including 'Uprising'. However, in 1980, Marley fell gravely ill. The cancer in his toe had spread upwards through his body and had infected his liver, stomach and brain. In September, Bob nearly fainted during a concert in New York City.

The next day, he collapsed while jogging through a park and was rushed to the hospital. The doctors revealed that the tumor in his brain had greatly enlarged and that Bob had less than a month to live.

Bob wanted to continue the tour though, and he performed a spectacular show in Pittsburgh on 22 September. Rita was not happy with his decision to spend his final days touring though, and the concert was canceled the next day. Bob then went to Miami where he was baptized at the Ethiopian Orthodox Church on 4 November.

Five days later, in a last attempt to save his life, Bob flew to a controversial treatment center in Germany with Rita. Three months later, on 11 May 1981, Bob Marley transitioned to the ancestral realm at the young age of thirty-six.

Bob Marley's funeral was held in Jamaica on 21 May, and hundreds of thousands of people attended, including the prime minister of Jamaica. Bob's body was taken back to his birth place in Nine Miles where it now rests in a mausoleum.

Piankhi

The Nubian king Piankhi (reigned ca. 741–ca. 712 B.C.) began the conquest of Lower Egypt which resulted in the establishment of the twenty-fifth, or 'Ethiopian', dynasty of pharaohs.

Piankhi was the hereditary ruler of the kingdom of Cush on the Upper Nile in what is now the northern Sudan. About 741 B.C., he succeeded his father, Kashta, who founded this Nubian Kingdom. By this time, Lower Kamit (Egypt) had been in full decline for almost half a millennium. The Egyptian state was torn by internal power struggles among petty rulers, so the situation was ripe for a strong invader to take over.

Piankhi moved steadily down the Nile, conquering towns one by one. By 721 B.C., he was in possession of Heracleopolis, and finally he captured Heliopolis in the Delta. Being descended from the original black founders of Egypt, Piankhi was accepted and his rule legitimized.

At this point, Piankhi regarded the conquest of Egypt as complete, and he returned home to his Cushite capital in Napata after placing the Egyptian rulers in tributary status. He was received in Napata with much acclaim for having humiliated the former Egyptian overlords of Nubia, but the tributary states which he left soon fell under the sway of a local ruler named Tefnakht, who reasserted Egyptian independence.

A great deal is known about the details of Piankhi's campaign because he built a huge stele in Amon with a lengthy inscription. This account is regarded as unusually rational and lively by modern egyptologists.

Just like the Nubian rulers who followed him, Piankhi was culturally very conservative, and he sought to strengthen some of the institutions which were undergoing decline in Egypt. In the brief time he was in Lower Egypt, he oversaw the restoration of some crumbling temples. Upon his return to Cush, he had a great pyramid built for himself in Kuru, south of Napata on the Nile.

He rebuilt the temple at Jebel Barkal and also built a number of other temples in the Egyptian style.

Curiously, all the Egyptian sources dwell on Piankhi's love of fast horses. He instituted the practice of decorating teams of horses to pull royal chariots, and the remains of a team of horses were found in his tomb at Kuru. The great king who reclaimed Egypt for its original and legitimate blacks transitioned peacefully, and his legacy was the last autonomous and authentic dynasty that ruled over Egypt in its golden age.

Cetawayo

Cetawayo kaMpande (IPA: [kletjwajo kampande], circa 1826–8 February 1884) was the King of the Zulu Kingdom from 1872 to 1879 and their leader during the Anglo-Zulu War (1879). His name has been transliterated as Cetawayo. Cetawayo was a son of Zulu king Mpande and Queen Ngqumbazi, half-nephew of Zulu king, Shaka, and grandson of Senzangakhona kaJama. In 1856, he defeated and killed in battle his younger brother, Mbuyazi, Mpande's favorite, and became the effective ruler of the Zulu people. He did not ascend to the throne, however, as his father was still alive.

His other brother, Umtonga, was still a potential rival. In 1861, Umtonga fled to the Boers' side of the border and Cetshwayo had to make deals with the Boers to get him back. In 1865, Umtonga did the same thing, apparently making Cetshwayo believe that Umtonga would try to replace him in the same manner as his father had replaced his predecessor, Dingane.

Mpande died in 1873 and Cetawayo became king on 1 September. Theophil present at Cetawayo's coronation, turned on the Zulus as he felt he was undermined by Cetawayo's skillful negotiating for land area compromised by encroaching Boers. As was customary, he created a new capital for the nation and called it Ulundi (the high place).

He expanded his army and readopted many methods of Shaka. He also equipped his impis with muskets. He banished European missionaries from his land. He also incited other native African peoples to rebel against Boers in Transvaal for freedom.

In 1878, Sir Henry Bartle Frere, British commissioner for South Africa, began to demand reparations for border infractions. They mainly angered Cetshawayo who kept his calm until Frere demanded that he should effectively disband his army. Cetshawayo laughed in his face, and when he was threatened by missionaries that he would burn in hell if he did not convert to Christianity, he lit a fire and had one of his warriors eat the fire, telling the missionary that we do the same thing with his threatened hell fire.

He led a brave Zulu army, trained in the powerful Afrikan martial arts, and defeated the British guns with spears several times also utilizing esoteric science. He proclaimed himself invincible and said that he was immune to bullets, to prove this to his warriors, he had them fire at him and the bullets fell to the ground. After being shamed, the British sent a great force to Zululand that included the heir to the French throne, Prince Napoleon.

Cetshawayo once again defeated them several times, killing the crowned prince, however the British villainy was such that they kept on bringing reinforcements until the great Zulu army finally fell. Cetshawayo was deposed and exiled to London, returning only in 1883.

From 1881, his cause had been taken up by Lady Florence Dixie, correspondent of the *London Morning Post*, who wrote articles and books in his support.

By 1882, differences between two Zulu factions—pro-Cetawayo uSuthus and three rival chiefs UZibhebhu—had erupted into a blood feuds and civil war. In 1883, the British tried to restore Cetawayo to rule at least part of his previous territory but the attempt failed. With the aid of Boer mercenaries,

Chief UZibhebhu started a war contesting the succession, and on 22 July 1883, he attacked Cetawayo's new kraal in Ulundi.

Cetawayo was wounded but escaped to Nkandla, KwaZulu-Natal forest. After pleas from the Resident Commissioner, Sir Melmoth Osborne, the king moved to Eshowe, where he transitioned to the ancestral realm a few months later. His body was buried within sight of the forest, to the south near Nkunzane River. The remains of the wagon which carried his corpse to the site was placed on the grave, and its remains may be seen at Ondini Museum, near Ulundi.

This great man was one of the greatest military minds of all times and his great courage is a source of inspiration for lovers of justice worldwide.

Empress Taitu

Taitu Betul was born on 11 February 1851, and she was empress of Ethiopia from 1889–1913.

Taitu is known to have wielded considerable political power as the wife of Menelik, both before and after they were crowned emperor and empress in 1889.

Deeply suspicious of European intentions toward Ethiopia, she was a key player in the conflict over the Treaty of Wuchale with Italy, in which the Italian version made Ethiopia an Italian protectorate, while the Amharic did not do so.

The empress held a hard line against the Italians, and when talks eventually broke down—and Italy invaded the Empire—she marched north with the emperor and the Imperial Army, commanding a force of cannons at the historic Battle of Adwa, which resulted in a humiliating defeat for Italy in March 1894.

Not only was she the first lady of Ethiopia behind the mighty emperor as a proud Afrikan history was being made at Adwa, she was also alongside the Ethiopian Army at the frontier of the battlefield serving her country. In 1889, she collaborated with Emperor Menilik to found Addis Ababa as the nation's capital. And it was Taitu who named Addis Ababa, Addis Ababa (beautiful flower).

When Menilik's health began to decline around 1906, Taitu started making decisions on his behalf.

After Menilik's death, Taitu banished to the old palace at Entoto, next to the St. Mary's church she had founded years before, and where Menilik had been crowned emperor.

Taitu lived out the rest of her life at Entoto Maryam Church near Addis Ababa, where she transitioned to the ancestral realm on 11 February 1918. Taitu and Menelik did not have any children.

Taitu was a remarkable and powerful Ethiopian who is best remembered for her love of Ethiopia, which makes her a true credit to her country and all humanity.

Lat Dior

Lat Dior Ngone Latyr Diop (1842–1886) was a 19th century Damel (king) of Cayor, a Wolof state that is today in south central Senegal.

A great resistance hero of Senegalese history, famed for his defiance and battles against the French, Lat Dior was deposed twice, in 1869 and 1879.

He converted to Islam around 1861, and made common cause with other Wolof and Fulani states to resist French colonialism. Instrumental in his conversion was the Almamy of Saloum, Maba Diakhou Ba. An ally of the Toucouleur empire's El Hadj Umar Tall, Maba convinced Lat-Dior both to convert, and to aid non-Wolof Islamic states of the region against their common foes.

Dior led his troops beside Maba in the battle of Rip on 30 November 1865, at the battle of Pathe Badiane in 1864 and Ngol Ngol in 1865. With Lat Dior, Maba took part in the conquests of the states of Sine, Baol and Djolof.

At Kaolack in 1865, they combined forces with soldiers from Waalo, Ndiambour and Ndiander to face the French fortifications of Governor Emile Pinet-Laprade but were repulsed.

After the French conquered Waalo (re-appointed), Governor Louis Faidherbe invaded Cayor in 1865 in order to stop the Damel's opposition to the construction of the Dakar to Saint-Louis railway. Dior is reported to have told the French Governor Servatius:

"As long as I live, be assured, I shall oppose, with all my might the construction of this railway."

But the French defeated Lat Dior's forces at the battle of Dekheule on 26 October 1868, after Faidherbe's retirement. Lat Dior struck a deal for limited autonomy and re-installment in 1871. In response to further French expansion, Cayor rose up again with Dior at their head, only to be defeated and be annexed again in 1879.

The great king transitioned to the ancestral realm in 1886, never undaunted by imperialist encroachment. Faidherbe is reputed to have said of Dior's troops: "*Ceux-la, on les tue on ne les deshonore pas*" (They can be killed but not dishonored). This has been adapted as the motto of the Senegalese Army: "*On nous tue, on ne nous deshonore pas.*"

In Dakar, there is a giant statue of Maalaw, the legendary horse of Lat Dior, near the great mosque.

Mogho Naba Wobgho

The territory of Burkina Faso today was traversed by numerous migrations. From the eleventh century.

The first kingdoms of Mossi were formed: the Gourma, the Mamprousi, the Dagomba, the Yatenga, the Kingdom of Boussoum and the kingdom of Ouagadougou. The latter quickly became the most influential. It was led by the Mogho Naba, both king and a magician. During the 13th and 14th centuries, these kingdoms opposed to large empires of the loop of the Niger (Mali and Songhay), they did not hesitate to attack and raid their neighboring states when they felt they were threatened.

The power of their armies allowed the Mossi kingdoms to preserve most of their independence. But at the end of the 15th century, the Songhai empire established its supremacy over the Niger bend, ending the dominion of the Mossi empire. Jealous of their power, the Mossi kings always opposed to unification of the Songhai.

The Mossi kingdoms had a remarkable social cohesion and political stability and religious autonomy. They maintained this until the French conquest in the late 19th century.

Mossi participated little trans-Saharan trade: the major trade flows bypassed the region. The Mossi were much less affected than its neighbors by the slave trade because they protected their citizens well. On the eve of the French colonization, the center of the territory was controlled by the confederation of kingdoms Mossi combining four sets policy, Yatenga the Wogodogo (Ouagadougou), the Kingdom of Boussoum and the Kingdom of Tenkodogo.

To the east had been built the kingdom of Gourma, and west, dominated by rulers Dioula of Kong in the 18th century, was fought over several kingdoms. The Mogho Naba Wbgho defended his kingdom with great merit against the French and taught his people a lesson of self-determination. His title is still used until this day.

Nina Simone

Eunice Kathleen Waymon was born on 21 February 1933 in Tryon, North Carolina, U.S.A.; the sixth of eight children, four boys and four girls. Early on in life, she revealed a prodigious musical talent playing the piano and singing in the local church with her sisters in their mother's choir. At the age of six, in 1939, a benefactor paid for her first piano lessons.

Eunice made so much progress that in 1943, when she was ten, she gave her first piano recital at the town library. There she not only experienced her first applause, but also had her first encounter with racism: during the recital her parents were removed from the first rows to accommodate some whites. This episode was a traumatic experience for her and may be the origin of her commitment to the fight for freedom and civil rights.

With the financial help of some local supporters, Eunice left North Carolina in 1950 to continue her musical education at the Juilliard School of Music in New York, the same school that Miles Davis attended. After New York, her family moved to Philadelphia. She tested for a scholarship at the prestigious Curtis Institute in Philadelphia but was rejected, ostensibly for musical reasons, but probably for her color.

Feeling discouraged, in order to support herself and pay for further lessons, she became an accompanist for a singing teacher. Later, in 1954, she took a job as a singer-pianist in the Midtown Bar and Grill in Atlantic City, adopting the stage name of Nina Simone. Nina (nina means 'girl' in Spanish) from a pet name that a boyfriend gave her, and Simone (from the French actress Simone Signoret) for its dignified sound.

It was at Midtown Bar, where Nina Simone sang, played and improvised, that her career took off. Subsequently, she played in several Philadelphia clubs. Recognized as a talented pianist, she was given a recording session with Bethlehem Records in 1957; in this session she recorded fourteen tracks.

Simone's first album Jazz as played in an Exclusive Side Street Club (eleven tracks), published in 1958, and by then also known as Little Girl Blue, was a great success, selling over a million copies.

Thanks to the success of her first recordings, in 1959, Simone signed with Colpix (Columbia Pictures Records), a collaboration that lasted until 1964. Nina recorded ten albums while signed to Colpix: six studio and four 'live' albums. She recorded some songs of Columbia film soundtracks (including *Wild Is The Wind*, *Sayonara*, *Samson and Delilah*) as well as a new version of the Bethlehem hit *I Loves You Porgy*.

In 1961, Nina married Andy Stroud, a New York detective, and in 1962, their daughter, Lisa Celeste Stroud, was born.

In 1964, Nina Simone began her association with Philips, a Mercury subsidiary. This collaboration lasted for three years, during which Nina recorded seven albums. One of the first songs recorded during the Philips period is *Don't Let Me Be Misunderstood*, from then associated with her name.

The songs is covered by the Animals in 1965, the same year where Nina published *I Put a Spell on You*, a 1956s song by Screamin' Jay Hawkins. Also this song is immediately covered (August 1965) by the Alan Price Set, the group founded by organist Alan Price after his departures from Animals.

During her association with Philips, Nina made protest songs also (after the jazz and black periods) and wrote *Mississippi Goddam*! This is her first song of protest, written after the murders of Medgar Evers in Mississippi (June 1963) and four black schoolchildren in Alabama (September 1963).

In 1966, Nina switched to RCA (she will stay until 1974: to date her last long-term affiliation with an American label) a deal negotiated by her husband, who acted as her manager and to whom some compositions are credited. From the summer of 1968 through the end of 1969, "all of her recordings were produced by her husband-manager, although we can assume that it was really Nina who was making the final selections of repertoire and essentially masterminding the sessions," according David Nathan.

Embittered by racism, Nina renounced her homeland in 1969 and became a wanderer, roaming the world. She lived in Liberia, in Barbados, Switzerland, France, Trinidad, the Netherlands, Belgium and UK at various times. In 1970, she and Stroud split up, and Nina attempt to manage herself and work with her brother, Sam Waymon. In 1974, she left RCA.

In 1978, Nina was arrested, and soon released, for withholding taxes in 1971–73, in protest at her government's undeclared war in Vietnam. The same year she made the LP Baltimore for the CTI label and in 1982, the LP Fodder on my Wings for a Swiss label. In 1985, she recorded Nina's back and Live and Kickin in U.S.

In 1987, her previously-mentioned European success with *My Baby Just Cares For Me* brought Nina back into the public eye; her music was featured in 1992 movie *Point Of No Return*, with the lead character using Nina as inspiration. The same year she recorded *Let It Be Me at The Vine Street Bar & Grill* in Hollywood for Verve Records.

She moved to the southern French town of Bouc-Bel-Air near Aix-en-Provence in 1993.

The greatest jazz singer of all times transitioned to the ancestral realm peacefully in her sleep on 21 April 2003.

W. E. Dubois

William Edward Burghardt DuBois was one of this country's most distinguished educators. Born in a small village in Massachusetts on 13 February 1868, DuBois first came face to face with the realities of racism in 19th century America while attending Fisk University in Nashville. It was while completing his graduate studies at Harvard that DuBois wrote an exhaustive study of the history of the slave trade, which is still considered the most comprehensive on the subject.

In 1895, he was the first African-American to earn a Ph.D. from Harvard University.

In 1897, DuBois took a position with Atlanta University. During his tenure there, he conducted extensive studies of the social conditions of blacks in America. At the 1900 Paris World's Fair, DuBois created a full-scale exhibit of Afrikan-American achievement since the Emancipation Proclamation in industrial work, literature, and journalism. It included photo-documentation on educational institutions such as Tuskegee, Fisk, and Howard.

Congress approved $15,000 for installation, and it was installed—off midway and in the Social Economy section of the Liberal Arts building, where it languished compared with the negative Midway exhibits.

In 1903, he wrote *The Souls of Black Folk*, which serves as the underpinning of access to many of his ideas.

In 1905, W. E. B. DuBois, John Hope, Monroe Trotter and twenty-seven others met secretly in the home of Mary B. Talbert, a prominent member of Buffalo's Michigan Street Baptist Church, to adopt the resolutions which lead to the founding of the Niagara Movement. The Niagara Movement would renounce Booker T. Washington's accommodation policies set forth in his famed 'Atlanta Compromise' speech ten years earlier.

The Niagara Movement's manifesto is, in the words of DuBois, "We want full manhood suffrage and we want it now. We are men! We want to be treated as men. And we shall win." The movement was a forerunner of the NAACP.

Despite the establishment of thirty branches and the achievement of a few scattered civil-rights victories at the local level, the group suffered from organizational weakness and lack of funds, as well as the lack of a permanent headquarters or staff, and it never was able to attract mass support. After the Springfield (Ill.) Race Riot of 1908, however, white liberals joined with the nucleus of Niagara 'militants' and founded the NAACP the following year, 1909.

The Niagara Movement disbanded in 1910, with the leadership of DuBois forming the main continuity between the two organizations. Throughout the first half of the 20th century, W. E. B. DuBois continued to work as an author, lecturer and educator. His teachings were an important influence on the civil rights movement of the 50s and 60s.

Due to his disappointment with the progress of blacks in the U.S., he migrated to a newly independent Ghana and became an honorary citizen, thanks to his friend, Kwame N'Krumah. Ironically, DuBois transitioned to the ancestral realm on the eve of the historic march on Washington in 1963. Actor and playwright Ossie Davis read an announcement of his death to the 250,000 people gathered the next day at the Washington Monument.

He passed away on 27 August 1963 in Accra, Ghana. Having been one of the brightest people of Afrikan descent in the 21st century.

Fard Mohammed

Master Fard Muhammad was born on 26 February 1877 in the Holy City of Mecca. He studied for forty-two years to prepare him for his mission among the Lost-Found Original Blackman in America. He was in and out of America for twenty years before he began his mission. Master Fard Muhammad taught at Berkeley University in California from 1910–1930. He started selling silk door to door in Detroit Michigan, teaching Islam in the homes of his customers.

On 4 July 1930, Master Fard Muhammad established the Nation of Islam in America. In 1931, the Most Honorable Elijah Muhammad heard the teachings of Master Fard Muhammad for the first time and accepted Islam as the true nature and religion of the Blackman.

Fard Muhammad taught the Most Honorable Elijah Muhammad intensely for 3.5 years (1931–1934) on the Theology of Time, God, the devil, the knowledge of self and others, the origin of life and the creation of the universe, the period of time of the rule of the White race, the coming of Allah, the resurrection and the judgment.

Master Fard Muhammad gave the Most Honorable Elijah Muhammad, the Maulana Muhammad Ali and the Yusef Ali translations of the Holy Quran to read and study. He also recommended 104 books for him to read out of the Library of Congress to help prepare him for his mission. Master Fard Muhammad appointed the Most Honorable Elijah Muhammad as the head or leader of the Nation of Islam in 1934 and left him to begin his phase of the mission.

It is not known when Master Fard passed away, but his legacy lives on in today's Nation of Islam all over the world.

March

Massinissa

Masinissa or Massinissa c.238–148 B.C., king of Numidia. He succeeded (c.207 B.C.) his father as king of E Numidia. Brought up in Carthage, he fought in a Carthaginian campaign in Spain in the Second Punic War, but eventually went over to the Roman side due to his love for a beautiful queen.

After defeating his old rival Syphax, king of W Numidia, he joined Scipio Africanus Major and led his cavalry in a decisive charge at the battle of Zama, which ended the war. Rome awarded him the Punic territory E of Carthage. His tragic relationship with Sophonisba at the end of the Second Punic War showed how far he was prepared to go for the sake of love, almost as far as sacrificing his own life.

During his long reign, he extended his power and converted his land of turbulent tribes-people into a very strong and prosperous kingdom. He goaded Carthage into resisting Numidian encroachments; the resistance furnished

Rome with a pretext for beginning the Third Punic War. This enabled him to further extend his territory.

Ancient accounts suggest Masinissa lived beyond the age of ninety, and was still personally leading the armies of his kingdom until he transitioned to the ancestral realm. This was in great part due to his highly nutritious vegetarian diet. Through his life he exemplified great cunning, longevity and great health practices which if we resurrected, would help us live long healthy lives even today.

Candace of Meroe

In the kingdom of Kush (called Ethiopia by classical authors), particularly during the Meroitic period, women played prominent roles in affairs of the state, occupying positions of power and prestige, the natural outgrowth of which was the development of a line of queens. Unlike some of the queens of Kamit (Egypt) who derived power from their husbands, the Queens of Kush were independent rulers, to the extent that it was often thought that Meroe never had a king.

Four of these queens—Amanerinas, Amanishakhete, Nawidemak and Maleqereabar—became distinctively known as Candaces, a corruption of the word Kentake.

The word is a transcription of the Meroitic ktke or kdke, which means 'queen mother'. All royal consorts were by definition Kdkes. The queen mother played two important roles, which ensured the line of succession and also consolidated her power. She played a prominent role in the choice and coronation of the new king and, unique to Meroitic society, she officially adopted her daughter-in-law.

Basically, some of the traits of the matriarchs of Meroe correspond to those of the queen mother in matrilineal societies in other parts of Africa.

The Candaces showed great power and leadership. One of them is mentioned in the Acts of the Apostles (8:28–39) where, on the road from Jerusalem to Gaza, Philip converted "an Ethiopian eunuch, a court official of the Candace, that is, the queen of the Ethiopians, in charge of her entire treasury…"

Pliny, who provided valuable details of the great city of Meroe, which have been borne out by subsequent excavations, states that, "The queens of the country bore the name Candace, a title that had passed from queen to queen for many years."

The Candaces have repeatedly appeared in the writings of classical authors. Alexander visited Candace, Queen of Meroe; she would not let him enter Ethiopia and warned him not to try to conquer her people as they were unconquerable. It is true that in the golden age of Alexander, he was able to go as far as Kamit in his conquest. He dared not try to conquer Meroe due to its brave and fearless leadership by the Candaces.

The Candaces resisted the Roman empire as well. After Petronius' punitive invasion of Napata, the Candace waited until most of his troops went off to another campaign and attacked the Romans. Petronius returned and a standoff ensued between the two armies until the Ethiopian ambassadors were allowed to negotiate a peace treaty with Augustus Caesar. The tribute exacted from the Meroites was renounced and a border was demarcated between Roman territory and the kingdom of Kush.

We know that, for a period of 1250 years (ending in 350 CE), the kingdom of Kush flourished as a unique civilization and remained profoundly African just like ancient Kamit (Egypt); and that the title of Candace existed for five hundred years. However, without a concerted effort in archaeology and a breakthrough in deciphering the Meroitic script, the world will never know the true glory of the kingdom of Kush and the magnificence of the Candaces.

It is clear, however, that these queens were great and second to no man. They were the archetype from which the Amazon warriors were based.

Harriet Tubman

Harriet Tubman is perhaps the most well-known of all the Underground Railroad's 'conductors'. During a ten-year span, she made nineteen trips into the South and escorted over three hundred enslaved Afrikans to freedom. And, as she once proudly pointed out to Frederick Douglass, in all of her journeys she 'never lost a single passenger'.

Tubman was born enslaved in Maryland's Dorchester County around 1820. At age five or six, she began to work as a house servant. Seven years later, she was sent to work in the fields. While she was still in her early teens, she suffered an injury that would follow her for the rest of her life. Always ready to stand up for someone else, Tubman blocked a doorway to protect another field hand from an angry overseer.

The overseer picked up and threw a two-pound weight at the field hand. It fell short, striking Tubman on the head. She never fully recovered from the blow, which subjected her dizzy spells for the rest of her life.

Around 1844, she married a free black man named John Tubman and took his last name. (She was born Araminta Ross; she later changed her first name to Harriet, after her mother.) In 1849, in fear that she, along with the other enslaved Afrikans on the plantation, was to be sold, Tubman resolved to run away.

She set out one night on foot. She followed the North Star by night, making her way to Pennsylvania, and soon after to Philadelphia, where she found work and saved her money. The following year she returned to Maryland and escorted her sister and her sister's two children to freedom. She made the dangerous trip back to the South soon after to rescue her brother and two other men.

On her third return, she went after her husband, only to find he had taken another wife. Undeterred, she found other enslaved Afrikans seeking freedom and escorted them to the North. Tubman returned to the South again and again.

She devised clever techniques that helped make her 'forays' successful, including using the master's horse and buggy for the first leg of the journey; leaving on a Saturday night, since runaway notices couldn't be placed in newspapers until Monday morning; turning about and heading south if she encountered possible slave hunters; and carrying a drug to use on a baby if its crying might put the fugitives in danger.

Tubman even carried a gun which she used to threaten the fugitives if they became too tired or decided to turn back, telling them, "You'll be free or die."

By 1856, Tubman's capture would have brought a $40,000 reward from the South. On one occasion, she overheard some men reading her wanted poster, which stated that she was illiterate. She promptly pulled out a book and feigned reading it. The ploy was enough to fool the men.

Tubman had made the perilous trip to slave country nineteen times by 1860, including one especially challenging journey in which she rescued her seventy year-old parents. Of the famed heroine, who became known as 'Moses', Frederick Douglass said, "Excepting John Brown—of sacred memory—I know of no one who has willingly encountered more perils and hardships to serve our enslaved people than [Harriet Tubman]."

And John Brown, who conferred with 'General Tubman' about his plans to raid Harpers Ferry, once said that she was "one of the bravest persons on this continent."

Becoming friends with the leading abolitionists of the day, Tubman took part in antislavery meetings. On the way to such a meeting in Boston in 1860, in an incident in Troy, New York, she helped a fugitive slave who had been captured.

During the Civil War, Harriet Tubman worked for the Union as a cook, a nurse, and even a spy. After the war, she settled in Auburn, New York, where she would spend the rest of her long life. This brave undefeated soul transitioned tour ancestral realm peacefully in 1913.

Garrett Morgan

Garrett Morgan, an African-American inventor, is recognized for his wide range of interests and inventions. He was born on 4 March 1877. He is best known for his development of the gas mask and the automatic traffic signal, but he also gained recognition for perfecting a hair-straightening cream and a belt fastener device for sewing machines.

Born in Paris, Kentucky, the seventh of eleven children, Morgan, like other indigents in the poverty belt, quit school at age fourteen and went to the city to look for work. Morgan moved first to Cincinnati, where he worked at odd jobs for four years. Then he moved on to Cleveland and found a job at a sewing machine repair company.

In 1907, Morgan opened his own sewing machine sales and repair shop. Two years later, he opened his own tailoring shop, and employed thirty-two people to make coats, suits, and dresses. Morgan encountered a problem in his sewing business: The heat and friction of the needles would often scorch wool cloth. He decided to solve the problem himself, and worked on a chemical solution to coat the needles and so reduce the friction.

Morgan discovered that this solution would also straighten curly hair. After testing it on himself and a neighbor's, Airedale, Morgan launched his G. A. Morgan Hair Refining Cream in 1909. The company he set up to manufacture and market his hair straightener did very well, and Morgan was alleged to be the first black man in Cleveland to own a car.

Morgan received a patent for his most important invention in 1914. This was his Safety Hood, a breathing device that evolved into the modern gas mask. It consisted of an airtight canvas hood worn over the head and connected to a breathing tubes that hung to the ground. Morgan won a gold medal at the Second International Exposition of Sanitation and Safety in New York City in 1914 for his invention, which he marketed for fire fighters, engineers, chemists, and others working with dangerous fumes.

But it wasn't until Morgan proved the usefulness of his device himself that his gas mask really caught on. In 1916, Morgan and his brother, Frank, donned the life-saving mask and rescued more than twenty workers trapped in a tunnel 228 feet (70 m) beneath Lake Erie at the Cleveland Water Works. For this rescue, Morgan won a second gold medal, and he began to receive many more orders for the mask.

His mask proved effective in World War I, and eventually became standard issue for soldiers. Morgan eventually set up his own company to manufacture gas masks. The product sold well until the public learned that the manufacturer was black. Even after he disguised himself as Big Chief Mason, a Canadian Indian, and hired white demonstrators as marketing representatives, sales of the gas mask faltered.

To occupy his talents, he turned to the development of the automatic three-stage electric traffic light. Before Morgan's invention, traffic signals indicated only Go or Stop, and they were frequently ignored. Morgan's light had arms that could be raised or lowered, and when they were in the halfway position, they indicated that drivers were to slow down. This was the precursor to the red, yellow and green lights in use today. Morgan patented his traffic light in 1923, and then sold the rights to General Electric for $40,000.

In the 1920s, he organized a newspaper, *the Cleveland Call*. As civil rights activist, he took part in the formation of the NAACP, and in 1931, ran unsuccessfully for Cleveland's city council on a platform of fair housing, employment, and representation for all people. His declining years were marred by glaucoma, but he maintained an interest in inventions until his transition to the ancestral realm in 1963. He was one of the greatest inventors of our times.

Moshoeshoe

For the greater part of the 19th century, conflict among the Afrikans, British and Boers pervaded in southern Africa. The British sought to expedite their imperial cause by intensifying their efforts to control the Afrikans and contain the Boers. As a result, the Boers trekked northwards, encroaching and eventually settling on lands where Bantu-speaking peoples had lived for centuries.

Political and economic disputes resulted in war between the British and the Boers, with the ultimate impact on Afrikans being the colonization of their traditional kingdoms by the British.

Meanwhile, the rise of the Zulu kingdom under Shaka dislocated neighboring states and widespread migrations created refugees in all directions. One group of Sotho people, led by Moshoeshoe, fled to the mountains.

Born in 1786, Moshoeshoe emerged as a militarist and diplomat, forging a nation out of the chaos created by Shaka's military campaigns. Considered one of Africa's greatest statesmen, Moshoeshoe merged the displaced with his own people into a unitary state with defined borders and one language.

The Basuto originated as a people around 1820 and eventually settled on the mountain Thaba Bosiu. By 1840, the Basuto kingdom increased from 2,000 to 40,000. Although, they based their military on the Zulu model, Basutoland was not a centralized state, but rather a federation of semi-independent states.

Moshoeshoe instilled a sense of identity and unity that inspired his people to defend the kingdom against any external threat to their independence and was able to resist the Zulus and the Boers. Moshoeshoe resorted to diplomacy to avert the Zulu threat, while he sought British protection to forestall the Boers from colonizing Basutoland.

Also, Moshoeshoe invited missionaries to Basutoland to gain information about the outside world, particularly about Christianity and literacy.

Moshoeshoe felt that if his people became Christians, the British would reduce their aggression toward 'fellow' Christians. The upside of the missionaries' sojourn was the development of the Basuto's written language. However, although Moshoeshoe could readily quote passages from the Bible, he never converted to Christianity.

In the late 1830s, Boer trekkers from the Cape Colony showed up on the western borders of Basutoland and subsequently claimed land rights. The next thirty years were marked by conflicts, highlighted by one war in 1858 where Moshoeshoe defeated the Boers, and another in 1865 where Moshoeshoe lost a great portion of the western lowlands.

In the interim, Moshoeshoe signed a treaty with the British. He then attacked the Boers, who had also signed a treaty with the British. As expected, the British launched an attack on Basutoland, but they were soundly defeated.

In 1868, Moshoeshoe realized that continued pressure from the Boers would lead to the destruction of his kingdom and he placed himself under British protection.

In 1869, the British signed a boundary treaty with the Boers. Moshoeshoe, expecting to recover all his lands, had to relinquish yet more land, which effectively reduced his kingdom to half its previous size. These boundaries have lasted to this day.

In 1870, Moshoeshoe, warrior and statesman extraordinaire, transitioned to the ancestral realm.

In 1966, Basutoland gained independence from Britain and was renamed Lesotho.

Mansa Musa

Mansa Musa is mostly remembered for his great hajj, or pilgrimage, to Mecca with hundred camel-loads of gold, each weighing 300 lbs.; five hundred servants, each carrying a 4 lb. gold staffs; thousands of his subjects; as well as his senior wife, with her five hundred attendants. Mansa Musa and his retinue "gave out so much gold that they depressed its value in Egypt and caused its value to fall."

However, attention should be focused on the effects of the hajj, rather than the pilgrimage itself.

The hajj planted Mali in men's minds and its riches fired up the imagination as El Dorado did later. In 1339, Mali appeared on a 'Map of the World'. In 1367, another map of the world showed a road leading from North Africa through the Atlas Mountains into the Western Sudan. In 1375, a third map of the world showed a richly attired monarch holding a large gold nugget in the area south of the Sahara. Also, trade between Egypt and Mali flourished.

Mansa Musa brought back with him an Arabic library, religious scholars, and most importantly, the Muslim architect al-Sahili, who built the great mosques at Gao and Timbuktu and a royal palace. Al-Sahili's most famous work was the chamber at Niani. It is said that his style influenced architecture in the Sudan where, in the absence of stone, the beaten earth is often reinforced with wood which bristles out of the buildings.

Mansa Musa strengthened Islam and promoted education, trade, and commerce in Mali. The foundations were laid for Walata, Jenne, and Timbuktu becoming the cultural and commercial centers of the Western Sudan, eclipsing those of North Africa and producing Arabic-language black literature in the 15th and 16th centuries. Diplomatic relations were established and ambassadors were exchanged between Mali and Morocco, and Malinke students were sent to study in Morocco.

For the forty-seven years between the time of the death of his grandfather's brother, Sundiata, and Mansa Musa's accession to the throne, Mali endured a period of political instability. Mansa Musa ruled for twenty-five years, bringing prosperity and stability to Mali and expanding the empire he inherited.

Mali achieved the apex of its territorial expansion under Mansa Musa. The Mali Empire extended from the Atlantic coast in the west to Songhai, far down the Niger bend to the east: from the salt mines of Taghaza in the north to the legendary gold mines of Wangara in the south.

Mansa Musa transitioned to the ancestral realm in 1337. He had brought stability and good government to Mali, spreading its fame abroad and making it truly "remarkable both for its extent and for its wealth and a striking example of the capacity of the blacks for political organization" (E. W. Bovill, 1958, The Golden Trade of the Moors). He was without contest the greatest sovereign of his time.

Amina of Zaria

The seven original states of Hausaland: Katsina, Daura, Kano, Zazzau, Gobir, Rano, and Garun Gabas cover an area of approximately five hundred square miles and comprise the heart of Hausaland in contemporary Nigeria. In the 16th century, Queen Bakwa Turunku built the capital of Zazzau at Zaria, named after her younger daughter.

Eventually, the entire state of Zazzau was renamed Zaria, which is now a province in present-day Nigeria.

However, it was her elder daughter, the legendary Amina (or Aminatu), who inherited her mother's brave and bold nature. Amina was sixteen years old when her mother became queen and she was given the traditional title of magajiya. She honed her military skills and became famous for her bravery and military exploits, as she is celebrated in song as 'Amina daughter of Nikatau, a woman as capable as a man'.

Amina is credited as the architect who created the strong earthen walls around the city, which was the prototype for the fortifications used in all Hausa states. She built many of these fortifications, which became known as ganuwar Amina or Amina's walls, around various conquered cities.

The objectives of her conquests were twofold: extension of Zazzau beyond its primary borders and reducing the conquered cities to vassal status. Sultan Muhammad Bello of Sokoto stated that, "She made war upon these countries and overcame them entirely so that the people of Katsina paid tribute to her and the men of Kano [and]...also made war on cities of Bauchi till her kingdom reached to the sea in the south and the west."

Likewise, she led her armies as far as Nupe and, according to the Kano Chronicle, "The Sarkin Nupe sent her [the princess] 40 eunuchs and 10,000 kola nuts. She was the first in Hausaland to own eunuchs and kola nuts."

Amina was a preeminent gimbiya (princess). She reigned from approximately 1536 to 1573. Over a thirty-four-year period, her many conquests and subsequent annexation of the territories extended the borders of Zaria, which also grew in importance and became the center of the North-South Saharan trade and the East-West Sudan trade. The Great Queen transitioned peacefully, having been a great trend-setter all her life.

Yakub Al-Mansur

Yakub Ibn Yusuk, better known as Al-Mansur, was the most powerful of the Moorish rulers who dominated Spain for five hundred years. His surname, Al-Mansur, means 'The Invincible'. He defeated all of his enemies, never having lost a battle.

Al-Mansur's father was Black and Arab, but his mother was a pure Afrikan, believed to have been from Timbuctoo or Senegal.

Al-Mansur, came to the throne after his father was killed in Portugal in 1184. He promised revenge for his father's death, but fighting with the Almohads, who were ousted from the throne, delayed him in Africa. After defeating the Almohads again, he headed out for Spain to avenge his father's death and restore his dynasty to its European throne.

Landing in Spain, he defeated the Europeans and captured all major cities, Al-Mansur, returned to Afrika with three thousand Christian captives, young women and children.

When the Christians in Spain, most of whom were white, and of German descent, heard of Al-Mansur's absence to Africa, they revolted, capturing many of the Moorish cities, including Silves, Vera, and Beja. When Al-Mansur heard this news, he returned to Spain, and defeated the Christians again. This time, many were taken in chained groups of fifty each, and later sold in Afrika as slaves.

Again, while Al-Mansur was away in Africa, the Christians mounted the largest army of that time period, of over 300,000 men, to defeat Al-Mansur. Immediately upon hearing this, Mansur returned to Spain and defeated Alphonso's army, killing 150,000 rebel-rousers, taking money, valuables and other goods beyond calculation.

In addition to being one of the greatest military leaders in history, Al-Mansur was a lover of the arts. His reign was responsible for the building of the famous Mosque at Granada and Cordova, which still stands today. As does the model he built of undefeatable Afrikan fervor.

Walter Rodney

Walter Rodney was born in Georgetown, British Guiana, on 23 February 1942. From an early age, he was involved in anti-colonial and nationalist politics. He was an excellent scholar and won a scholarship to study history at the University of the West Indies. His combination of commitment and skills encouraged Rodney to think about the ways in which history could be used to help ordinary working people.

He went to England to study Afrikan history, where he also experienced the crude racism of the period. At the same time, he gained a better understanding of the world-wide nature of the struggle against racism and how he could assist it.

Rodney tried to put his ideas into practice when he accepted a job teaching Afrikan History at the University of Dar es Salaam in Tanzania. Here, he became involved in discussions around the role of the university in making a more just and equal society. His belief that universities should contribute to making a better society for working people was also evident when he left Tanzania to teach at the University of the West Indies.

In Jamaica, he gave lectures about Afrikan history and Black Power to anyone who would listen and took time to get to know and learn from the poorest communities of the island, especially the Rastafarians.

Through his educational work and political organization, Rodney became a leader of the Black Power movement in Jamaica, which he defined to include Caribbean people of both Afrikan and East Indian heritage. The government banned Rodney's re-entry on his return from a Black writers conference in Canada and he returned to the University of Dar es Salaam.

At the time, Dar es Salaam was the center for a great deal of political thinking and activity. This environment inspired Rodney to think more deeply about solving practical political, economic and cultural problems. He lectured and published extensively on Afrikan history, contemporary Afrikan affairs and imperialism during this period, which also saw the publication of his best known work, *How Europe Underdeveloped Africa.*

However, he came to realize that there was only so much he could do as a foreigner in Tanzania and decided to commit himself to working for change in Guyana.

In 1974, Rodney and his family returned to Guyana with the promise of a teaching post at the university. However, the government of Forbes Burnham did not let Rodney take up the job because it did not want him to use his skills to help popular resistance against it. Even so, Rodney helped set up the Working Peoples' Alliance (WPA), which was committed to the removal of Burnham and the system of government which he had installed with help from both Britain and the U.S.

Rodney and the WPA believed that only the people could achieve this goal and encouraged people toward mass action against the government. The government began a campaign to destroy the WPA and the movement was energizing. One aspect of that campaign was to eliminate the WPA leadership. On 13 June 1980, Walter Rodney was assassinated by a bomb.

News of his murder sparked outrage around the world, and a massive funeral procession in Guyana in defiance of the government, as people mourned the great activist and scholar whose memory and courage remain entrenched in our memory.

Empress Menen

Empress Menen Asfaw (Baptismal name Wolete Giyorgis) (25 March 1889–15 February 1962) was the wife and consort of Emperor Haile Selassie I of Ethiopia. According to both published and unpublished reports, the then Woizero Menen Asfaw was given in marriage by her family, to the prominent Wollo nobleman, Dejazmach Ali of Cherecha, and bore him a daughter, Woizero Belaynesh Ali, and a son, Jantirar Asfaw Ali.

This first marriage ended in divorce, and Woizero Menen then married Dejazmach Amede Ali Aba-Deyas, another very prominent nobleman of Wollo. She bore her second husband two children as well, a daughter, Woizero Desta Amede, and a son, Jantirar Gebregziabiher Amede.

Following the sudden death of her second husband, Woizero Menen's grandfather, Negus Mikael, arranged her marriage to Ras Leul Seged Atnaf Seged, a prominent Shewan nobleman, who was considerably older than Woizero Menen, sometime in late 1909 or early 1910.

The account given in the autobiography of the emperor, *My Life and Ethiopia's Progress*, mentions no previous marriage or children of Empress Menen and no such order by Iyasu, but states only that at the age of twenty, they were married by their own mutual consent, and describes her as 'a woman without any malice whatsoever'. When Tafari Makonnen became emperor of Ethiopia as Haile Selassie I, Menen Asfaw was crowned as Empress at his side. Empress Menen had no children by Ras Leul Seged.

Empress Menen was active in promoting women's issues in Ethiopia, was Patroness of the Ethiopian Red Cross, and the Ethiopian Women's Charitable Organization. She was also patroness of the Jerusalem Society that arranged for pilgrimages to the Holy Land. She founded the Empress Menen School for Girls in Addis Ababa, the first all-girls school which had both boarding and day students.

Girls from all over the empire were brought to the school to receive a modern education, encouraged by the empress who visited it often and presided over its graduation ceremonies. The empress gave generously, as well as sponsored programs for the poor, ill and disabled. She was also a devoutly religious woman who did much to support the Ethiopian Orthodox Tewahedo Church.

When the empress was exiled from Ethiopia during the Italian occupation from 1936 to 1941, she made a pledge to the Virgin Mary at the Church of the Nativity in Bethlehem, promising to give her crown to the church if Ethiopia were liberated from occupation. The empress made numerous pilgrimages to Holy Sites in then British-ruled Palestine, in Syria and in Lebanon, during her exile to pray for her occupied homeland.

Following the return of Emperor Haile Selassie and his family to Ethiopia in 1941, a replica of the crown was made for future empresses, but the original crown that Empress Menen was crowned with at her husband's side in 1930 was sent to the Church of the Nativity in Bethlehem. Empress Menen, although often seen wearing a tiara at public events that called for it, would never again wear a full crown.

Empress Menen performed perfectly in the role of empress-consort. In her public role, she combined religious piety, concern for social causes, and support for development schemes with the majesty of her imperial status. Outwardly, she was the dutiful wife, visiting schools, churches, exhibitions and model farms, attending public and state events at her husband's transition to the ancestral realm in 1962.

The empress was buried in the crypt of Holy Trinity Cathedral in Addis Ababa among the tombs of her children. Prime Minister Aklilu Hapte-Wold delivered her eulogy paying tribute to her charity, her piety, and her role as advisor and helpmate to the emperor, as well as her personal kindness and goodness.

On the third day of memorial and commemoration after the funeral, the emperor himself paid tribute to his wife by saying that although, the prime minister had aptly described what kind of person his late wife had been, he wanted to say that during their five decades of marriage, not once had it been necessary to have a third party mediate between him and his wife, and that their marriage had been one of peace and mutual support.

Later, the emperor built a pair of grand sarcophagi in the north transept of Holy Trinity Cathedral's nave, in order to transfer his wife's remains there and eventually be buried at her side himself. But due to the revolution, the emperor was not buried there after his death, and the empress remained in her original tomb in the crypt.

During the ceremonial burial of her husband's remains in November 2000, the remains of Empress Menen were also disinterred from the crypt tomb, and placed in the sarcophagus next to her husband in the nave of the Cathedral, as he had originally intended.

Yaa Asantewaa

Yaa Asantewaa was the queen mother of the Edweso tribe of the Asante (Ashanti) in what is modern Ghana.

At the time, the Gold Coast (west-central Africa) was under the British protectorate. The British supported their campaigns against the Asante with taxes levied upon the local population. In addition, they took over the state-owned gold mines thus removing considerable income from the Asante government. Missionary schools were also established and the missionaries began interfering in local affairs.

When the Asante began rebelling against the British rule, the British attempted to put down the unrests. Furthermore, the British governor, Lord Hodgson, demanded that the Asante turn over to them the Golden Stool, i.e. the throne and a symbol of Asante independence. Capt. C. H. Armitage was sent out to force the people to tell him where the Golden Stool was hidden and to bring it back.

After going from village to village with no success, Armitage found at the village of Bare only the children who said their parents had gone hunting. In response, Armitage ordered the children to be beaten. When their parents came out of hiding to defend the children, he had them bound and beaten too.

This brutality was the instigation for the Yaa Asantewaa War for Independence which began on 28 March 1900. Yaa Asantewaa mobilized the Asante troops, and for three months laid siege to the British mission at the fort of Kumasi. In a famous speech to encourage the men of Asante to fight, Yaa Asantewaa was noted to have said to the men that if the men don't fight, then the women will.

The British had to bring in several thousand troops and artillery to break the siege. Also, in retaliation, the British troops plundered the villages, killed much of the population, confiscated their lands and left the remaining population dependent upon the British for survival. They also captured Queen Yaa Asantewaa whom they exiled along with her close companions to the Seychelle Islands off Afrika's east coast, while most of the captured chiefs became prisoners-of-war.

Yaa Asantewaa remained in exile until her transition to the ancestral realm twenty years later. Her courage and leadership made her the jewel of the Asante crown and a figure who lives internally in the memory of proud Afrikans worldwide.

April

Neith-Hotep

Neith-Hotep was the first queen of ancient Egypt or Kamit in approximately 3000 B.C.E. She started the first ancient Egyptian dynasty (family) along with her husband who was the first Shekhem Ur Shekhem (Pharaoh) named Narmer. The unity of Upper (southern) and Lower (northern) Egypt was brought about by this great marriage.

Queen Neith-Hotep who hailed from the North found value in uniting ancient Egypt together, because she knew that unity was strength, therefore she agreed to be married with Narmer who he himself had decided that war was not the best way to unite Egypt.

Together, Neith-Hotep and Narmer went on to rule a very prosperous Egypt that was governed by the laws of truth and justice. She advocated living a holy life, and it was no surprise that her name Neith-Hotep actually means in Metu Neter (Ancient Egyptian) 'God is pleased'.

The children of Neeith-Hotep and Narmer were Heru-Aa and BennuReBa, and they went on to consolidate the unity of Egypt after their parent's transition. Neith-Hotep was buried with all the funerary rites of a great queen, on her tomb was the Metu Neter inscription that indicated God was pleased. She was a true African queen after which lots of other queens modeled themselves.

Ptah-Hotep

Ptah-Hotep was the first documented philosopher of history. He lived during the 5th dynasty of Kamit (Ancient Egypt) and was known to have a plurality of skills and talents. After going through manhood rites of passage and then being initiated to the mysteries of ancient Egypt, he authored a book called The Instruction of Ptahhotep. This book instructed young men in proper behavior and behavior that would lead them to being peaceful and joyful beings.

These instructions were given in order for men to cultivate their higher selves and to stray away from crime and any other unsociable behavior.

Ptah-Hotep went on to be a city administrator and Vizier (Prime Minister) under the King Djedkare Isesi. He was a very wise leader that used the divine oracle of Tehuti in order to create sayings that could be used to instruct people and teach them how to behave in different situations.

Ptah-Hotep lived around 2800 B.C.E., and therefore his book is the oldest book that has ever been recovered of all times. Ptah-Hotep was also a High

Priest in Kamit and specifically a priest that negotiated issues that surrounded divine law and inter-relationships between people animals and things. For this reason, he was fond of dogs and wrote volumes on their nature.

He transitioned peacefully after having a full life and later on his grandson compiled a collection of his teaching which he put together in a book called *The Maxims of Ptahhotep*, which is the oldest book of wisdom and behavioral instructions still used until this day.

Malik Andeel

BENEVOLENT SULTAN OF BENGAL, INDIA (d. 1494)

Among the many Ethiopians who attained to high power in eastern India was Malik Andeel, possibly the greatest of their number. Born in bondage, he ultimately became commander-in-chief of the armies of the rich and potent kingdom of Bengal under the rule of Sultan Futteh Khan, and was later sultan himself.

In the course of a rebellion in 1473, Futteh Khan was killed. The throne was seized by Bareek, chief eunuch, who compelled Malik Andeel to take an oath of allegiance promising that he would never attack him 'while he was on the throne'. Malik Andeel, however, cherished plans of becoming sultan. Ingratiating himself into the favor of Bareek until he had won his complete confidence and was permitted to come and go in the palace at will, he conspired with Bareek's attendant, another Ethiopian eunuch.

The plan was to get Bareek thoroughly drunk, and when this was achieved, Malik Andeel was called. Malik found the intoxicated Bareek lolling on a chair, not upon the throne, and taking advantage of the occasion, he construed this as a condition not covered by his oath, and stabbed the sultan. Bareek, however, was large and powerfully built, and in the rough and tumble fight that followed, might have beaten Malik Andeel had not the latter's attendants come to his rescue.

Even then they did not know where to strike, as the room was pitch dark, the lights having been extinguished in the scuffle, but Malik Andeel, who was underneath and covered by the sultan's huge body, ordered them to stab. Bareek was killed and Malik Andeel emerged unhurt.

Malik Andeel was then elected sultan by the people of Bengal with the official title of Feroze Shah. He was an able ruler. His Ethiopian compatriots backed him so effectively that none of the white Turkish or Afghan chiefs dared to rebel against him. Malik Andeel was noted for his generosity.

On one occasion, he ordered that a sum of money be distributed among the poor, which his ministers thought to be far too much. To impress this upon him, they heaped up the money in a room through which the sultan was bound to pass. Learning of the intent, Malik Andeel said when he saw it, “Is that all? Double it!”

After a peaceful reign of thirteen years, Malik Andeel transitioned to the ancestral realm in 1494. He was succeeded by his son, Mdahrratad. The remains of a mosque, a minaret, and a reservoir built by Malik Andeel were still in evidence in 1813. Malik Andeel governed his people with ‘strict justice and munificent liberality’.

Billie Holiday

Billie Holiday was a true artist of her day and rose as a social phenomenon in the 1950s. Her soulful, unique singing voice and her ability to boldly turn any material that she experienced into her own music made her a superstar of her time. Today, Holiday is remembered for her masterpieces, creativity and vivacity, as many of Holiday's songs are as well known today as they were decades ago.

Holiday's poignant voice is still considered to be one of the greatest jazz voices of all time. Holiday (born Eleanora Fagan) grew up in jazz talent-rich Baltimore on 7 April 1915. As a young teenager, Holiday served the beginning part of her so-called 'apprenticeship' by singing along with records by Bessie Smith or Louis Armstrong in after-hours jazz clubs. When Holiday's mother, Sadie Fagan, moved to New York in search of a better job, Billie eventually went with her.

She made her true singing debut in obscure Harlem nightclubs and borrowed her professional name—Billie Holiday—from screen star Billie Dove. Although, she never underwent any technical training and never even so much as learned how to read music, Holiday quickly became an active participant in what was then one of the most vibrant jazz scenes in the country. She would move from one club to another, working for tips.

She would sometimes sing with the accompaniment of a house piano player while other times she would work as part of a group of performers.

At the age of eighteen, and after gaining more experience than most adult musicians can claim, Holiday was spotted by John Hammond and cut her first record as part of a studio group led by Benny Goodman, who was then just on the verge of public prominence. In 1935, Holiday's career got a big push when she recorded four sides that went on to become hits, including *What a Little Moonlight Can Do* and *Miss Brown to You*.

This landed her a recording contract of her own, and then, until 1942, she recorded a number of master tracks that would ultimately become an important building block of early American jazz music. Holiday began working with Lester Young in 1936, who pegged her with her now-famous nickname of 'Lady Day'. When Holiday joined Count Basie in 1937, and then Artie Shaw in 1938, she became one of the very first black women to work with a white orchestra, an impressive accomplishment of her time.

In the 1930s, when Holiday was working with Columbia Records, she was first introduced to the poem *Strange Fruit*, an emotional piece about the lynching of a black man. Though Columbia would not allow her to record the piece due to subject matter, Holiday went on to record the song with an alternate label, Commodore, and the song eventually became one of Holiday's classics.

It was *Strange Fruit* that eventually prompted Lady Day to continue more of her signature, moving ballads. Holiday recorded about hundred new recordings on another label, Verve, from 1952 to 1959. Her voice became more rugged and vulnerable on these tracks than earlier in her career. During this period, she toured Europe, and made her final studio recordings for the MGM label in March of 1959.

Despite her lack of technical training, Holiday's unique diction, inimitable phrasing and acute dramatic intensity made her the outstanding jazz singer of her day. White gardenias, worn in her hair, became her trademark. "Singing songs like *The Man I Love* or *Porgy* is no more work than sitting down and eating Chinese roast duck, and I love roast duck," she wrote in her autobiography. "I've lived songs like that."

Billie Holiday, a musical legend still popular today, transitioned to the ancestral realm in an untimely way at the age of forty-four on 17 July 1959. Her passionate voice, innovative techniques and touching songs will forever be remembered and enjoyed.

Paul Robeson

Paul Robeson was born in Princeton, New Jersey on 9 April 1898, to a former enslaved African, the Rev. William Robeson. His mother, a teacher, died not long thereafter when he was only five years old. Three years later, the Robeson family moved to Westfield, New Jersey. In 1910, Robeson's father became pastor of St. Thomas A.M.E. Zion Church and the Robeson family moved to Somerville, New Jersey.

Paul Robeson attended Somerville High School. There, Robeson excelled in sports, drama, singing, academics, and debating. He graduated from Somerville High School in 1915.

Robeson was awarded a four year academic scholarship to Rutgers University in 1915, the third black student in the history of the institution. Despite the openly racist and violent opposition he faced, Robeson became a twelve letter athlete excelling in baseball, basketball, football, and track. He was named to the All American Football team on two occasions.

In addition to his athletic talents, Robeson was named a Phi Beta Kappa scholar, belonged to the Cap & Skull Honor Society, and graduated valedictorian of his class in 1919.

He went on to study law at Columbia in New York and received his degree in 1923. There he met and married Eslanda Cardozo Goode, who was the first black woman to head a pathology laboratory. Robeson worked as a law clerk in New York, but once again faced discrimination, and soon left the practice because a white secretary refused to take dictation from him.

At this point in his life, Paul returned to his childhood love of drama and singing. He starred in Eugene O'Neill's 'All God's Chillun Got Wings' in 1924, creating the starring role. While the racial subject matter of the play spurred controversy and protest, he went on to star in another play by O'Neill, 'Emperor Jones'. Perhaps he is most widely recognized from the musical Showboat, where he changed the lines of the song *Old Man River*. His eleven films included *Body and Soul*, *Jericho*, and *Proud Valley*.

His concert career reads like a world traveler's passport: New York, Vienna, Prague, Budapest, Germany, Paris, Holland, London, Moscow, and Nairobi. His travels taught him that racism was not as prevalent in Europe as it was back home. In the United States, he couldn't enter theaters through the front door or sing without intimidation and protest, but in London, he was welcomed with open arms and standing ovations.

Robeson believed in the universality of music and that by performing Negro spirituals and other cultures' folk songs, he could promote intercultural understanding. As a result, he became a citizen of the world, singing for peace and equality in twenty-five languages.

During the 1940s, Robeson continued to have success on the stage, in film, and in concert halls, but remained face to face with prejudice and racism. After finding the Soviet Union to be a tolerant and friendly nation, he began to protest the growing Cold War hostilities between the United States and the USSR. He began to question why Afrikan-Americans should support a government that did not treat them as equals.

At a time when dissent was hardly tolerated, Robeson was looked upon as an enemy by his government. In 1947, he was named by the House Committee on Un-American Activities, and the State Department denied him a passport until 1958. Events such as these, along with a negative public response, led to the demise of his public career.

Paul Robeson, the great and accomplished thespian, transitioned to the ancestral realm on 23 January 1976, in Philadelphia, Pennsylvania, after living in seclusion for ten years. Robeson's legacy has been an inspiration to millions around the world. His courageous stance against oppression and inequality in part led to the civil rights movement of the 1960s.

Through his stage and film performances, he opened doors to inter-racial performances. With his travels across America and abroad, he opened the world's eyes to oppression. Robeson stood tall and proud against powerful governmental and societal forces. He remains in our memory a successful scholar, athlete, performer, and activist.

Julius Nyerere

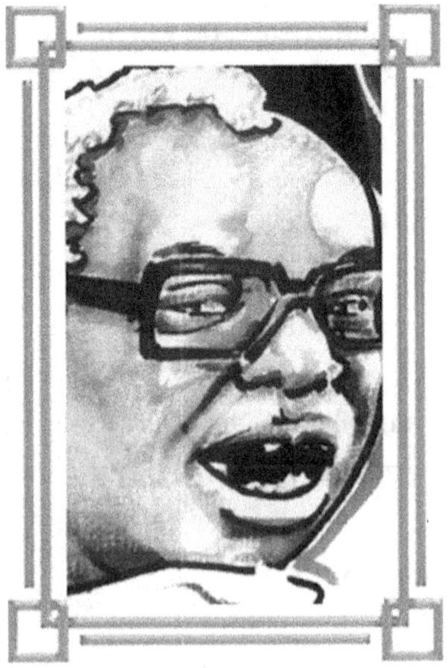

One of Africa's most respected figures, Julius Nyerere (1922–1999) was a politician of principle and intelligence. Known as Mwalimu or teacher, he had a vision of education that was rich with possibility.

Julius Kambarage Nyerere was born on 13 April 1922 in Butiama, on the eastern shore of lake Victoria in north west Tanganyika. His father was the chief of the small Zanaki tribe. He started school at twelve (he had to walk twenty-six miles to Musoma to do so). Later, he transferred for his secondary education to the Tabora Government Secondary School.

His intelligence was quickly recognized by the Roman Catholic fathers who taught him. He went on, with, to train as a teacher at Makerere University in Kampala (Uganda). On gaining his certificate, he taught for three years and then went on a government scholarship to study history and political economy for his Master of Arts at the University of Edinburgh (he was the first

Tanzanian to study at a British university and only the second to gain a university degree outside Africa).

On his return to Tanganyika, Nyerere was forced by the colonial authorities to make a choice between his political activities and his teaching. He was reported as saying that he was a schoolmaster by choice and a politician by accident. Working to bring a number of different nationalist factions into one grouping, he achieved this in 1954 with the formation of TANU (the Tanganyika African National Union).

He became President of the Union (a post he held until 1977), entered the Legislative Council in 1958 and became chief minister in 1960. A year later, Tanganyika was granted internal self-government and Nyerere became premier. Full independence came in December 1961, and he was elected President in 1962.

Nyerere's integrity, ability as a political orator and organizer, and readiness to work with different groupings was a significant factor in independence being achieved without bloodshed. In 1964, following a coup in Zanzibar (and an attempted coup in Tanganyika itself), Nyerere negotiated with the new leaders in Zanzibar and agreed to absorb them into the union government. The result was the creation of the Republic of Tanzania.

As president, Nyerere had to steer a difficult course. By the late 1960s, Tanzania was one of the world's poorest countries. Like many others, it was suffering from a severe foreign debt burden, a decrease in foreign aid, and a fall in the price of commodities.

His solution, the collectivization of agriculture, villagization (ujima) and large-scale nationalization was a unique blend of socialism and communal life. The vision was set out in the Arusha Declaration of 1967 (reprinted in Nyerere 1968):

"The objective of socialism in the United Republic of Tanzania is to build a society in which all members have equal rights and equal opportunities; in which all can live in peace with their neighbors without suffering or imposing injustice, being exploited, or exploiting; and in which all have a gradually increasing basic level of material welfare before any individual lives in luxury." (Nyerere 1968: 340)

The focus, given the nature of Tanzanian society, was on rural development. People were encouraged (sometimes forced) to live and work on a co-operative basis in organized villages or ujamaa (meaning 'familyhood' in

Kishwahili). The idea was to extend traditional values and responsibilities around kinship to Tanzania as a whole.

Within the Declaration, there was a commitment to raising basic living standards (and an opposition to conspicuous consumption and large private wealth). The socialism he believed in was 'people-centered'. Humanness in its fullest sense rather than wealth creation must come first.

Societies become better places through the development of people rather than the gearing up of production. Unlike many other politicians, he did not amass a large fortune through exploiting his position.

The policy met with significant political resistance (especially when people were forced into rural communes) and little economic success. Nearly 10 million peasants were moved and many were effectively forced to give up their land. The idea of collective farming was less than attractive to many peasants.

A large number found themselves worse off. Productivity went down. However, the focus on human development and self-reliance did bring some success in other areas notably in health, education and in political identity.

A committed pan-Africanist, Nyerere provided a home for a number of African liberation movements including the African National Congress (ANC) and the Pan African Congress (PAC) of South Africa, Frelimo when seeking to overthrow Portuguese rule in Mozambique, Zanla (and Robert Mugabe) in their struggle to unseat the white regime in Southern Rhodesia (now Zimbabwe).

He also opposed the brutal regime of Idi Amin in Uganda. Following a border invasion by Amin in 1978, a 20,000-strong Tanzanian army along with rebel groups, invaded Uganda. It took the capital, Kampala, in 1979, restoring Uganda's first president, Milton Obote, to power. The battle against Amin was expensive and placed a strain on government finances.

In 1985, Nyerere gave up the presidency but remained as chair of the party, Chama Cha Mapinduzi (CCM). He gradually withdrew from active politics, retiring to his farm in Butiama. In 1990, he relinquished his chairmanship of CCM but remained active on the world stage as Chair of the Intergovernmental South Center.

One of his last high profile actions was as the chief mediator in the Burundi conflict (in 1996). He transitioned to the ancestral realm in a London hospital of leukemia on 14 October 1999. He had proven to been one of the most insightful politicians of his time.

Marie Joseph Angelique

Canada has been shown in history as a haven that contradicted the ills of enslavement, especially lauded as a safe haven for runaway slaves. Portrayed as the opposite of the American South, Canada's (then known as New France) version of the 'peculiar institution' has been described as benevolent enslavement. Benevolent or otherwise, it was still slavery with the ultimate consequence of one man or one race dominating another.

Marie-Joseph Angelique was an enslaved Afrikan born in the Azores Island of the northeastern coast of Afrika. At first, she was enslaved to the Portuguese, who sent her to New France, were she became and enslaved house maid. Held in captivity by Francois Poulin of Montreal in the early 1730s, and being in her prime, she was expected to procreate with male captives as well as provide sexual services to her master.

Angelique had other plans, such as freedom and having a normal relationship with her apparent lover, Claude Thibault, a white indentured servant from France.

On 10 April 1734, Angelique learned that she was about to be sold and therefore, attempted to escape. During her escape, a fire was set to Montreal, which she was blamed for without clear evidence. The fire spread and the final damage was forty-six buildings, including the famed L'Hotel Dieu hospital. The conflagration resulted solely in property damage. No lives were lost.

After this, Angelique was captured and brought to trial. The trial, in accordance with the French justice system, was a systematic process that took two months. First, the chief investigator extracted her 'confessions' which in essence was a narrative of her entire life. Later, she endured another round of confession, this time under torture, where she admitted her guilt due to the barbary of her torturers.

On 21 June, the day of her execution, she was driven through the streets on a scavenger's cart, with a rope tied around her neck and signs bearing the word 'incendiaire' (arsonist) on her chest and back. On arrival at the parish church at Place d'Armes, she was made to kneel and beg for forgiveness from the King, God, and her fellow citizens. Then her hand was cut off.

Placed back in the wagon, she was taken to the gallows where she was publicly hanged by the crown executioner. She was summarily burned at the stake and her ashes were 'cast to the four corners of the earth'.

Enslavement in New France was tacitly condoned by the church, which sat silent when benevolence became brutality. The case of Marie-Joseph Angelique, a Azores-born enslaved woman, who was tortured and hanged for burning a large portion of Montreal, illustrates the hypocrisy of the church and the nature of slavery in New France which, when removing the facade of benevolence, was equivalent to the vicious acts perpetrated against the enslaved in the southern United States.

Queen Mutemwia

Queen Mutemwia was a Kamitic (ancient Egyptian) Queen of the middle 18th dynasty, who was in the lineage of Queen Tiye, the mother of Akenaton and also of Tutankhamen. She was a great queen, who alongside her husband TehutiMes IV known as Thutmose IV, gave Kamit its largest land mass, conquering most of what is now the Middle East and Sudan. TehutiMes was known for his wisdom and consulted the oracle regularly in order to be successful.

Mutemwia had many titles, one of which was that of Great Royal Wife. She used this title at her husband's death, after which their son, Amenhotep III, took over the throne of Kamit at the early age of ten. During the reign of her son, Mutemwia was very powerful and he usually consulted her prior to making important decisions on matters of state.

She continued to be very influential well into her son's reign and was a source of inspiration for him. She fulfilled the destiny of her name well since her name meant 'Mother' on a barque. Indeed she was a great mother who traveled fluently to help her progeny.

When she transitioned into the ancestral realm, she was buried with full royal honors and a solid granite statue of a sacred boat was erected in the honor of this queen that led from behind and always remained devoted to her family's well-being.

Mumia Abu-Jamal

Political activist and journalist Mumia Abu-Jamal was born in Philadelphia, Pennsylvania on 24 April 1954. Born Wesley Cook, he took the name Mumia ('Prince') in high school while taking a class on Afrikan cultures. In 1971, he added Abu-Jamal ('father of Jamal') after the birth of his first son, Jamal. He has been married three times.

Abu-Jamal's first encounter with the police came when he was fourteen. He was beaten by a white Philadelphia police officer for disrupting a 'George Wallace for President' rally in 1968. Eventually, he dropped out of high school and joined the Philadelphia chapter of the Black Panther Party.

Jamal was appointed BPP's 'Lieutenant of Information', putting him in charge of the organization's media relations and placing him on the radar for surveillance by the Federal Bureau of Investigation (FBI). He eventually earned his graduate equivalency high school degree (GED) and briefly attended Goddard College in Vermont.

In 1975, Abu-Jamal began working for a series of radio stations, using his commentary on issues of the day to advocate for social change. Due to his growing popularity, he was elected president of the Philadelphia Association of Black Journalists. Despite his popularity, Abu-Jamal was forced to take a second job as a taxi driver to supplement his income.

Abu-Jamal became nationally prominent, however, then he was arrested for the murder of Philadelphia policeman, Daniel Faulkner. On December 9, 1981, Faulkner was shot and killed during a routine traffic stop involving Jamal's brother, William Cook. During the scuffle between Faulkner and Cook, Abu-Jamal also was shot and taken to Thomas Jefferson University Hospital.

He was treated and then arrested and charged with first-degree murder. In June 1982, Abu-Jamal was tried. Despite conflicting testimony from key witnesses, Abu-Jamal was found guilty and sentenced to death. In 1994, Abu-Jamal returned to radio once again as a commentator for Prison Radio and for National Public Radio. His NPR commentaries were compiled in 1995 as part of Live from Death Row, which resulted in Abu-Jamal's punishment of solitary confinement for engaging in entrepreneurship from prison.

In 1999, Arnold Beverly admitted that he and an unnamed assailant, not Abu-Jamal, had shot Faulkner as part of a contracted killing because the officer was interfering with graft and payoff to corrupt police. Soon afterwards some prosecutors' witnesses in the trial came forward and admitted that they lied under oath. Abu-Jamal and his supporters pressed for a new trial based on these recent developments.

On 27 March 2008, a three-judge panel issued a majority 2-1 opinion upholding that there were irregularities in his case. If the Commonwealth of Pennsylvania chooses not to hold a new hearing, Abu-Jamal will be automatically sentenced to life in prison. On 22 July 2008, Abu-Jamal's formal petition seeking reconsideration of the decision by the full Third Circuit panel of twelve judges was denied.

On 6 April 2009, the United States Supreme Court also refused to hear Abu-Jamal's appeal. On 19 January 2010, the Supreme Court ordered the appeals court to reconsider its decision to rescind the death penalty, with the same-constituted appeal panel duly convening in Philadelphia on 9 November 2010, to hear submissions for that purpose.

Abu-Jamal has been made an honorary citizen of about twenty-five cities around the world, including Paris, Montreal, Palermo and Copenhagen. In 2001, he received the sixth biennial Erich Muhsam Prize, which recognizes outstanding activism on behalf of a liberatory vision of human society in keeping with that of its anarchist namesake; in particular, most of its awardees have been activists in the cause of social justice for persecuted minorities.[106]

In October 2002, he was awarded honorary membership of the Berlin-based Association of Those Persecuted by the Nazi Regime—Federation of Antifascists and Antifascist Groups VVN-BDA. On 29 April 2006, a newly-paved road in the Parisian suburb of Saint-Denis was named Rue Mumia Abu-Jamal in his honor.

Ella Fitzgerald

Few artists stand as the very definition of the art they practice, but Ella Fitzgerald is one of them. No jazz singer can avoid being influenced by her, or at least taking into account the comprehensiveness of her work.

Fitzgerald didn't have the darkness of Billie Holiday, the bravura of Sarah Vaughan or the acidity of Carmen McRae, but what she did have was a effervescence, a childlike joy and a classic command of her craft that audiences connected with right away. Originally inspired by Connie Boswell, she also swung like mad, and was one of the few singers deeply respected by jazz instrumentalists. Her scat singing was flexible, creative and a sure crowd-pleaser.

Fitzgerald's career spanned sixty years. Born in Newport News, VA, on 25 April 1918, she broke into the music business by winning a 1934 talent show at Harlem's Apollo Theater, then she joined Chick Webb's driving band, becoming his featured singer at the Savoy Ballroom. In 1938, she had her first great hit, a novelty tune based on a nursery rhyme, *A Tisket A Tasket*, followed by *Undecided*, in 1939. When Webb died that year, Fitzgerald led the band until 1942, then started a solo career.

Beginning in 1946, she was the star vocal attraction on the fabled Jazz At The Philharmonic shows, organized by Norman Granz, who also became her manager. Fitzgerald's albums on Granz's labels (Verve, Pablo), beginning in 1956, led her to the popular 'songbook' projects, in which she devoted each set to an American songwriter, such as Duke Ellington, George Gershwin, Irving Berlin and Harold Arlen.

The albums widened her appeal, making her one of a handful of jazz musicians who became a household name in America, as well as helping to define, what is now referred to as, the Great American Songbook. Her duo albums with guitarist Joe Pass are among the greatest jazz recordings ever made.

Though she sang solidly in a swing-to-bop mode, Fitzgerald never seemed to go out of style, gathering fans from each succeeding generation. In the 1960s, she filled college auditoriums full of student rebels and appealed to lounge lizards in the 90s. Fitzgerald transitioned to the ancestral realm on 15 June 1996.

In 1979, Fitzgerald was elected by the Readers into the Down Beat Hall of Fame. She was one of the most decorated singers of all times.

Hannibal Barca

In 219 B.C., Hannibal Barca, perhaps the best known personality in Carthaginian history, seized Saguntum in Spain. Polybius, the Roman historian, reported that this breached an existing treaty and was interpreted by the Romans as a declaration of war. A year later, the second Punic War commenced. In May of that year, Hannibal raised an armed force of 90,000 men on foot and 12,000 men on horseback.

By the summer, they reached Rhone. However, they were now a much-reduced force of 50,000 soldiers, 9,000 horsemen, and 37 elephants. Celts and Gauls flocked to his standard, however, and increased their numbers. They hated Roman imperial rule and saw the Carthaginian campaign as a way of getting back at the Romans.

Hannibal's forces crossed the Alpine passes at the end of the year. This great general was to first to maneuver elephants across the alps.

From the north they marched on Italy, however. Penetrating deep into Italian territory, they seized Cann^ in 216 B.C., killing 70,000 Roman soldiers. Carthage, on the other hand, lost 5,500 soldiers and 200 horsemen in the same campaign. Next, they marched on Rome but were unable to breach the walls. They camped there for years.

Sir James Frazer, the author of *The Golden Bough* wrote, Hannibal "hung with his dusky army like a storm-cloud about to break, within sight of the sentinels of Rome." In 215 B.C., he sent two officers to Sicily to seduce the local rulers to break their loyalties to Rome.

The Romans, however, made inroads. By 210 B.C., they destroyed Carthage's new allies in Sicily and the following year, Scipio, the Roman general, commanded an invasion of Spain. A year later, the Roman army seized the gold and silver mines of that land which was the basis of Carthage's wealth. In around 206 B.C., a King of Numidia, an African state to the west of Carthage, changed alliances as Carthage began to lose.

Allying himself with Rome, he persuaded Scipio to bring the war to Africa. In 204 B.C., Scipio invaded Africa causing Hannibal and Mago, his brother, to leave Italy and return home. The Romans engaged them at the Battle of Zama in 202 B.C. Assisted by 10,000 horsemen, supplied by Numidia, the Romans triumphed. Scipio had planned for and frustrated Hannibal's secret weapon—the use of elephants.

The terms of the peace treaty of 201 B.C. were harsh. Carthage was obliged to return lands that once belonged to Numidia. They were forbidden to make war on any people without the consent of Rome. They were also forced to hand over their war elephants and not acquire others. Finally, they were forced to pay a huge reparation of 10,000 talents over fifty years. Following the treaty, Scipio had the Carthaginian fleet burned.

Carthage made some sort of recovery during this period with Hannibal still at the helm. "The business of that city was again as flourishing as it had ever been," a British historian said. "Again ships sailed to the coasts of Cornwall and Guinea; again the streets were lined with the workshops of industrious artisans."

The archaeological finds support the notion that the city recovered. Carthage even proposed to pay off the reparation due to Rome in 10 years. The Romans, however, refused. Eventually, the Romans demanded that the Carthaginians hand over Hannibal. Instead, he fled into exile in 196 B.C.

Before transitioning to the ancestral realm, he left behind a letter declaring, "Let us relieve the Romans from the anxiety they have so long experienced, since they think it tries their patience too much to wait for an old man's death." Hannibal transitioned in 181 B.C., but he was the most brilliant military strategist of all times, and up until today, the most leading edge military schools worldwide study his strategy of war as a model of brilliance.

May

Tehutimes, The Great

TehutiMes 3rd was the sixth King of the 18th Dynasty of Kamit (Ancient Egypt). His name in Metu Neter (Hieroglyphs) meant 'wisdom born' and his life was a testament of this axiom.

TehutiMes 3rd was a great ruler and it was during his reign that Kamit reached its most extraordinary heights occupying its greatest land mass. He ruled Kamit with great wisdom and unrivaled strategy for almost fifty-four years from 1479 B.C.E to 1425 B.C.E.

Being the only son of TehutiMes 2nd, TehutiMes 3rd took over the throne when his father transitioned. However, since he was too young to rule, his Stepmother HetShepsu-t was given regency over the empire. HetShepsu-t soon took over Kamit for herself and declared herself Shekhem Ur Shekhem (Pharaoh).

She had a very successful rulership and eventually transitioned to the ancestral realm. Upon her transition, TehutiMes 3rd took full control of Kamit and was declared king.

As King, TehutiMes used oracles to plan his military strategies. He consolidated all of Syria, except Phoenicia into the Kamitic Empire and enriched Kamit with great wealth and power. Over 350 cities fell to Kamit under TehutiMes 3rd's rule and this was shown on his stele. His numerous campaigns were very successful and it is clear that his strategies were studied by Europeans, such as Napoleon.

During his reign, he also led Kamit as far south as it had ever been since the migration from the source of the river Hapi (Nile). He reconnected Kamit with its source and bonded it with its Nubian fathers and mothers.

In architecture, he set about building two great Tekhens (obelisks) the Tekhen Waty which today has been stolen by Europeans and stands in Rome and TehutiMes' Tekhen. The Tekhen Waty was the tallest tekhen ever cut. He also commissioned architects to build the Tekhen of TehutiMes which today was also stolen and stands in Istanbul, Turkey formally known as Constantinople.

This great Shekhem Ur Shekhem (Pharaoh) was the archetype of a king for centuries after he passed in Kamit and the world over. He transitioned to the ancestral realm after fifty-four years of divine leadership and empowering governance. He was given full funerary rites and his sarcophagus entered into the valley of Kings with other great kings and queens from Kamit's glorious past.

Elijah Mccoy

Elijah McCoy was born on either 2 May 1843 in Colchester, Ontario. He was the third of twelve children. His parents were self-emancipated Afrikan-Americans from Kentucky who had escaped via the Underground Railroad.

When McCoy was a child, his family returned across the border, settling near Ypsilanti, Michigan, where his father worked in the logging industry. As a boy, Elijah showed exceptional mechanical abilities. At the age of fifteen, his parents decided to send him to Edinburgh, Scotland, to pursue a Mechanical Engineering apprenticeship. This was at a time when it was difficult for blacks to obtain the same kind of training in the United States of America.

On his return to the United States, McCoy realized that as qualified as he was, he could not get a job as a mechanical engineer. The only type of job he could get was as a fire or oil man. The oil man job led him to become interested in the problems of lubricating machinery that were in motion. He perfected a method for over two years to steadily supply oil to machinery in intermittent drops from a cup.

McCoy eliminated the process of shutting down machinery to lubricate them. Little did he know at that time that his name would one day become synonymous with perfection.

During his lifetime, Elijah McCoy was awarded over fifty-seven patents. He was known throughout the world. His inventions were used on engines, train locomotives, on Great Lake steam ships, on ocean liners and on machinery in factories. He patented inventions in France, Austria, Germany, Great Britain, Russia, Canada and the United States.

The expression 'The Real McCoy' probably sounds familiar. Machine buyers used to insist on getting the real McCoy. They would not accept anything else but the inventions of McCoy. Hence, they wanted the real McCoy. To this day, McCoy's name is still associated with authenticity.

Because of his inventions, Elijah McCoy became mechanical consultant to several firms, including the Detroit Lubricating Company. Many were not aware of his race and were often surprised that to see that this so-called genius was an Afrikan. He faced racial prejudice and there were times when his scheduled appearances were canceled at the last moment.

McCoy left many legacies. Most of his inventions were in the field of automatic lubrication but his genius even went further, and he made inventions such as the Ironing Table and a Lawn Sprinkler. Today, his lubrication processes are used in machinery such as cars, locomotives, ships, rockets and many other machinery. He is credited with having helped modernize the industrial world with his inventions.

Elijah McCoy transitioned to the ancestral realm in Detroit in 1929 at the age of eighty-six, still suffering from injuries from a car accident seven years earlier that killed his second wife.

Abraha

‘Abraha (Ge’ez: ‘Abreha) also known as ‘Abraha al-Asram or Abraha b. as-Saba’h, was an Aksumite Christian ruler Abyssinia (Ethiopia). He was a proud Afrikan from modern day Ethiopia, ‘Abraha also seized control of Yemen from Esimiphaeus, the Christian Himyarite viceroy appointed by Kaleb, his superior king, with the support of dissident elements in the Ethiopian occupation force eager to settle in the Yemen, then a rich and fertile land.

‘Abraha seized power, establishing himself at Sana’a and proclaiming Christianity. He aroused the wrath of Kaleb, however, by withholding tribute and Kaleb sent his general, ‘Ariat, once again to take over the governorship of Yemen. ‘Abraha rid himself of the latter by a strategic move in a duel in which ‘Ariat was killed and ‘Abraha suffered the injury which earned him the nickname of al-Asram, ‘scar-face’.

After this, Kaleb had to accord him recognition. ‘Abraha’s rule was confirmed by Kaleb successor, Emperor Beta-’Esra’el, in return for a tribute and he went on to become an outstanding figure in Yemeni history, ruling efficiently and promoting the cause of Christianity in the face of the Judaism prevalent in Yemen and the pre-Islamic religions of Central Arabia.

Abraha also led an expedition against Mecca. At this period, Mecca was the thriving center of the pre-Islamic religion of the Ka'aba and the pilgrim traffic was in the hands of the powerful Qurays family. Fired with Christian zeal, 'Abraha set out to build a magnificent church at Sana'a to serve as a counter-attraction to the surrounding pre-Islamic peoples. This aroused the hostility of the Qurays who feared that the pilgrim traffic with its rich offerings would be moved to Sana'a.

It is sometimes said that one of their followers succeeded in defiling the church and this led 'Abraha to embark upon a campaign against Mecca. This event is associated in Islamic tradition with the year of the Prophet's birth, c. 570 A.D. 'Abraha is said to have used elephants in the campaign and the date is celebrated as the Year of the Elephant, 'am al fil'. An indirect reference to the event is found in Surah 105 of the Quran.

'Abraha's expedition probably failed due to the successful delaying tactics of the Qurays and sickness that broke out in the camp, which killed most of his army and forced him to withdraw Abraha also had an inscription on the Marib Dam in Yemen on which he did major repairs. He received envoys of Kings from Byzantium, from Persia and from Harith.

Abraha's rule was a period of prosperity and security in Ethiopia. The royal title adopted by 'Abraha is similar to that of his immediate predecessors and to that of Emperor Kaleb, 'King of Saba'.

The date of 'Abraha's transition to the ancestral realm was immediately after his expedition to Mecca. He was succeeded on the throne by two of his sons, Yaksum and Masruq, born to him by Raihana, a Abyssinian noblewoman whom 'Abraha had wed. Abraha was one of the most reputed rulers of his time.

Martin Delany

(Born 6 May 1812, Charles Town, Virginia, U.S.—died 24 January 1885, Xenia, Ohio), African-American abolitionist, physician, and editor in the pre-Civil War period; his espousal of black nationalism and racial pride brought forward expressions of such views a century later.

In search of quality education for their children, the Delanys were a family descended from Afrikan royalty. They moved to Pennsylvania when Martin was a child. At nineteen, while studying nights at an Afrikan-American church, he worked days in Pittsburgh. Embarking on a course of militant opposition to slavery, he became involved in several racial improvement groups.

Under the tutelage of two sympathetic physicians, he achieved competence as a doctor's assistant as well as in dental care, working in this capacity in the South and Southwest (1839).

Returning to Pittsburgh, Delany started a weekly newspaper, *the Mystery*, which publicized grievances of blacks in the United States and also championed women's rights. The paper won an excellent reputation, and its articles were often reprinted in the white press. From 1846 to 1849, he worked in partnership with the abolitionist leader Frederick Douglass in Rochester, New York, where they published another weekly, *the North Star*.

After three years, Delany decided to pursue formal medical studies; he was one of the first blacks to be admitted to Harvard Medical School and became a leading Pittsburgh physician.

In the 1850s, Delany developed an overriding interest in foreign colonization opportunities for Afrikan-Americans, and in 1859–60, he led an exploration party to West Africa to investigate the Niger Delta as a location for settlement.

In protest against oppressive conditions in the United States, Delany moved in 1856 to Canada, where he continued his medical practice. At the beginning of the Civil War (1861–65), he returned to the United States and helped recruit troops for the famous 54th Massachusetts Volunteers, for which he served as a surgeon.

To counter a desperate Southern scheme to impress its enslaved Afrikans into the military forces late in the war, in February 1865, Delany was made a major (the first black man to receive a regular army commission and be an officer in the U.S. army) and was assigned to Hilton Head Island, South Carolina, to recruit and organize former slaves for the North. When peace came in April, he became an official in the Freedmen's Bureau, serving for the next two years.

In 1873, Delany became a customs inspector in Charleston and was an active supporter of the Liberian Exodus Joint Stock Exchange Company, an organization which arranged the transport of emigrants to Liberia. In 1874, Delany ran unsuccessfully for lieutenant governor as an Independent Republican in South Carolina; thereafter his fortunes declined. He was the author of many books.

Martin Robinson Delany transitioned to the ancestral realm in Wilberforce, Ohio, on 24 January 1885. He was an Afrikan pioneer who stayed true to his dignified royal lineage.

Queen Kahina

In 639 A.D., a new conquering force swept into Africa. The Arabians seized Egypt, Cyrenaica, Tripoli, and pushed on to Carthage and Numidia. The invasion swept away 600 years of Roman occupation.

The new conquerors spread Islam from Egypt to Morocco and also into Spain. The Spanish conquest was achieved with Afrikan help. The invaders also destroyed many Afrikans, enslaved many, and caused others to flee further south to evade their clutches. Kuseila of Mauritania resisted but he was defeated and killed in 688 A.D. Dahia al-Kahina (cf) became leader of the Afrikan resistance. She followed the old Carthaginian religion.

This differs from Judaism but also shares some affinities with it. There are, of course, Afrikan Jews in many parts of Africa such as the Falasha of Ethiopia and the Lemba of South Africa. Arab records describe her as having 'dark skin, a mass of hair and huge eyes'—the comment referring to her hair may refer to an afro or perhaps dreadlocks.

Dr. John Clarke describes her as a nationalist who favored no particular religion. This may explain her effectiveness in bringing together a united front against the invaders.

She counterattacked the invaders and drove them into Tripolitania. This was so effective that some Arabs doubted whether Afrika could be taken. As one Afrikan army was beaten, another replaced them. The Arabs seized Carthage in 698 A.D. Dahia defeated them and instituted a scorched earth policy to prevent the Arabs from being able to find crops to feed on in the region. That desolation can be seen even today in southern Tunisia.

Eventually, however, the Arabs returned. Dahia was finally defeated in battle in 705 A.D. North Africa was overrun. Today, Black people are a large minority in North Africa, with most of the population being of mixed white and black ancestry.

Kahina demonstrated a great strength of conviction and she was never defeated, and never let anyone force her to change her religion and beliefs. She is a great hero to this day in Northern Africa and around the world.

King Narmer

Narmer was the first king of the First Dynasty of Kamit (Ancient Egypt) in about 3200 B.C.E. It was due to his wise ways that Kamit united. Upper Kamit in the south and Lower Kamit in the north had always been separated, and prior to Narmer, they had been ruled by a lineage of Kings called the Scorpion Kings.

Narmer knew in order to have a great civilization that the brothers and sisters of Upper and Lower Kamit would have to come together, therefore he sought the hand of Neith-Hotep, a princess of Lower Kamit, in order for this union to occur. Once the union was allowed, being a King from Upper Kamit, this meant that the lineages of both Lower and Upper Kamit where now one. Due to this, both of the regions came together without any need of war, but due to family relationships.

Narmer, whose secondary name was Menes, went on to be the first ruler of ancient Kamit, setting an example of leadership that was modeled by rulers after him. He was a pious man that sought wisdom from the sages, and his elders and with his wife, they showed themselves to be very family-oriented. Being the first king to unite the two lands enabled him to be the first king to wear both the White Crown of Upper Egypt (looks like a bowling pin), and the Red Crown of Lower Egypt.

His rule marked the beginning of written history and the era of dynasties, which followed in succession until the 30th Dynasty. It was during his reign that Metu Neter (Hieroglyphics) were devised and Egypt commenced its pyramid building following in the tradition of Nubia. He established an army and a fleet with distinctive banners.

After his great divine work had been done, Narmer peacefully transitioned to the ancestral realm leaving his son, Heru-AA, to rule Kamit. His name was left on an ancient Kamitic Palette that testified to us of the true greatness of this father of ours, who was also a father of the greatest civilization humanity has ever seen.

Ahhotep

Ahhotep was a great Queen of Kamit's 17th Dynasty. Her name meant that "peace is great" and she was a testimony to this as she lived a life in which inner peace was highly revered and valued most.

Like her mother, Tetisheri, and daughter, Ahmose-Nefertari, she was long revered as one of the ancestors of the 18th Dynasty. When her husband, King Seqenenre Tao, was killed on the battlefield while fighting the Hyksos, the relatively unknown Kamose succeeded him for an undetermined number of years.

After the latter's death, Ahmose was proclaimed king. Ahmose was a son of Queen Ahhotep and King Seqenenre Tao. Too young to undertake the full responsibilities of kingship, Ahmose was supported by Ahhotep as acting regent until he reached maturity. An inscription on a doorway at the Nubian fortress of Buhen links the cartouches of Queen Ahhotep and King Ahmose, implying such a co-regency.

Given the troubled nature of this period, the Queen-Regent played an active military role. This is confirmed in a stela, raised by King Ahmose in his 18th regnal year at the temple of Amun at Karnak, in which he praises her part in the safe-keeping of Egypt. The king describes Queen Ahhotep as:

"She is one who has accomplished the rites and taken care of Egypt; she has looked after her soldiers; she has brought back her fugitives and collected together her deserters; she has pacified Upper Egypt and expelled her rebels." In the same text, she is described as King's Daughter, King's Mother, and intriguingly as 'mistress of the land' and 'mistress of Haw-nbwt' as well.

While 'Haw-nbwt' is often translated as 'the shores of distant lands'. Queen Ahhotep was the first royal lady to hold the important function of 'God's Wife'.

Queen Ahhotep apparently ceded pride of place to her daughter, Ahmose-Nefertari, around the time when the Donation Stela was raised. She lived to see (her grandson) Amenhotep I become king. The Queen was rewarded with divine honors, and a long-surviving cult was established in her memory.

Her last resting place was discovered in 1859 by an excavation team working for Auguste Mariette at Dra Abu el-Naga. Sadly enough, its exact location is no longer known. In her tomb was an exclusive retinue of weapons.

The discovered weaponry would tend to further underline the military role Ahhotep fulfilled while being the country's Queen Regent, although the presence of military equipment in a royal lady's tomb outfit was not exceptional during the period of transition between the 17th and 18th Dynasties. Her life was testimony to the strength of conviction and the value of a great woman.

William Grant Still

Long known as the 'Dean of American Negro Composers', as well as one of America's foremost composers, William Grant Still has had the distinction of becoming a living legend. On 11 May 1895, he was born in Woodville (Wilkinson County) Mississippi, to parents who were teachers and musicians. They were of Afrikan, Native-American, Spanish, Irish and Scotch bloods.

When William was only a few months old, his father died and his mother took him to Little Rock, Arkansas, where she taught English in the high school. There his musical education began—with violin lessons from a private teacher, and with later inspiration from the Red Seal operatic recordings bought for him by his stepfather.

In Wilberforce University, he took courses leading to a B.S. degree, but spent most of his time conducting the band, learning to play the various instruments involved and making his initial attempts to compose and to orchestrate. His subsequent studies at the Oberlin Conservatory of Music were financed at first by a legacy from his father, and later, by a scholarship established just for him by the faculty.

At the end of his college years, he entered the world of commercial (popular) music, playing in orchestras and orchestrating, working in particular with the violin, cello and oboe. His employers included W. C. Handy, Don Voorhees, Sophie Tucker, Paul Whiteman, Willard Robison and Artie Shaw, and for several years he arranged and conducted the Deep River Hour over CBS and WOR.

While in Boston playing oboe in the Shuffle Along orchestra, Still applied to study at the New England Conservatory with George Chadwick, and was again rewarded with a scholarship due to Mr. Chadwick's own vision and generosity. He also studied, again on an individual scholarship, with the noted ultra-modern composer, Edgard Varese.

In the 20s, Still made his first appearances as a serious composer in New York, and began a valued friendship with Dr. Howard Hanson of Rochester. Extended Guggenheim and Rosenwald Fellowships were given to him, as well as important commissions from the Columbia Broadcasting System, the New York World's Fair 1939–40, Paul Whiteman, the League of Composers, the Cleveland Orchestra, the Southern Conference Educational Fund and the American Accordionists Association.

In 1944, he won the Jubilee prize of the Cincinnati Symphony Orchestra for the best Overture to celebrate its Jubilee season, with a work called Festive Overture. In 1953, a Freedoms Foundation Award came to him for his To You, America! Which honored West Points Sesquicentennial Celebration. In 1961, he received the prize offered by the U.S. Committee for the U.N., the N.F.M.C. and the Aeolian Music Foundation for his orchestral work, The Peaceful Land, cited as the best musical composition.

After moving to Los Angeles in the early 1930s, citations from numerous organizations, local and elsewhere in the United States, came to the composer.

Along with them came honorary degrees like the following: Master of Music from Wilberforce in 1936; Doctor of Music from Howard University in 1941; Doctor of Music from Oberlin College in 1947; Doctor of Letters from Bates College in 1954; Doctor of Laws from the University of Arkansas in 1971; Doctor of Fine Arts from Pepperdine University in 1973; Doctor of Music from the New England Conservatory of Music, the Peabody Conservatory and the University of Southern California.

Some of the awards that Still received were: the second Harmon Award in 1927; a trophy of honor from Local 767 of the Musicians Union A.F. of M., of which he was a member; trophies from the League of Allied Arts in Los Angeles (1965) and the National Association of Negro Musicians; citations from the Los Angeles City Council and Los Angeles Board of Supervisors (1963); a trophy from the A.P.P.A. in Washington D.C. (1968); the Phi Beta Sigma George Washington Carver Award (1953); the Richard Henry Lee Patriotism Award from Knotts Berry Farm, California.

Also, a citation from the Governor of Arkansas in 1972; the third annual prize of the Mississippi Institute of Arts and Letters in 1982. He also lectured in various universities from time to time.

In 1939, Still married journalist and concert pianist, Verna Arvey, who became his principal collaborator. They remained together until Still transitioned to the ancestral realm of heart failure on 3 December 1978. ASCAP took care of all of Dr. Stills hospitalization until his transition.

Dr. Still's service to the cause of brotherhood is evidenced by his many firsts in the musical realm: Still was the first Afro-American in the United States to have a symphony performed by a major symphony orchestra. He was the first to conduct a major symphony orchestra in the United States, when in 1936, he directed the Los Angeles Philharmonic Orchestra in his compositions at the Hollywood Bowl.

He was the first Afro-American to conduct a major symphony orchestra in the Deep South in 1955, when he directed the New Orleans Philharmonic at Southern University. He was the first of his race to conduct a White radio orchestra in New York City. He was the first to have an opera produced by a major company in the United States, when in 1949, his Troubled Island was done at the City Center of Music and Drama in New York City. He was the first to have an opera televised over a national network.

With these firsts, Still was a pioneer, but, in a larger sense, he pioneered because he was able to create music capable of interesting the greatest conductors of the day: truly serious music, but with a definite American. Still wrote over hundred and fifty compositions (well over two hundred if his lost early works could be counted), including operas, ballets, symphonies, chamber works, and arrangements of folk themes, especially Negro spirituals, plus instrumental, choral and solo vocal works.

Auset-Nefer-T (Isetnofret)

Queen Auset-Nefer-t was a principle wife of Ramses the great, who was the ruler that ruled Kamit (Ancient Egypt) for the second longest period of time. Her name meant beautiful mothering and her life went far in proving her names meaning. During her reign, Kamit was the most marvelous of all the civilizations on Earth and it was during this time that it reached its zenith.

She lived during the Golden Age of the Golden Age of Kamit and was dearly loved by her husband and family. She gave birth to the heir to the throne of Kamit. Isetnofret gave birth to at least four children. Her eldest son, Ramesses, was named after his father and great-grandfather.

Ramesses rose to the rank of Generalissimo in the Egyptian army, and after the death of his older half-brother, became crown prince of Egypt. Isetnofret's second son, Khaemwaset, served in the army for a short time, but he is most famous for the work he did as a priest. Khaemwaset first became a semi-priest of Ptah in Memphis. In this capacity, he officiated at some of the burials of the Apis bulls.

Later, he became the High Priest of Ptah in Memphis and after the transition of his brother, Ramesses, he served as crown-prince for five years. Isetnofret's third son, Merenptah, also a significant figure in Egypt. He was destined to become the next Pharaoh. Isetnofret's daughter, Bint-Anath, became a great royal wife in the year 25 of her father's reign. This daughter became an important lady at the royal court.

Isnofret transitioned to the ancestral realm peacefully, and even though it was never known where she was buried, her value as queen and mother were always remembered and treasured.

Mary Seacole

Mary Seacole was a Jamaican nurse who treated sick and injured soldiers during the Crimean War. Mary Seacole was born Mary Jane Grant in Kingston Jamaica on 14 May 1805 (At that time Jamaica was part of the British Empire). Her mother was of Afrikan descent and her father was a white Scottish soldier in the British army.

Her mother ran a boarding house for army officers and their families. Mary's mother made her own medicines and Mary learned from her.

Twice, when she was a teenager, Mary visited London. Then in 1836, she married Edwin Horatio Seacole. Unfortunately, he soon died. Afterward, Mary ran a boarding house. In 1850, she treated people in Kingston suffering from cholera. She then went to Panama to help her brother run a hotel. She helped sick people there too. However, Mary eventually returned to Jamaica.

In 1854, war began between Britain and Russia, and British force was sent to Crimea. Mary sailed to England and volunteered to go to Crimea as a nurse but she was told she was not needed due to racism. However, Mary Seacole was not so easily put off. She traveled to Crimea herself in 1855.

To support herself, Mary ran a boarding house called the British Hotel. She also sold provisions and when she was not working there Mary worked tirelessly treating sick and injured soldiers. They called her Mother Seacole. When the war ended in 1856, Mary returned to England. In 1857, she wrote a book called *Wonderful Adventures of Mrs. Seacole*.

Mary Seacole transitioned to the ancestral realm on 14 May 1881 at Paddington, London. She was buried in Kensal Green cemetery.

In 1991, Mary Seacole was awarded the Jamaican Order of Merit. She was a great example of devotion, care and mothering.

Hampate Ba

Amadou Ba Hampate is a Malian writer and ethnologist, born in Bandiagara (Mali) in 1900 (or 1901), and died 15 May 1991 in Abidjan (Cote d'Ivoire).

Amadou Hampate Ba was born in May 1900 or 1901 in Bandiagara, capital of the Dogon country and former capital of the Empire of Macina Toucouleur. Hampate Ba was a descendant of a noble Fulani family. After the death of his father, he was adopted by the second husband of his mother, Amadou Ali Thiam Tidjani, a man from the Toucouleur ethnic group.

He first attended Koranic School of Tierno Bokar, and became a dignitary of the brotherhood tidjaniyya before being commandeered to act for the French school Djenne in Bandiagara then. In 1915, he ran away to join his mother, Kati, where he resumed his studies. In 1921, he refused to enter the Normal School in Goree.

As punishment, the governor assigned him to Ouagadougou, as a 'temporary writer'. From 1922 to 1932, he held various positions in the colonial administration in Upper Volta (now Burkina Faso) and until 1942 in Bamako. In 1933, he obtained a leave of six months that he spent with Tierno Bokar, his spiritual leader.

In 1942, he was posted at the French Institute of Black Africa (IFAN) in Dakar. He conducted professional comprehensive research at this time and collected oral traditions. He then devoted fifteen years to research on oral traditions in West Africa that lead him to write the Fulani empire of Macina. In 1951, he was awarded a UNESCO fellowship enabling him to travel to Paris and meet the Afrikanist community, including Marcel Griaule.

In 1960, Mali got its independence from the imperialist French and Hampate Ba founded the Institute for Human Sciences in Bamako and represented his country at the General Conference of UNESCO. In 1962, he was elected to the Executive Board of UNESCO. In 1966, he participated in the development of a unified system for the transcription of Afrikan languages.

In 1970, his term expired at UNESCO. After this, Amadou Ba Hampate devoted himself entirely to his research and writing. In the last years of his life, he went to Abidjan to classify its records accumulated during his life on the oral traditions of West Afrika as well as writing his memoirs, *Amkoullel child Fulani Yes sir!*, which was published after his transition to the ancestral realm on 15 May 1991.

His life was a true testimony of the greatness of the Afrikan storytelling traditions of which he was a standard-bearer.

Senmut

Senmut was a Kamitic (Ancient Egyptian) architect and government official who lived during the era of the 18th Dynasty in Kamit. He was a polymath who had multiple talents, and he used his talents to manifest his great genius.

Senmut was the son of Kamitic intellectuals in the persons of Ramose and Hatnofret. His name actually meant 'the healer of the great mother' and this was perfectly in line with his destiny. Initially, during the reign of TehutiMes 2nd, Senmut was given the title of Steward of the God's Wife and also the title of Steward of the King's Daughter.

As an owner of this title, he was a close associate of Hatshepsut, teaching her the way of the world and also cosmology and leadership skills. Due to his great work in this position, he became highly trusted by Hatshepsut and he was her confidante.

When TehutiMes 2nd transitioned, Hatshepsut was given regency over Kamit and eventually went on to become its full ruler, Shekhem Ur Shekhem

(King). She took unto herself the title of king and Senmut was her vizier (prime minister) and architect. Senenmut supervised the quarrying, transport, and building of twin Takhnes (obelisks), at the time the tallest in the world, at the entrance to the Temple of Karnak.

One still stands today; the other broke in two and toppled centuries ago. Karnak's Red Chapel, or Chapelle Rouge, was intended as a barque shrine and originally stood between the two obelisks. Senmut also built the Djeseru-Djeseru Temple for Hatshepsut in 'The Valley of The Kings'.

He defended the honor of his queen at any extent, and did all that was possible to construct great monuments that testified to her great rule as the first female absolute ruler of Kamit. Being advanced in age, Senmut transitioned to the ancestral realm peacefully in the late 'our story' as one of the greatest architects of all time.

Sebekneferu

Sebekneferu was a Kamitic Shekhem Ur Shekhem (Pharaoh) of the 12th Dynasty. Her name virtually meant that 'intelligence is beautiful' and her life was a testament to this saying. She was the daughter of Amennemhat III. Her family life was great, but her parents did not have any male children, therefore at their transition her sister, NefruPtah, was meant to take over. However, she transitioned at an early age and therefore, Sebekneferu who was next in line for the double crown of Kamit and took over as ruler.

When she took over, she was one of the first female absolute rulers of Kamit and she ruled with great dignity and pride. During her reign, the river Hapi (Nile) that usually flooded Kamit, flooded Kamit at a height of 1.83 meters. This was a testament that she initiated a great era of renewal in the destiny of Kamit.

She oversaw a period of great prosperity in the 'our story' of Kamit in which Kamit was the light of the world and was a high site of civilization, learning and architecture. As a woman, she was highly respected since Kamitic culture was matriarchal.

She transitioned peacefully after four years of sound governance and the end of her rule spelled the end of the 12th Dynasty in Kamit. Since she had no heirs, what followed was an era of relative instability in Kamit. Nevertheless, this woman will go down in history as one of the first female monarchs to effectively rule the greatest empire of her times.

Bhambatha

Bambata or Bambatha kaMancinza (ca. 1860–1906), also known as Mbata. Bhambatha, was a Zulu chief of the amaZondi clan in the Colony of Natal in modern day South Africa.

He was the eldest son of Cheif Mancinza. He is famous for his role in an armed rebellion in 1906 when the poll tax was raised from a tax per hut to per head (£1 tax on all native men older than eighteen) increasing popular hardship during a severe economic depression.

In 1906, the British colonialists in Zululand imposed an unfair poll tax on the Zulu. Some Zulu chiefs accepted this tax and acted as tax-collectors for the greedy British, but being the caretaker of his people's welfare, Bambata refused to impose this tax on his people and openly defied the British exploiters.

The Natal Police believed Bambata was going to resist the tax with force and sent about hundred and fifty men to arrest him. Instead, the police were ambushed and four policemen killed. Thousands of colonial troops were then sent after him, including cavalry and heavy artillery, leading to 3,500 innocent people being killed by the British. Bambata continued to struggle with his people, refusing to give in.

His struggle was protracted and reached the scale of a full out war. Many battles were fought with Bambata being victorious occasionally. At the apex of the struggle, Bambata faced the British in the Battle of Mome Gorge. Being outnumbered and overpowered by the sophisticated technology of the British, Bambata fought bravely and fell in battle.

He transitioned to the ancestral realm without ever having given up. He is often credited as an inspiration to native South African resistance and as a precursor of the anti-apartheid movement.

Malcolm X

"We're not Americans, we're Africans who happen to be in America. We were kidnapped and brought here against our will from Africa. We didn't land on Plymouth Rock—that rock landed on us."

Malcolm X was born Malcolm Little in Omaha, Nebraska, on 19 May 1925. His father, Earl, a Baptist minister and follower of the black nationalist Marcus Garvey, was under continuous threat by the Ku Klux Klan. The family moved to Lansing, Michigan, where their house was burned by white racists in 1929, and in 1931, Earl was murdered. Malcolm's mother had a nervous breakdown and the eight children were sent to various foster homes.

The top student and only black in his eighth grade class, Malcolm dropped out of school after his teacher told him that a 'nigger' could never become a lawyer—his dream. He went to Boston to live with his sister, Ella, and turned to crime. He became a street hustler and in 1946, he was arrested and sentenced to ten years.

While in prison, though, he began a period of education and self-transformation. He joined the Nation of Islam, a black nationalist group headed by Elijah Muhammad. He took 'X' as his last name, signifying his unknown Afrikan tribal name that had been lost when his family was given the enslaved name 'Little'.

After his parole in 1952, Malcolm X became a brilliant and charismatic speaker, building the Nation of Islam from 400 to 30,000 members. In 1964, Malcolm broke with the Nation and formed the Organization of Afro-American Unity. Journeying to Mecca, the holiest of Muslim shrines, he took the name El-Hajj Malik El-Shabazz, and began speaking of international black consciousness. His change of views targeted him for assassination by some members of the Nation of Islam.

While preparing to speak in a Harlem ballroom on 21 February 1965, Malcolm X was shot and killed by three assassins from the Nation of Islam. It is still unclear what role the FBI, which had Malcolm X under surveillance, may have played in his transition.

Historians consider Malcolm X among the half-dozen most influential Afrikan-American leaders in history. His book, *The Autobiography of Malcolm X*, written with Alex Haley and published posthumously, is considered one of the most important non-fiction books of the 20th century. Many black people felt that Malcolm X, by voicing the truth of their frustration and anger, gave them courage and self-respect.

He told Afrikan-Americans that they had to stop defining themselves as whites had defined them in terms of subservience and inferiority. His message was strength and pride and truth.

Toussaint De Louverture

Toussaint Louverture, the great Haitian Hero and leader of the Black Jacobins. He was born on 20 May 1743. Toussaint Louverture is considered the father of Haiti. Inspired by the French Revolution, the gens de couleur pressed the colonial government for expanded rights. In October 1790, 350 revolted against the government.

On 15 May 1791, the French National Assembly granted political rights to all blacks and mulattoes who had been born free—but did not change the status quo regarding enslavement. On 22 August 1791, abducted Afrikans in the north rose initially at Bois-Caiman against their masters near Cap-Frangais (now Cap-Haitien). This revolution spread rapidly and came under the leadership of Toussaint Louverture.

He soon formed alliances with the gens de couleur and the maroons, whose rights had been revoked by the French government in retaliation for the uprising. Toussaint's armies defeated the French colonial army, but then joined forces with it in 1794, following a decree by the revolutionary French government that abolished slavery. Under Toussaint's command, the Saint-Domingue army then defeated invading Spanish and British forces.

This cooperation between Toussaint and French forces ended in 1802, however when Napoleon sent a new invasion force designed to subdue the colony, many islanders suspected the army would also re-impose slavery. Napoleon's forces initially were successful at fighting their way onto the island, and persuaded Toussaint to a truce. He was then betrayed, captured and transitioned to the ancestral realm in a French prison of pneumonia in 1803, but his spirit forever animated his brave people.

Jean-Jacques Dessalines and Henri Christophe, leaders of separate military factions, resumed the rebellion. Napoleon's forces were defeated by Dessalines at the Battle of Vertieres on 18 November 1803. On 1 January 1804, the nation declared its independence, securing its position as the second independent country in the New World, and the only successful slave rebellion in world history, led by a great general who even in death lived on.

Eugene Chen

Eugene Chen, four times foreign minister of Chinese government and one of the most dynamic political figures of the 20th century, was born of Afrikan-Chinese-Spanish parentage in British West Indies. His family name was Akam. Educating for the law in England, he then returned to Trinidad where but because of minor disagreements with the island he decided to cast his lot with the Chinese and left for where he became legal adviser to the Ministry of Communications in 1912.

Two years later, he founded The Peking Gazette, and being a polemist and fighter who knew but one tactic, a vigorous attack, he selected as his chief target the strongest foe possible: the North China Daily News, chief spokesman of British interests in the Far East, the defender of capital, and the prestige and power Britain had built up in that region.

At that commerce was centered in Shanghai, then a so-called settlement, but this commerce was chiefly for Britain's to some extent that of Japan, then an ally of financial power was centered in the British Hong Kong Bank. As a result of his onslaughts, Chen was arrested in 1916 and thrown into a narrow cell with five lice-covered wall. However, because he was still a British subject and because extraterritoriality yet existed in China, he asserted that he was being illegally held and was released, apparently because of this, in 1917.

Undaunted, he now entered the enemy's stronghold, Shanghai, where he joined Dr. Sun Yat-sen, founder of Nationalist China, and became his personal adviser and private secretary, a position he held until Sun Yat-sen's death in 1925. He also founded The Shanghai Gazette, in which he renewed his attacks on British interests and was again thrown into prison, but was later freed.

In 1919, he was a delegate to the Versailles Conference where he formulated China's demands in clear, unmistakable terms. He demanded, among other things, the abolition of concession territories, insisting that all such be placed under a mixed Chinese and foreign administration with Chinese predominant. This demand later paved the way for China's victory over the extraterritorial powers formerly held by the white governments.

In 1922, he founded the Ming Pao, or People's Tribune, and became chief adviser to the Southern Government of China. In an effort to build up Chinese commerce, not for the benefit of the whites and the Japanese, but the Chinese, he led a strike and a boycott principally against British interests. He asked the Chinese not to speak English and not to use English ships nor to buy and sell British-made goods.

This had such effect that in 1926, the British yielded and asked for a conference, in which most of Chen's demands were granted and out of which came the Chen-O'Malley Agreement in which Britain returned to China the rich port of Hankow.

In 1927, while foreign minister, he was instrumental in preventing war between China on one hand and Britain and the United States on the other. White people had been mobbed by the Chinese in Nanking and from southern China had come terrible rumors of the violation of white women. The result was a great outcry for military intervention and the world "stood at the eve of a war in which the Russian-Asiatic and the capitalistic-western powers would clash."

President Coolidge had already dispatched American marines to the scene, but Chen stepped into the breach and in an eloquent note to the white powers expressed China's willingness for peace. He said that he was willing to have the disturbances thoroughly investigated, asking only that the verdict, whether it be for or against China, be just. This frankness had such an effect on President Coolidge that he recalled the marines, and in a public address, declared for peace to the great discontent of the interests who wanted war in order to gain greater power in China.

The same year, however, due largely to European intrigue, there was a split between the Nanking and the Wuhan governments, and Chen retired to France, but returned in 1931 to become foreign minister of the Canton Government. While in China, Chen married Miss Chang Tsing-ying, daughter of Chang Chen-kiang, head of the Cheking Provincial Government.

The New York Times in its obituary of Chen (21 May 1944) says:

"Eugene Chen, British-born Chinese publisher and politician, was four times foreign minister in various Chinese governments and twice was a refugee when his political fortunes were at low ebb. When Chiang Kai-shek was friendly with the Soviet Union, Mr. Chen was Foreign Minister of the Russian-dominated Hankow Government, unofficially run by Borodin and Bluecher."

"In 1927, after the collapse of the Hankow Government, Mr. Chen fled to Russia when Borodin staged his famous 'retreat across the Gobi Desert', and with him went other Chinese leaders with left-wing tendencies. He transitioned to the ancestral realm one year before the start of World War II, having helped China began a strong diplomatic force."

Samuel Sharpe

Samuel Sharpe was the main instigator of the 1831 Freedom Rebellion, which began on the Kensington Estate in St. James and which was largely instrumental in bringing about the abolition of slavery.

Because of his intelligence and leadership qualities, Sam Sharpe became a 'daddy', or leader of the native Baptists in Montego Bay. Religious meetings were the only permissible forms of organized activities for the enslaved Afrikans. Sam Sharpe was able to communicate his concern and encourage political thought, concerning events in England which affected the slaves and Jamaica.

Sam evolved a plan of passive resistance in 1831, by which the slaves would refuse to work on Christmas Day of 1831, and afterwards, unless their grievances concerning better treatment and the consideration of freedom, were accepted by the state owners and managers.

Sam explained his plan to his chosen supporters after his religious meetings and made them kiss the Bible to show their loyalty. They, in turn, took the plan to the other parishes until the idea had spread throughout St. James, Trelawny, Westmoreland, and even St. Elizabeth and Manchester.

Word of the plan reached the ears of some of the planters. Troops were sent into St. James and warships were anchored in Montego Bay and Black River, with their guns trained on the towns.

On 27 December 1831, the Kensington Estate Great House was set on fire, as a signal that the Slave Rebellion had begun. A series of other fires broke out in the area and soon it was clear that the plan of non-violent resistance, which Sam Sharpe had originated, was impossible and impractical.

Armed rebellion and seizing of property spread mostly through the western parishes, but the uprising was put down by the first week in January.

A terrible retribution followed. While fourteen whites died during the Rebellion, more than five hundred enslaved Afrikans lost their lives—most of them as a result of the trials after.

Samuel Sharpe was hanged on 23 May 1832. In 1834, the Abolition Bill was passed by the British Parliament, and in 1838, slavery was abolished.

Sharpe had said: “I would rather die upon yonder gallows than live enslaved.”

Betty Shabazz

(Born 28 May 1936, Detroit, Mich., U.S.—died 23 June 1997, Bronx, N.Y.)

Born Betty Dean Sanders, she was an American educator and civil rights activist, who is perhaps best known as the wife of slain black nationalist leader, Malcolm X.

Shabazz was raised in Detroit by adoptive parents in a comfortable middle-class home and was active in a Methodist church. Upon high school graduation, she left Detroit to study elementary education at Tuskegee Institute (now Tuskegee University) in Alabama. There, she experienced racism for the first time in her life, and after two years, she left for New York City, where she became a registered nurse.

In 1956, Sanders met Malcolm X at a Nation of Islam lecture in Harlem, and in 1958, she converted to Islam and married him. The assassination of her husband (who by this time had changed their last name to Shabazz) in 1965 was witnessed by Shabazz, who was pregnant with twins at the time, and their four daughters. After his transition, Shabazz dedicated herself to raising her children and continuing her education, eventually receiving a Ph.D. (1975) in education administration from the University of Massachusetts.

In 1976, Shabazz began working at Medgar Evers College in Brooklyn, first as a professor, then as the director of its department of communications and public relations. She also lectured occasionally, addressing such topics as civil rights and racial tolerance. Shabazz transitioned to the ancestral realm from severe burns suffered in a fire set by her twelve year old grandson. She is honored and revered as a great woman.

Maurice Bishop

Maurice Bishop, the son of Rupert and Alimenta Bishop, was born on 29 May 1944.

An intelligent pupil, Bishop won a scholarship to the Roman Catholic Presentation Boys College. While at this school, he won the gold medal for 'outstanding academic and all round ability'. As a young man, Bishop developed an interest in politics and in 1962, joined with Bernard Coard to form the Grenada Assembly of Youth After Truth. Twice a month Bishop and Coard led debates on current events in the Central Market Place in Grenada.

Maurice Bishop studied law in England and also visited Eastern Europe where he was instructed in the tenants of Marxism. He returned to Grenada in 1969 and immediately sought to make a positive change for his people. Soon afterward, he helped form the Movement for Assemblies of the People (MAP) and the Movement for the Advance of Community (MACE).

In 1973, these organizations merged with Joint Endeavor for Welfare, Education and Liberation (JEWEL) to establish the New Jewel Movement (NJM).

In 1979, a rumor began going around that PM Eric Gairy planned to use his 'Mongoose Gang' to assassinate leaders of the New Jewel Movement while he was out of the country.

On 13 March 1979, Bishop and the NJM took over the nation's radio station. With the support of the people, the NJM was able to take control of the rest of the country forming the People's Revolutionary Government (PRG) and the People's Revolutionary Army (PRA).

He received aid from the Soviet Union and Cuba and with this money constructed the Grenada International Airport to improve tourism, and started Argro industries among other things. Bishop attempted to develop a good relationship with the United States and allowed private enterprise to continue on the island. Bernard Coard, the Minister of Finance, disagreed with this policy. He also disliked Bishop's ideas on grassroots democracy.

On 19 October, with the support of the army, Coard overthrew the government. Maurice Bishop was then unjustly executed. He had fought all his life for freedom and self-determination for his people. He is well loved by many till this day and his truth lives on.

King Njoya

Njoya, the Great was the King of The Bamoun Kingdom in modern day Cameroun. He was born in 1876 to the royal family of the Bamoun people. During his childhood years, he excelled in intelligence and was very sportive.

After the transition of his father, he was the legitimate heir to the throne, but his brother tried to usurp the throne. At this point, Njoya rallied forces with the Peul people and rightfully annulled the threat of his brother. He was then the only natural ruler of the Bamoun Kingdom.

King Njoya started nation-building after he had stabilized his empire and reinforced his army as well as the Bamoun religion.

At the end of the 19th century, he evolved an independent system of writing for his own language as well as for a secret 'court language'. He was inspired by a dream, in which he was told to draw a man's hand on a board and then to wash off his drawing and drink the water. After doing this, he asked his subjects to draw different objects and to name them.

Armed with their results, he experimented until he had created the first writing system containing some 466 pictographic and ideographic symbols. He then set up a series of schools or 'book houses' throughout his kingdom, at which hundreds of his subjects learned to read and write. An important and varied collection of literature was compiled, only some of which has been preserved.

Among other works, Njoya compiled a volume on the history and customs of his kingdom, a book of rules of conduct at his court, a pharmacopoeia and a collection of maps of his kingdom. He created a library and ethnographic collection at his palace and encouraged the development of traditional weaving and dyeing under his patronage.

After the World War I, Njoya's schools and achievements were destroyed by the French colonial authorities and he was deposed in 1931 and exiled to Yaounde, where he transitioned to the ancestral realm, disowned but never defeated as his written text and the pride of his people demonstrate until this day.

Imhotep

Imhotep was one of the greatest Kamau (Ancient Egyptians) to be recorded into the annals of history. His name meant 'To come in peace' and his life was a testimony to this adage. Born on 31 May 2665 B.C.E. to a family of commoners in Men-Nefer (Memphis), Imhotep became the world's first recorded polymath.

Imhotep is credited with being the founder of medicine and with being the author of a medical treatise the so-called Edwin Smith papyrus containing anatomical observations, ailments, and cures.

As one of the officials of the Pharaoh, Djoser, he designed the Pyramid of Djoser (the Step Pyramid) at Saqqara in Egypt in 2630–2611 B.C.E. He was been responsible for the first known use of columns in architecture. As an instigator of Egyptian culture, Imhotep's idealized image lasted well into the Ptolemaic period.

The Egyptian historian, Manetho, credited him with inventing the method of a stone-dressed building during Djoser's reign. It is true that a building of the Step Pyramid's size and made entirely out of stone had never before been constructed. Before Djoser, pharaohs were buried in mastaba tombs.

As a Vizier (prime minister) and High Priest of Pharoah Djoser, Imhotep excelled in statesmanship The Upper Egyptian Famine Stela, dating from the Ptolemaic period, bears an inscription containing an account about a famine of seven years during the reign of Djoser. Imhotep is credited with having been instrumental in ending it. One of his priests explained the connection between the god Khnum and the rise of the Nile to the king, who then had a dream in which the Nile energy spoke to him, promising to end the drought.

Imhotep transitioned to the ancestral realm at a grand old age. It is clear that he was one of the greatest figures of all time. His memory is enduring and today when doctors take their medical oath they swear by Aescupulous, which is a Greek translation of the name Imhotep.

June

Shamba Bolongongo

Shamba Bolongongo was one of the best-known African Kings of Bakuba. Bakuba is still in modern day Afrika. He was the 93rd king of Bakuba in Central Afrika. Shamba Bolongongo was a peaceful ruler because his main objective was making sure that peace was kept throughout his kingdom. It was said that his reign brought about 'The Golden Age' of the Bushongo people of the Southern Congo.

One of the things Shamba Bolongongo did was that he went out of his way to use all the things he had been taught while he traveled. He helped the farmers of Bakuba by bringing three plants that came from the Americas: maize, cassava, and tobacco. The farmers made good use of those crops to feed the people of Bakuba. Shamba also brought in some iron tools and better farming techniques, making it possible for the farmers of Bakuba to double their output and to enhance the diet of the Bakuba.

King Bolongongo worked to make all his people feel as important and respected as he did, not just people with 'power' but also the common people. He made his people feel important by entitling them to special titles and giving them different responsibilities with those titles. His kingdom also consisted of some bantu inhabitants. He gave titles to people as judges, officers, treasurers, bodyguards and more.

They all played a role in the rituals that imprinted the political life of the kingdom. Bright and colorful parades were then celebrated for the season of the harvest and when the new or rare merchandise arrived at the market.

Now when King Shamba Bolongongo transitioned, his aunt's son succeeded him due to the matriarchal nature of the Congo society. Unlike Shamba, his successor was a warrior who led the Bakuba and their army into various wars against their neighbors.

Shamba was the most popular of the Bakuba kings. Under his rule, Bakuba was peaceful and rich. It is said that almost everything the Bakuba possess or do have originated during the leadership of this great and peace-loving monarch: Shamba Bolongongo.

Samory Toure

Samory Toure, who was a great leader and nationalist from West Africa, fought the French from taking possession of his homeland for over eighteen years. He fought with such mastery that the French military leaders referred to him as 'The Black Napoleon'. He frustrated the Europeans to the degree that they suffered large losses of manpower and money. Samory's expert military strategy and tactics caused even greater insecurity for the French.

Samory was born of humble means in Manyambaladugu, modern day Guinea. The son of a poor Black merchant and a Senegalese female servant, Samory had become an idol of the other soldiers. Being provoked by jealousy, the king demanded Samory be removed from the army and sent back to his homeland, Bissandugu, where he became king of the ethnic group.

Samory's homeland was attacked by the neighboring King Sori Bourama. His mother was captured during this raid. Samory was unable to pay his mother's ransom, so he freed her by taking her place.

Samory, always desiring to be a free man, became a favorite of the king because of his splendid physique, his ability to throw a spear, and his knowledge of the Arabic language. Soon he became a bodyguard for the king, and later advanced to counselor of the group. He freed himself and his mother and lead an army.

Samory defied all of his opponents and even conquered his former capturer, King Sori Bourama. Samory expanded his empire to an area of over 100,000 sq. miles or more, making him the most powerful native ruler in West Africa.

On 29 September 1898, while Samory was on his knees, outside of his tent praying, a French sergeant and a French scout crept upon him from behind, captured and exiled him to an island for life. He transitioned to the ancestral realm, but was always remembered as a fearless king who defied all odds and rose to greatness in the face of adversity. His great-grandson became the first president of an independent Guinea.

Charles Drew

Charles Drew (1904–1950) was born 03 n June 1904 in Washington D.C. Charles Drew excelled in academics and sports during his graduate studies at Amherst College in Massachusetts. Charles Drew was also a honor student at McGill University Medical School in Montreal, where he specialized in physiological anatomy.

Charles Drew researched blood plasma and transfusions in New York City. It was during his work at Columbia University where he made his discoveries relating to the preservation of blood. By separating the liquid red blood cells from the near solid plasma and freezing the two separately, he found that blood could be preserved and reconstituted at a later date.

Charles Drew's system for the storing of blood plasma (blood bank) revolutionized the medical profession. Dr. Drew also established the American Red Cross blood bank, of which he was the first director, and he organized the world's first blood bank drive, nicknamed 'Blood for Britain'. His official title for the blood drive was Medical Director of the first Plasma Division for Blood Transfusion, supplying blood plasma to the British during World War II.

The British military used his process extensively during World War II, establishing mobile blood banks to aid in the treatment of wounded soldiers at the front lines. In 1941, the American Red Cross decided to set up blood donor stations to collect plasma for the U.S. armed forces.

After the war, Charles Drew took up the Chair of Surgery at Howard University, Washington D.C. He received the Spingarn Medal in 1944 for his contributions to medical science. Charles Drew transitioned to the ancestral realm at the early age of forty-six from injuries suffered in a car accident in North Carolina. He, like Imhotep before him, was one of the most influential figures in the history of medicine.

Josephine Baker

Born Freda Josephine McDonald in St. Louis, Missouri, on 3 June 1906, she later took the name Baker from her second husband, Willie Baker, whom she married at age fifteen.

Surviving the 1917 riots in East St. Louis, Illinois, where the family was living, Josephine Baker ran away a few years later at age thirteen and began dancing in vaudeville and on Broadway. In 1925, Josephine Baker went to Paris where, after the jazz revue La Revue Negre failed, her comic ability and jazz dancing drew attention of the director of the Folies Bergere.

Virtually an instant hit, Josephine Baker became one of the best-known entertainers in both France and much of Europe. Her exotic, sensual act reinforced the creative images coming out of the Harlem Renaissance in America.

During World War II, Josephine Baker worked with the Red Cross, gathered intelligence for the French Resistance and entertained troops in Africa and the Middle East.

After the war, Josephine Baker adopted, with her second husband, twelve children from around the world, making her home a World Village, a 'showplace for brotherhood'. She returned to the stage in the 1950s to finance this project.

In 1951 in the United States, Josephine Baker was refused service at the famous Stork Club in New York City. Yelling at columnist Walter Winchell, another patron of the club, for not coming to her assistance, she was accused by Winchell of communist and fascist sympathies. Never as popular in the U.S. as in Europe, she found herself fighting the rumors begun by Winchell as well.

Josephine Baker responded by crusading for racial equality, refusing to entertain in any club or theater that was not integrated, and thereby breaking the color bar at many establishments. In 1963, she spoke at the march on Washington at the side of Martin Luther King Jr.

Josephine Baker's World Village fell apart in the 1950s and in 1969, she was evicted from her chateau which was then auctioned off to pay debts. Princess Grace of Monaco gave her a villa. In 1973, Baker married an American, Robert Brady, and began her stage comeback.

In 1975, Josephine Baker's Carnegie Hall comeback performance was a success, as was her subsequent Paris performance. But two days after her last Paris performance, she transitioned to the ancestral realm of a stroke on 12 April 1975. She left behind a legacy of creativity and talent that up until this day are idolized by many.

John Carlos

John Carlos was born in Harlem, New York, on 5 June 1945. Carlos graduated from the Machine Trade and Medal High School and was awarded a full track and field scholarship to East Texas State University. He won the university's first track Lone Star Conference Championship. From East Texas, Carlos went to San Jose State University.

Here he met Harry Edwards and they became friends. Edwards was a member of the Olympic Project for Human Rights (OPHR) which attempted to get an athletes boycott of the Mexico games. The boycott did not materialize but the stance of OPHR had made an impression on both John Carlos and Tommy Smith.

Carlos won the bronze medal in the 200 meters final. During the medal ceremony, he raised his left arm in the air (with the hand in a black glove) in what was a Black Power salute. Along with Smith, who had done the same, Carlos was expelled from the games and had to return to America.

However, both men had been seen across the world making this stand and it must have aroused curiosity among some as to why they had done this in what was seen as an apolitical event. The so-called 'Silent Protest' was voted the sixth most memorable television event of the 20th century.

When Carlos and Smith returned to the U.S.A., they were greeted as heroes by some and as unpatriotic troublemakers by others. However, they had made civil rights in America an international topic. Carlos was with Martin Luther King just ten days before King was assassinated in 1968.

However, the athlete who had achieved international fame in Mexico found that it counted for nothing once the games were over. Carlos had to do a succession of menial jobs just to financially survive. He claims that money was so tight that on cold nights, he had to chop up furniture and use it as fire wood to keep out the cold.

After leaving athletics, John Carlos had a short career in the NFL. After this, he joined PUMA and also worked for the city of Los Angeles. This brave living legend gave a consequence to sports and currently works as a track and field coach for Palm Springs High School in California.

Alexander Pushkin

In a sense, Alexander Pushkin is the beginning of real Russian drama. He was born on 6 June 1799. With his first play, Boris Godunov (written in 1825), he broke, or perhaps we should say, established, several precedents. First of all, his plot was chosen from a somewhat legendary incident of Russian history. His characters were real Russians, thinking, speaking, living as Russians. Instead of following French or German examples, as writers for the stage had done heretofore, he experimented with romantic tragedy after the style of Shakespeare. As a reading play, *Boris Godunov* is, in spots, superb. Its influence on later dramatic writers was considerable however.

Alexander Pushkin on his father's side was descended from one of the oldest families of the Russian gentry. His mother was the grand-daughter of Peter, the Great Abyssinian Afrikan Engineer-General. The young Alexander's first poems appeared when he was but fifteen, and by the time he left school, he was regarded as a rival by the acknowledged literary leaders of the day.

After Pushkin left school, he lived a riotous life in St. Petersburg as a member of the most brilliant and dissipated crowd in the capital. Seditious utterances in certain of his writings caused his banishment from St. Petersburg, and finally what was almost an incarceration on his mother's estate. When somewhat later, he was pardoned and permitted to return to the capital, he found that under the pretense of favoring him, the Czar was in reality curtailing both his personal and literary liberty.

When later on he was appointed to a court position, simply so that the Czar could invite his beautiful wife to the court balls, Pushkin's bitterness knew no bounds. He was powerless to change the situation however, and in 1837, challenged one of his wife's admirers to a duel which resulted in the writer's death.

Pushkin's greatest contemporary successes with the general public were his two poems, *The Captive of the Caucasus* and *The Fountain of Bakhchisaray*, and the drama, *Boris Godunov*. Viewed from a critical angle, however, his real masterpieces are the poem, *The Bronze Horseman*, and the drama, *The Stone Guest*, which concerns itself with the closing love intrigue and tragic ending of the Spanish Don Juan.

It has been left for later generations of Russians to appreciate Pushkin's true worth. It is significant that he was practically the only writer of pre-Revolutionary Russia who escaped the general condemnation of the Bolsheviks of everything that smacked of aristocratic culture. He alone had made the Russian language move from merely an oral language to a literate one.

Tommie Smith

Tommie Smith began life quietly, born to Richard and Dora Smith on June 6, 1944, in Clarksville, Texas, the seventh of twelve children. Tommie Smith survived a life-threatening bout of pneumonia as an infant. Today, his historic achievements make him a nationally and internationally distinguished figure in Afrikan-American history.

He is the only man in the history of track and field to hold eleven world records simultaneously. As a college student, Tommie amazingly tied or broke a total of thirteen world records in track. Tommie Smith received his Bachelor of Arts degree from San Jose State University in Social Science, with double minors in Military Science and Physical Education.

Tommie received his Master's Degree in Sociology from Goddard Cambridge in Boston, Mass. In May 2005, Honorary Doctorate Degree of Humane Letters from San Jose State University. During the historic 19th Olympiad held in Mexico City, in the summer of 1968, Tommie Smith broke the world and Olympic records with a time of 19.83 seconds and became the 200-meter Olympic champion.

As the Star Spangled Banner echoed in the wind, at the Mexico City Summer Olympic Games, Tommie Smith and John Carlos stood on the victory podium, draped with their Olympic medals, each raised a clinched fist, covered in a black leather glove in a historic stand for human rights, liberation and solidarity. This courageous, unexpected worldwide event propelled Tommie Smith into the spotlight as a human rights spokesman, activist, and symbol of Afrikan pride at home and abroad.

Cheered by some, jeered by others, and ignored by many more, Tommie Smith made a commitment to dedicate his life, even at great personal risk, to champion the cause of oppressed people. The story of the "silent gesture" is captured for all time in the 1999 HBO TV documentary, *Fists of Freedom.*

Tommie Smith's courageous leadership, talent, and activism have earned him well-deserved acclaim athletic and humanitarian awards.

Some highlights have been: featured in periodicals, including *Sports Illustrated, Time, Newsweek*, and *Ebony*. In 1978, he was an inductee into the National Track & Field Hall of Fame; coaching staff of 1995 World Indoor Championship team in Barcelona, Spain; 1996 inductee into the California Black Sports Hall of Fame; 1999 Sportsman of the Millennium Award; May 1999 inductee into the Bay Area Hall of Fame.

Also, November 1999 inductee into the San Jose State University Sports Hall of Fame; 2000–2001 Commendation, Recognition and Proclamation Awards from the County of Los Angeles and the State of Texas, New York City to name a few. 2004 dedication of the Tommie Smith gymnasium in Saint-Ouen, France, 2005 the City of La Courneuve, France, dedicated the Tommie Smith Sports House.

Since the games of the XIX Olympiad, Tommie has enjoyed a distinguished career as a coach, educator, athletic director and activist.

At 6'3" and 185 pounds, Tommie Smith had the ideal build for a long sprinter, with trademark accelerations down the stretch that made him one of the most versatile sprinters in history. With all-time bests of 10.1 seconds for 100 meters, 19.83 seconds for 200 meters and 44.5 seconds at 400 meters, Smith still ranks high on the entire world all-time performance lists.

While a student at San Jose State, Smith was coached by Bud Winter. Smith began making waves in winning the national collegiate 220 yard title in 1967 before adding the Amateur Athletic Union furlong crown soon after. He repeated as AAU 200 meter champion in 1968, making the summer U.S. Olympic team for the Mexico City Games.

In the 200 meter Olympic final, Smith blazed home in a world's record time of 19.83 seconds—even while decelerating toward the finish line with fists of triumph held high as he realized a gold medal run into history.

During his career, Smith set seven individual world records and was a member of several world record relay teams while a student athlete at San Jose State.

Although, born in Clarksville, Texas, Tommie began his incredible career in Lemoore, California, when as a fourth grade student he was asked to race against the fastest runner in the school (his sister). He went on to become the only man in the history of track and field to hold eleven world records simultaneously. By the time he graduated from high school, he had been voted 'Most Valuable Athlete' three years straight, in basketball, football, and track and field.

Tommie was the 200 meter champion in the 19th Olympiad in Mexico City with a time of 19.83 seconds, which was a world record until 1979 and an Olympic record until 1984.

With God-given talent and encouragement to excel, Tommie Smith was propelled into human rights spokesman-ship long before it became a popular cause. His concern was for the plight of Afrikan-Americans and others at home and abroad. Since the 'Stand for Victory', Tommie Smith has remained as committed and as dedicated to principles that are helped Afrikans renew their pride and uplift themselves.

Al Jahiz

Lord of the golden age of Arab literature (A.D. 778–868).

"The most genial writer of the age, if not of Arabic literature, and the founder of the Arab prose style, was the grandson of a Afrikan servant, Amr ben Bahr, known as Al-Jahiz, 'The Goggle Eyed'," says Gibbs, Arabic scholar.

"Al-Jahiz," says Christopher Dawson, "was the greatest scholar and stylist of the 9th century." "An early representative of the zoological and anthropological sciences was Abu-Uthman Amr ibn Bahr Al-Jahiz…whose Kitab-al-Hawaya…contains germs of later theories of evolution, adaptation, and animal psychology."

"AL-Jahiz knew how to obtain ammonia from animal offal by dry distillation His influence over later zoologists…is manifest. But the influence of Al-Jahiz as a radical theologian and a man of letters if greater. He was one of the most productive and frequently quoted scholars in Arabic literature. His originality, wit, satire, and learning, made him widely known."

Al-Jahiz, who was a black Afrikan, started life in most humble surroundings but by studiousness, a prodigious memory, remarkable powers of assimilation, and unruffled good nature, he reached the highest rank of scholarship and esteem.

Born at Basra in Asia Minor in modern day Iraq, he studied philology, philosophy, and science there under the noted Mu'tazlite teacher, an-Nassam. Of an independent spirit, he was not long in striking out on an intellectual path of his own, and founded his own school of thought, known as the Jahizite. Such was his good-natured wit, his breadth of mind, and his impartiality, that he was beloved even by members of the fanatical religious sects that normally would have treated him as a heretic.

An indefatigable reader, Al-Jahiz would hire the shops of booksellers outright so that he could spend the whole night reading in them. His works are voluminous. Few writers were as industrious as he, and still fewer wrote over such a long period of time. He was prolific until he died in A.D. 868 at the age of ninety.

He wrote, as Gibbs says, "with a careless loquacity, alternately grave and gay, exalted and extravagant. His wit was ready and his industry was immense."

Al-Jahiz's masterpiece is *The Book of Animals*, in seven volumes. Among his other works are *The Merit of the Turks, In Praise o/Merchants and Dispraise of Officials, The Superiority of Speech to Silence, The Superiority in Glory of the Black Race over the White*, and *The Book of Eloquence and Rhetoric*. In his works, which contain the most varied and curious kinds of information, he presents all sides of the story.

Thus in his *Book of Animals,* we find him discussing animals pro and con, as, for instance, the good and the bad qualities of the dog. In personal appearance, Al-Jahiz was unprepossessing. It is related that Caliph Al-Mutawakkil engaged him to teach his son, but when he saw him, he was so repelled by his looks that he paid him a large sum and dismissed him.

Later, however, he recalled him and placed the young prince under his tutorship, although he strongly disagreed. This great literary mind transitioned peacefully to the ancestral realms. His plethora of books, however, are still pricelessly sought after by scholars worldwide up until today.

Taharqa

Taharqa (To place upon the spirit) was the brother of Shabaka who also was a King of Kamit. He was part of the 25th dynasty of ancient Kamit and ruled from 690–664 B.C.E. Upon Shabaka's transition, Taharqa was installed as Shekhem Ur Shekem (Pharoah/Thunderer of thunderers). Taharqa placed his rulership on a spiritual rebirth of his people and led them by example.

He was a humble and religious man whose main preoccupation in life was to become a God-Man and to declare himself as MaaKheru. His empire stretched from Palestine to the confluence of the Blue and White Hapi (Nile). In about 684 B.C.E., the Hapi rose in a great flood. Taharqa's kingdom brought an exceptional harvest that year, and the kingdom grew rich. He ordered many construction projects, and built or renewed many fine temples in Kamit. The early years of his reign were very prosperous.

Later on during his reign, the deceitful Assyrians disrupted Kamit's peace once again and attacked from the 'Middle East'. Taharqa had a few victories, but eventually was defeated by the Assyrian hordes who reclaimed Men-Nefer illegitimately once again. Taharqa withdrew to the city of Amen (Thebes) and led a pious life. He followed the wise counsel from the oracle and consolidated himself in the seed-place of his ancestry.

After twenty-six years of good governance, Taharqa transitioned peacefully in Nubia; due to his great wisdom and great achievements, a pyramid of over hundred and fifty feet high was erected to honor him and to have his descendants, such as your person and my person, testify to the immortality of his great deeds and great virtue of his struggle to restore us to spiritual, moral and physical greatness.

Bilal

Bilal ibn Rabah or Bilal al-Habashi (raa) was from the Habash (Abyssinia) area, now known as Ethiopia. He was also known as 'Bilal ibn Riyah', 'ibn Rabah', and sometimes he was called 'Bilal al-Habashi' (Bilal the one from Abyssinia).

Born in the late 6th century, Bilal (raa) was forty-three years old (579 AD) at the time of Hijra (622 AD) but it has been suggested by some that he could have been as old as fifty-three (569 AD).

One of the many emancipated Afrikans of Abu Bakr (raa). Prior to being emancipated from bondage, Bilal was asked who his master was and responded that his only master was Allah. Even after his slave master tortured him to try and make him say that he and not Allah was Bilal's master, Bilal persevered. This act of bravery and faith led to his release.

After his release, Bilal became one of Prophet Mohammed's followers. Bilal was known for his beautiful voice and was given the honor by the Holy Prophet Muhammad of being the first Muazzin of Islam. He would be the chosen one to call all the faithful of Islam to come and pray.

His beautiful voice resonated throughout the Islamic dominions of the time calling all the followers of the Prophet Mohammed to come and pray as was the routine five times a day. He was Prophet Mohammed's most faithful and dedicated follower.

Bilal ibn Rabah al-Habashi (raa) was believed to have transitioned to the ancestral realm sometime between 629 AD to 639 AD at the age of sixty and was known as one of the most trusted and loyal sahaba (companions) of the Prophet Muhammad as well as Ali ibn Abi Talib (raa) cousin and son in-law of the Prophet.

His respected stature during the birth of Islam is a perfect example of the importance Afrikans in the foundations of Islam.

Nehanda of Mashona

In the 14th century, as the state around Great Zimbabwe entered its twilight, some residents began moving northward. It is said that Prince Mutota left Great Zimbabwe with an army and, after a series of conquests on his northward trek, eventually settled down and founded the Mutapa state.

The Shona are monotheists, who venerate their ancestors and believe in spirit possession. The High God of the Shona, known by various names over time, is now usually referred to as Mwari. In the Mutapa state, they elevated ancestor veneration and spirit possession to astounding heights with the establishment of royal mhondoro cults.

It is said that Matope announced that his spirit was immortal and upon his death, it would enter a mhondoro, or lion. The mhondoro wandered the forests in the form of a lion until it found a suitable medium. Each mhondoro had its own 'spirit province' that may extend over one or more paramountcies, but the mhondoro had to reside within these delineated borders. Matope's sister-wife, Nehanda, who possessed supernatural powers, also became a guardian spirit.

The incursion by the British led to the destruction of the political, economic and religious order of the peoples of Southern Afrika. The imposition of the hut tax, forced labor, suppression of religious practices, and land alienation crystallized Afrikan resistance. The military campaign to drive out the British, called the Chimurenga or 'the war of liberation', was started by the Ndebele in May 1896, and their traditional enemies, the Shona, joined them in October of the same year.

The unique element of the Chimurenga was the leading roles played by three mhondoro: Mukwati in Matabeleland: Kagubi in western Mashonaland; and Nehanda, the sole woman, in Central and Northern Mashonaland. The mhondoro struck directly at the core of Shona beliefs and, in so doing, captured the minds of the people by effectively convincing them that Mwari blamed the whites for all their suffering and decreed that the whites should be driven from the land.

Nehanda Charwe Nyakasikana was considered to be the female incarnation of the oracle spirit Nyamhika Nehanda. Referred to as Mbuya Nehanda, she is commonly referred to as the grandmother of present day Zimbabwe. She exhorted the Shona people to expel the British from the land, encouraging them to intensify the struggle and rallying them on.

Using secret messages to communicate with each other, the mhondoro effectively coordinated their efforts. Kagubi was captured in October 1897, but Nehanda eluded the British a while longer, until she was eventually captured in December. They were both charged with murder—Kagubi for the death of an African policeman and Nehanda for the death of the Native Commissioner Pollard—and summarily sentenced to death by hanging.

Kagubi subsequently converted to Christianity, but Nehanda steadfastly refused, and went transitioned to the ancestral realm in defiance, denouncing the British. Nehanda's dying words, "My bones will rise again," predicted the Second Chimurenga, which culminated in the independence of present-day Zimbabwe.

Facing the superior technology of the British, the rebellion surprisingly lasted until the end of 1897 despite British acts of horror and brutality. Although, the British casualties were numerically less, they represented one-tenth of their population. The key elements of the mhondoro cults—ancestor veneration and spirit possession—persist among the people of present-day Zimbabwe.

During the Second Chimurenga, Ian Smith, then Prime Minister of Rhodesia (now Zimbabwe), in an airborne leaflet drop, invoked the names of royal mhondoro in a desperate effort to dilute popular support for ZANLA (Zimbabwe African National Liberation Army). In 1972, the spirit of Nyamhika Nehanda found a new medium in an elderly woman, who was whisked to safety by ZANLA guerillas.

She was consulted on military decisions and her prophecies provided valuable assistance to the revolutionary struggle. She transitioned to the ancestral realm in 1973.

The indomitable Mbuya Nehanda, revolutionary prophet and leader of the First Chimurenga in 1896, has now been rightfully buried in Zimbabwe's Heroes' Acre.

Eduardo Mondlane

Eduardo Mondlane was born on 20 June 1920, in the Gaza district of southern Mozambique. The son of a Tsonga chief and the only member of his large family to receive even a primary education, he later attributed his educational drive to the vision of a 'very determined and persistent' mother.

The colonial school system was almost exclusively for Europeans, but Mondlane gained entry into a Swiss mission school and went from it to an American Methodist agricultural school. He then served for two years instructing Afrikan peasants in techniques of dry farming.

Next, Mondlane obtained a scholarship and admission to a Presbyterian secondary school in the Transvaal, South Africa, and in 1948, he was admitted to Witwatersrand University of Johannesburg, the first African from Mozambique to enter a South African university. In 1949, the South African government declared him an unwanted 'foreign native' in a white university and revoked his student permit.

Returned to Lourengo Marques in Mozambique, Mondlane was arrested and interrogated about his role in the formation of a local Afrikan student association.

In June 1950, Mondlane entered the University of Lisbon as the only Afrikan student from Mozambique pursuing a higher education in Portugal. After a year, during which he complained of harassment by the political police, his Phelps Stokes scholarship was transferred to the United States, where he entered Oberlin College in Ohio at the age of thirty-one. After earning a bachelor's degree from Oberlin in 1953, he undertook graduate work at Northwestern University in Illinois and received a doctorate in 1960.

By this time, Mondlane had become Mozambique's best-known, best-educated, and most watched Afrikan. The uniqueness of his position can be appreciated when one notes that perhaps ten out of nearly six million Afrikans in Mozambique were attending secondary schools in 1955, while slightly over two hundred were enrolled in technical schools or seminaries.

In 1957, after a year as a visiting scholar at Harvard, where he worked on role conflict (the subject of his dissertation), Mondlane joined the trusteeship section of the United Nations Secretariat in New York as a research officer. In this capacity, he went to West Africa in 1960 as part of a UN team preparing and supervising a plebiscite in the British Cameroons. From the Cameroons, following an absence of eleven years and accompanied by his American wife and family, he revisited Mozambique in early 1961.

After renewing and expanding a wide assortment of personal contacts on his tour of Mozambique, he returned to the United States, resigned his post at the UN, and accepted a teaching position within the East African program at Syracuse University. At the same time, he began lecturing and writing on Portuguese colonialism and political and economic conditions in Mozambique.

In June 1962, Mondlane flew to Dar es Salaam, Tanzania, where he helped to unite several groups of exiled Mozambique nationalists into the Mozambique Liberation Front (FRELIMO). He was confirmed as the movement's first president at a congress held that September in Tanzania. He then returned to America to complete his obligations at Syracuse University.

During this last semester of teaching, he delivered a paper at the first American Negro Leadership Conference on Africa (Harriman, N.Y., November 1962). Early in 1963, he and his family moved to Dar es Salaam, where Mondlane assumed his new role as a revolutionary leader.

For some years, Mondlane had worked with American Protestants and others to funnel scholarship funds to Afrikans wishing to attend secondary school in Mozambique and to study abroad. It was only consistent, therefore, that he made education a principal concern of FRELIMO. He founded the Mozambique Institute in Dar es Salaam to receive refugee students, to obtain scholarships, and, ultimately, to develop a new Mozambique primary and secondary school curriculum.

FRELIMO sent volunteers for military training to Algeria and the United Arab Republic and to camps in Tanzania. By September 1964, Mondlane had a cadre of some 250 trained men, and guerrilla operations were launched that month in the northern Cabo Delgado and Niassa districts of Mozambique. By 1969, several thousand FRELIMO guerrillas were operating in those areas.

To equip and feed them, Mondlane circled the globe, raising funds and seeking arms. Money and training were made available by various African states, the Organization of African Unity (OAU), the Soviet Union, and China, and educational and humanitarian funds by the World Council of Churches (Geneva), Scandinavian countries, and various private groups in the United States.

Although, a new FRELIMO military front was opened in the Tete district of northwest Mozambique during 1968, Mondlane still warned soberly of a long, costly fight ahead. His leadership came under attack within the movement by would-be rivals and dissidents of the key northern Maconde community. In the face of Portuguese intransigence and military support for Portugal from Western countries, the struggle for independence was proving more costly and slower than some had hoped.

Despite criticism related to the difficulties and intrigues of exile politics, the Central Committee convened the second FRELIMO congress inside the Niassa district in July 1968. There Mondlane was reelected president by an overwhelming majority.

A sunny, didactic man with an open life-style, Mondlane was an easy target for political enemies. On 3 February 1969, he was killed by a bomb mailed to him marked as a book. His assassins remain unknown. Leaving behind a wife and three children and a weakened Mozambique liberation movement, Eduardo Mondlane immediately became a martyred symbol of the continuing Afrikan struggle for national independence.

He was succeeded as president of FRELIMO by the movement's military commander, Samora Machel, while his wife, Janet Mondlane, continued as director of the Mozambique Institute.

Mohammed Ahmad 'The Mahdi'

Muhammad Ahmad ibn 'Abd Allah, the man known to history as al Mahdi was born in the Sudan in 1844. Al Mahdi is an Arabic term meaning 'The Divinely Guided One' which has been claimed by a number of Islamic leaders, including the founder of the Ahmadist sect in Pakistan, but Muhammad Ahmad ibn 'Abd Allah is the most famous al Mahdi and he will be referred to this appellation in what follows.

The father of al Mahdi was a ship builder in the Dungulah district of the Sudan. The family moved south to a village near Khartoum shortly after the birth of al Mahdi.

As a boy and young man, al Mahdi was devoted to religious study. His devotion deviated from the orthodox toward a mystic Sufism. He aspired to strong self-discipline and an ascetic life. As a young man, he joined a religious order called the Sammanujah. He was given the status of shaykh.

Even as a very young man, al Mahdi's devoutness attracted a following. In 1870, he and some of his disciples journeyed 175 miles of Khartoum to an island in the White Nile called Abba. They went there to receive religious instruction from one of the teachers living on that island. But al Mahdi found fault with his teacher's worldliness and was expelled from the following. He then joined the following of another teacher on Abba Island.

In 1880–81, al Mahdi became convinced that the rulers of Egypt and the Sudan were all corrupt puppets of the infidel Europeans and that the ruling class in general had abandoned true Islam. He felt his mission was to destroy those defiling forces and agents.

On 29 June 1881, Muhammad Ahmad ibn 'Abd Allah assumed the title of al Mahdi, the Divinely Guided One. He and a small number of his followers began the insurrection. Quickly he gained followers and took control of territory. The government in Egypt sent troops to subdue the uprising. Two such expeditionary forces were wiped out.

The government then sent a force of eight thousand troops commanded by a British general. This too was wiped out, to a man. In 1884, al Mahdi forces besieged Khartoum. The defense was under the command of Charles Gordon, who recently had commanded British forces in the Chinese Empire.

The defenders of Khartoum withstood the siege for months and a military expedition under Lord Kitchener was sent to relieve the defenders but it was delayed. In January of 1885, the forces of al Mahdi overwhelmed the defenses. When Gordon's headquarters were stormed, he took up a sword to fight but Gordon was killed.

Al Mahdi was not to live long after his brilliant military victory over the Anglo-Egyptian forces in Khartoum. He transitioned to the ancestral realm about six months later on 22 June 1885. He was not quite forty-one years of age. It had taken not quite four years from his assumption of the title of al Mahdi to conquer the Sudan and establish theocratic rule over it. It was a truly meteoric rise to fame and power.

Before his transition, al Mahdi named three Khalifas to be his successors. One emerged as the dominant figure and ruled with the support of the Baqqara Arabs. His life showed that he had been divinely chosen to lead his people to freedom.

Adelaide Casely Hayford

Adelaide Smith Casely Hayford was a Afrikan woman who dedicated her life to the education of girls in Sierra Leone. Born on 2 June 1868 in Freetown, Sierra Leone, Casely Hayford was the second youngest of seven children of parents, William Smith Jr. and Anne Spilsbury. Her prosperous, educated family was part of the Freetown Krio elite.

When Adelaide was four years old, her family moved to England where she was raised and educated. Her mother died soon afterwards. Raised by her father, Hayford excelled in her studies. When she turned seventeen, she was sent to Germany to study music.

In 1888, Casely Hayford moved back to England where she joined her father and new English stepmother. In 1892, twenty-four year old Hayford moved to Freetown to try teaching as a career. This experience gave her an opportunity to study the education systems in West Africa. Casey married West Afrikan author, Joseph Ephraim Casely Hayford, after a courtship that lasted only a few weeks.

Their only daughter, Gladys, was born in 1904 with a malformed hip joint. Casely Hayford took her daughter to England for medical treatment and remained there for three years. Meanwhile, her marriage to Joseph Casely ended in divorce in 1909, and in May 1914, Casely Hayford returned to Sierra Leone where she would dedicate the rest of her life to educating Afrikan girls.

Embracing the middle class uplift ideology that was common in Victorian England, Casely Hayford believed that education would prepare young girls for their appropriate roles as wives and mothers and promote pride of racial identity. As president of the Young Women's Christian Association (YWCA) and as principal of the Girls' Vocational School in Freetown, Sierra Leone, which she founded, Casely Hayford promoted her educational principles throughout Sierra Leone and across West Africa.

She took two fund-raising trips to the United States, the first in 1920 and the second five years later. Each trip spread the word of her work to American audiences and raised funds to support the Girls' Vocational School in Freetown. Her travels also exposed Casely Hayford to the racial hierarchies and the exploitation of black female labor throughout the world.

Toward the end of her life, she began speaking and writing on both issues, although she never abandoned her goal of preparing young women for middle class domesticity. Casely Hayford continued as principal of the Girl's Vocational School until her retirement in 1940.

On 24 January 1960, Casely Hayford transitioned in her hometown of Freetown, Sierra Leone. She will be remembered through memoirs and letters as a single mother, an educator, a world traveler, an author, and an Afrikan patriot.

Chris Hani

Chris Hani, born Martin Thembisile Hani (28 June 1942–10 April 1993) was the leader of the South African Communist Party and chief of staff of Umkhonto we Sizwe, the armed wing of the African National Congress (ANC). He was a fierce opponent of the apartheid government. He was assassinated on 10 April 1993.

Hani was born on 28 June 1942 in the small town of Cofimvaba, in a rural village called kuSabalele Transkei. He was the fifth of six children. He attended Lovedale school and later studied modern and classical literature at the University of Fort Hare.

At age fifteen, Hani joined the ANC Youth League. As a student, he was active in protests against the Bantu Education Act. Following his graduation, he joined Umkhonto we Sizwe (MK), the armed wing of the ANC. Following his arrest under the Suppression of Communism Act, he went into exile in Lesotho in 1963. He received military training in the Soviet Union and served in campaigns in the Rhodesian Bush War in what is now Zimbabwe.

In Lesotho, he was the target of assassination attempts, and he eventually moved to the ANC's headquarters in Lusaka, Zambia.

He returned to South Africa following the unbanning of the ANC in 1990, and took over from Joe Slovo as head of the South African Communist Party in 1991. He supported the suspension of the ANC's armed struggle in favor of negotiations. However, he stated that he would not rule out violence in a speech on National television shortly before his death.

Chris Hani was assassinated on 10 April 1993 outside his home in Dawn Park, a racially-mixed suburb of Boksburg. He was accosted by a Polish far-right immigrant named Janusz Walus, who shot him in the head as he stepped out of his car. Walus fled the scene, but was arrested soon afterwards after Hani's neighbor called the police. Clive Derby-Lewis, a senior South African

Conservative Party M.P., who had lent Walus his pistol, was also arrested for complicity in Hani's murder.

Hani's assassination was part of a plot by the far-right in South Africa to derail the negotiations to end apartheid.

Both Janusz Walus and Clive Derby-Lewis were sentenced to death for the murder. Clive Derby-Lewis's wife, Gaye Derby-Lewis, also a senior Conservative Party figure, was acquitted. The two men's sentences were commuted to life imprisonment when the death penalty was abolished as a result of a Constitutional Court ruling in 1995.

Hani was a charismatic leader, with significant support among the radical anti-apartheid youth. At the time of his death, he was the most popular ANC leader after Nelson Mandela, and was sometimes perceived as a rival to the more moderate party leadership. Following the legalization of the ANC, Hani's support for the negotiation process with the apartheid government was critical in keeping the militants in line. For his great selfless work on behalf of oppressed Afrikans, he will always be remembered.

Kwame Ture

Stokely Carmichael was born in the Port of Spain, Trinidad, on 29 June 1941. Carmichael moved to the United States in 1952 and attended high school in New York City. He entered Howard University in 1960 and soon afterward, joined the Student Nonviolent Coordinating Committee (SNCC).

In 1961, Carmichael became a member of the Freedom Riders. After training in non-violent techniques, black and white volunteers sat next to each other as they traveled through the Deep South. Local police were unwilling to protect these passengers and in several places they were beaten up by white mobs. In Jackson, Mississippi, Carmichael was arrested and jailed for forty-nine days in Parchman Penitentiary. Carmichael also worked on the Freedom Summer project, and in 1966, became chairman of SNCC.

On 5 June 1966, James Meredith started a solitary March Against Fear from Memphis to Jackson, to protest against racism. Soon after starting his march, he was shot by sniper. When they heard the news, other civil rights campaigners, including Carmichael, Martin Luther King and Floyd McKissick, decided to continue the march in Meredith's name.

When the marchers got to Greenwood, Mississippi, Carmichael and some of the other marchers were arrested by the police. It was the 27th time that Carmichael had been arrested and on his release on 16 June, he made his famous Black Power speech. Carmichael called for "black people in this country to unite, to recognize their heritage, and to build a sense of community."

He also advocated that Afrikan-Americans should form and lead their own organizations and urged a complete rejection of the values of American society.

The following year, Carmichael joined with Charles V. Hamilton to write the book, *Black Power: The Politics of Liberation in America* (1967). Some leaders of civil rights groups such as the National Association for the

Advancement of Colored People (NAACP) and Southern Christian Leadership Conference (SCLC), rejected Carmichael's ideas and accused him of black racism.

Carmichael also adopted the slogan of 'Black is Beautiful' and advocated a mood of black pride and a rejection of white values of style and appearance. This included adopting Afro hairstyles and Afrikan forms of dress. Carmichael began to criticize Martin Luther King and his ideology of non-violence. He eventually joined the Black Panther Party where he became 'honorary prime minister'.

When Carmichael denounced United States involvement in the Vietnam War, his passport was confiscated and held for ten months. When his passport was returned, he moved with his wife, Miriam Makeba, to Guinea, where he wrote the book, *Stokely Speaks: Black Power Back to Pan-Africanism* (1971).

Carmichael, who adopted the name Kwame Ture, also helped to establish the All-African People's Revolutionary Party and worked as an aide to Guinea's prime minister, Sekou Toure.

Kwame Toure transitioned to the ancestral realm of complications due to cancer on 15 November 1998. His selfless global struggle for Afrikan people remains engraved in our hearts and minds.

Sengbe Pieh

Sengbe Pieh was a Mende rice farmer with a wife and three children. He was living in Mani, Sierra Leone, when he was captured in 1839 and placed aboard a ship bound for Havana, Cuba. There, he was sold at a slave auction, along with an estimated forty-eight other Sierra Leone (Salone) men and children to a Spanish farmer, Jose Ruiz. Ruiz placed Sengbe and his other Afrikan kidnapees aboard the Amistad for what he thought would be a short trip to his plantation.

Sengbe, however, had other plans.

On the 3rd day of the voyage, Sengbe loosened a spike from the ship's deck and once below, used it to free himself and his fellow captives from their chains. While some were Mende and understood his language, there were also members of other ethnic groups and though they didn't speak his language, his intent was clear—Let's take this ship and sail home!(translation, head back to Africa).

Armed with cane knives from the cargo hold, they stormed the deck, killing the captain and driving other crewmen to flee using a skift. He ordered the ship's navigator to sail back to Sierra Leone—which he did during the day, while at night, steering back toward Cuba. Eventually though, some believe because of a storm, they landed near Long Island, where Sengbe and the other captives were captured by the U.S. Navy and charged with murder and piracy.

A group of American abolitionists decided to come to their defense, assembling their own dream team to argue their case. Of course, the Spanish government wanted the kidnapees to be returned to Cuba, and President Martin van Buren was sympathetic but decided that the men would first be tried for murder. Lewis Tappan and James Pennington argued that while slavery was legal in Cuba, importation of these slaves was not.

Inexplicably, the judge ruled in their favor. He thought that the kidnapped Africans had the right to use violence to escape captivity. The U.S. government appealed the decision and the case went before the U.S. Supreme Court, where former President John Quincy Adams, moved by the story, joined the fight and his infamous eight hour speech led to their release.

After speaking out against slavery in the sympathetic North, Sengbe and the group returned to Salone in January 1842. Unfortunately, upon his return, he discovered that his wife and children had been killed. It is not known when or how he transitioned to the ancestral realm, but his struggle for freedom had great repercussions worldwide leading to the civil war in America and the emancipation of his Afrikan brethren and sistren who were held in North Afrikan illegal captivity.

July

Khama, The Good

In 1875, Khama III became king of the Bamangwato, modern day Botswana, when he expelled his father and brother, Sekgoma and Kgamane.

Known as Khama, the Good, Khama was a Christian convert and proved to be more pious than European missionaries. He abandoned all aspects of his traditional religion and imposed Christianity on his people. He was fixated with the evils of alcohol, enforcing its prohibition to the point where he attempted to abolish the brewing of African beer.

His strict adherence to Christian virtues somewhat alienated his people. The threat of civil unrest, in part, prompted his alliance with the missionaries. In addition, the Ngwato were the constant targets of Ndebele raids; the Boers were trekking into the interior and claiming African lands; and Cecil Rhodes' British South African Company (BSAC) had designs on the mineral wealth of the area.

Although, opposed to colonialism, Khama saw missionary alliances and British protection as essential to his survival. John Mackenzie, a missionary and close friend of Khama, launched a relentless campaign for British protection to stem the influx of the expansionist Boers. In 1885, the British Government relented and offered protection, which came at a price. Khama's interests were deemed secondary to the need to forestall the Boer expansion and the intrusion of other European powers, especially the Germans.

The British scheme resulted in Khama's Ngwato territory being reduced by half. The area south of the Molopo River became a Crown Colony called 'British Bechuanaland' and the area north of the Molopo River became the Bechuanaland Protectorate.

The British Government, however, remained indifferent to Bechuanaland. The British imperialists were split into two camps: the capitalist faction, led by Cecil Rhodes, who favored settler colonialism, and the "humanitarian" group of missionaries who dreaded the effect of settler colonialism on their Christian converts. By 1894, the British Government promised Rhodes that his BSAC would take control of the Protectorate.

Aware of the implications of this decision, Khama and two high-level chiefs, accompanied by a charitable missionary, W. C. Willoughby, traveled to England to lodge an appeal to Colonial Minister Joseph Chamberlain. They were instructed to discuss the matter with Rhodes, who was clearly adamant. Khama and the others enlisted the aid of the London Missionary Society to take the matter to the British public, who subsequently pressured Chamberlain to continue British protection of Bechuanaland.

Khama sought to maintain the sovereignty of his state by allying with the intruders. Influenced by the missionaries, Khama sought British protection to prevent being subjugated by the Boers or the Ndebele. Instead of confrontation, Khama actively pursued protectorate status, which restricted his sovereignty, but allowed him to maintain a nominal independence while being protected by the British.

In 1923, Khama died after contracting pneumonia.

In 1966, Bechuanaland, named the Republic of Botswana, became independent with Khama III's grandson, Sir Seretse Khama, as its first president.

Patrice Lumumba

Born on 2 July 1925 in Kasai province in the former Belgian Congo, Lumumba had a modest education in Protestant and Catholic schools, before undergoing clerical training at the post office training school where he passed with distinction. He rose to the regional headship of postal services in Kisangani. He worked in the then Leopoldville (Kinshasa) and Stanleyville (Kisangani) before becoming a beer salesman. He married Pauline Opangu in 1951.

At the time of his stint as the regional head of the post office, he had become well known all over the country and in Belgium. In 1955, when he joined the Liberal Party of Belgium and began distributing and editing party literature, his enemies sought to forestall his rising star by arresting and charging him with the embezzlement of post office funds. He was released when his lawyer appealed on the evidence that he had not taken the money.

In 1958, he founded the Mouvement National Congolais (MNC) through which he represented Congo at the All-African People's congress in Accra

Ghana in December of the same year. As his profile now rose across the continent and the world, he was arrested again on framed-up charges of inciting an anti-colonial riot in January 1960, where thirty people were killed. For this he was committed to six months in prison.

As it turned out, this was the time that a round-table conference was to be held in Brussels to finalize the future of Congo, and his arrest was meant to give room for manipulation of the talks.

But pressure from the delegates secured his release, and subsequently his attendance of the conference. From then onward, Lumumba and MNC became synonymous with the independence of Congo, and it was not surprising, therefore, that at only thirty-five years of age, Patrice Emery Lumumba became the Prime Minister of Congo after the 11–25 May 1960 elections. However, events leading to the independence celebrations, or prior to that, seemed to have sealed his fate.

At 30 June 1960 independence celebrations, which Belgian King Baudouin attended, the prime minister's name was deliberately omitted from the program. Somehow, he managed to deliver his now famous independence speech, in which he honestly refuted the harm of racism and colonialism. King Baudouin thought was this honest speech disrespectful to him. The writing was now clearly on the wall.

Soon afterward, Katanga province declared independence with Belgian support. Unknown to many Congolese, the CIA with covert Belgian support had blacklisted Lumumba as a communist. His arrest, torture and the seemingly laid-back attitude of the UN troops in Congo formed the backdrop that became the Congo crisis.

Not surprisingly, in January 1961, the rest of the world watched in disbelief as a popularly elected African leader was hounded, arrested and murdered by hooligans helped by Belgian connivance, as two super-powers engaged in sparring, on the sidelines. Lumumba's brave stance against imperialism was and remains a valiant example for freedom fighters worldwide.

Mary Mcleod Bethune

Mary McLeod Bethune was born on 10 July 1875. She was an African-American and one of the great educators of the United States. She was a leader of women, a distinguished adviser to several American presidents, and a powerful champion of racial equality.

Mary McLeod was born in Mayesville, S.C. Her parents, Samuel and Patsy McLeod, were formerly enslaved; Mary was the fifteenth of seventeen children. She helped her parents on the family farm and first entered a Presbyterian mission school when she was eleven years old. Later, she attended Scotia Seminary, a school for African-American girls in Concord, N.C., on a scholarship.

She graduated in 1893; there she had met some of the people with whom she would work closely. Though she had a serious turn of mind, it did not prevent her from being a lively dancer and developing a lasting fondness for music. Dynamic and alert, she was very popular and the acknowledged leader of her classmates. After graduating from Scotia Seminary, she attended the Moody Bible Institute.

After graduation from Moody Institute, she wished to become a missionary in Africa; however, she was unable to pursue this end. She was an instructor at the Presbyterian Mission School in Mayesville in 1896 and later an instructor at Haines Institute in Augusta, GA, in 1896–1897. While she was an instructor at Kindell Institute in Sumpter, S.C., in 1897–1898, she met Albertus Bethune, whom she later married.

Bethune began her career as an educator in earnest when she rented a two-story frame building in Daytona Beach, Fla., and began the difficult task of establishing a school for African-American girls. Her school opened in October 1904, with six pupils, five girls and her own son; there was no equipment; crates were used for desks and charcoal took the place of pencils; and ink came from crushed elderberries.

Thus began the Daytona Literary and Industrial School for Training Negro Girls, in an era when most African-American children received little or no education.

At first, Bethune was teacher, administrator, comptroller, and custodian. Later, she was able to secure a staff, many of whom worked loyally for many years. To finance and expand the school, Bethune and her pupils baked pies and made ice cream to sell to nearby construction gangs. In addition to her regular classes, Bethune organized classes for the children of turpentine workers. In these ways, she satisfied her desire to serve as a missionary.

As the school at Daytona progressed, it became necessary to secure an adequate financial base. Bethune began to seek financial aid in earnest. In 1912, she interested James M. Gamble of the Proctor and Gamble Company of Cincinnati, Ohio, who contributed financially to the school and served as chairman of its board of trustees until his death.

In 1923, Bethune's school for girls merged with Cookman Institute of Jacksonville, Fla., a school for boys, and the new coeducational school became known as Bethune-Cookman Collegiate Institute, soon renamed Bethune-Cookman College. Bethune served as president of the college until her retirement as president emeritus in 1942. She remained a trustee of the college to the end of her life. By 1955, the college had a faculty of hundred and a student enrollment of over a thousand.

In addition to her career as an educator, Bethune wrote numerous magazine and newspaper articles and contributed chapters to several books. In 1932, she founded and organized the National Council of Negro Women and became its president; by 1955, this organization had a membership of 800,000. Bethune gained national recognition in 1936, when President Franklin D. Roosevelt appointed her director of African-American affairs in the National Youth Administration and a special adviser on minority affairs.

She served for eight years and supervised the expansion of employment opportunities and recreational facilities for African-American youth throughout the United States. She also served as special assistant to the secretary of war during World War II. In the course of her government assignments, she became a close friend of Eleanor Roosevelt.

During her long career, Bethune received many honorary degrees and awards, including the Haitian Medal of Honor and Merit (1949), the highest award of the Haitian government.

Bethune died in Daytona Beach on 18 May 1955, of a heart attack. She was buried on the campus of Bethune-Cookman College.

Ramses, The Great

Ramses II (also known as Ramses, the Great and Ramesses II) was a Kamitic Shekhem Ur Shekhem (King) (lived c. 1314 B.C. to 1224 B.C.), reigned 1290 B.C.–1224 B.C. (sixty-six years). He became king at the age of twenty-four, and died in his ninetieth year. He, therefore, was the second longest ruler of Kamit. He was known to the Ancient Greeks as Sesostris.

He was the third king of the 19th Dynasty, and the son of Seti I and his Queen Tuya. The most memorable of Ramses' wives was Nefertari. Another of his wives was Istnofret and Maetnefrure, Princess of Khatti. It is said that Ramses II had over two hundred children. Some of his children were Bintah (Bintanath), Setakht (Sethnakhte), the Pharaoh Merenptah, and Kha'emweset (Prince).

Ramses led several expeditions north into the lands east of the Mediterranean (the location of the modern Israel, Palestine, Lebanon and Syria). At the Battle of Qadesh in the fourth year of his reign (1286 B.C.),

Kamitic forces under Rameses II engaged the forces of Muwatallis, king of the Hittites. Over the following years, neither power could effectively defeat the other, so in the 21st year of his reign (1269 B.C.), Ramses concluded an agreement with Hattusilis III, the earliest known surviving peace treaty.

Ramses also campaigned south of the first cataract into Nubia. He constructed many impressive monuments, and more statues of him exist than of any other Egyptian Pharaoh. Ramses was indeed a strong believer in the work of those living in Deir el Medina.

He transitioned to the ancestral realm peacefully after a long and prosperous reign over the land of Kamit. The great man had ushered in some of the greatest years of the ancient Kamitic civilization.

Ahmose

Egyptian army officer, tutor of princess Neferura, 18th Dynasty, during the reigns of Ahmose, Amenhotep I, Thutmose I, Thutmose II and Thutmose III. During the regency of Hatshepsut, Ahmose Pen-Nekhbet started his military career at the end of the 17th Dynasty, probably around the same time as Ahmose, son of Abana. It would seem that he was a bit younger than his namesake.

King Ahmose, under whom both served at first, was not shy of decorating Ahmose, son of Abana, with various honors, whereas Ahmose Pen-Nekhbet could not mention any rewards for his military efforts since the reign of King Amenhotep I. This would imply he had a younger age or a negligible military rank or function under King Ahmose.

Ahmose Pen-Nekhbet continued to serve under the four kings, immediately succeeding Ahmose. "I was not separated from the King upon the battlefield, from [the time of] King Nebpehtire (Ahmose) (...) to King

Akheperenre (Thutmose II)." He remained "in favor of the King's presence, until King Menkheperre (Thutmose III)."

Ahmose Pen-Nekhbet probably died or at least retired from public life around the time when Queen Hatshepsut took on the full royal regalia, in the 7th regnal year of the nominal King Thutmose III. Ahmose Pen-Nekhbet stated that "the God's Wife repeated favors for me, the Great King's Wife, Maat-ka-ra."

While using the Queen's royal title, Ahmose did not include her in the list of kings under whom he served. The last public act he described was that he "educated her (Hatshepsut's) eldest daughter, Neferura (…), while she was a child at the breast," as a tutor either previous to or jointly with Senmut.

Just like the earlier mentioned Ahmose, son of Abana, Ahmose Pen-Nekhbet originally came from Nekheb (modern day El Kab) in Upper Kamit (Southern Kamit), at the time of his birth a region under the rule of the Theban Kings. Following the undoubted example of many of his neighbors and relatives, he joined the Theban forces in their struggle against the Hyksos for power over Lower Kamit. Ahmose Pen-Nekhbet's military exploits started off with a campaign under King Ahmose in the land of Djahi (northern Palestine).

The timing, range or importance of this campaign are hard to make out, as Ahmose Pen-Nekhbet's account is the only source so far, mentioning this expedition. The earlier mentioned lack of rewards for Ahmose Pen-Nekhbet during King Ahmose's reign could further simply the relative unimportance of this campaign.

As Amenhotep I succeeded King Ahmose, Ahmose Pen-Nekhbet followed the King into Nubia and to "the north of Iamu in the land of Kehek (or Iamu-Kehek)." While the location of such a 'land of Kehek' to the west of the Nile Delta.

After the Nubian expedition, the army of King Thutmose I went on a campaign through the Levant, going as far as Naharin (Western Mesopotamia), all the way up to the Euphrates River. Ahmose Pen-Nekhbet further accompanied the Egyptian army for one last time under King Thutmose II against the Shasu (SAsw) nomads in the Sinai. The enemy casualties and booty from these campaigns far exceeded those of the Hyksos war.

The growth of wealth in Ancient Kamit during this timeframe is apparent in the ever growing rewards, bestowed on Ahmose Pen-Nekhbet by the successive kings under whom he served.

Ida B. Wells

Ida B. Wells (1862–1931) was a newspaper editor and journalist who went on to lead the American anti-lynching crusade. Working closely with both African-American community leaders and American suffragists, Wells worked to raise gender issues within the 'Race Question' and race issues within the 'Woman Question'.

Wells was born the daughter of enslaved Afrikans in Holly Springs, Mississippi, on 16 July 1862. During Reconstruction, she was educated at a Missouri Freedman's School, Rust University, and began teaching school at the age of fourteen. In 1884, she moved to Memphis, Tennessee, where she continued to teach while attending Fisk University during summer sessions.

In Tennessee, especially, she was disgusted at the poor treatment she and other African-Americans received. After she was forcibly removed from her seat for refusing to move to a 'colored car' on the Chesapeake & Ohio Railroad, her suit against the railroad for violating her civil rights was rejected by the Tennessee Supreme Court in 1877. This event and the legal struggle which followed it, however, encouraged Wells to continue to oppose racial injustice toward African-Americans.

She took up journalism in addition to school-teaching, and in 1891, after she had written several newspaper articles critical of the educational opportunities afforded African-American students, her teaching contract was not renewed. Effectively barred from teaching, she invested her savings in a part-interest in the *Memphis Free Speech* newspaper.

In 1892, Wells wrote a scathing series of editorials following the lynching of three prominent African-American Memphis businessmen, friends of Wells'. In the aftermath of the lynching and her outspoken criticism of it, her newspaper's office was sacked. Wells then moved to New York City, where she continued to write editorials and exposes against lynching, which was at an epidemic level in the years after Reconstruction.

Joining the staff of The New York Age, Wells became a much-sought-after lecturer and organizer for anti-lynching societies made up of men and women of all races. She traveled throughout the U.S. and went to Britain twice to speak about anti-lynching activities.

In 1895, Wells married Ferdinand L. Barnett, a Chicago lawyer, public official, and publisher of *the Conservator*. She settled in Chicago and adopted as her married name Ida Wells-Barnett. After 1895, she limited her activities to Chicago, but she was quite active in Chicago's rapidly-growing African-American community.

In Chicago, she wrote for *the Conservator*, published a book length expose of lynching (*The Red Record*, 1895), and organized Chicago women regarding several causes, from anti-lynching to suffrage. From 1898 to 1902, Wells served as secretary of the National Afro-American Council, and in 1910, she founded and became the first president of the Negro Fellowship League.

Throughout her life, Wells was militant in her demands for equality and justice for African-Americans, and insisted that the African-American community must win justice through its own efforts. She attended the 1909 meeting of the Niagara Movement, but she would not take part in the less radical National Association for the Advancement of Colored People which grew out of the conference. After a life of organizing and writing, she transitioned to the ancestral realm in Chicago on 25 March 1931.

Assata Shakur

Born on 17 July 1947, Assata Shakur was a leader in the Black Liberation Movement and a member of the Black Panther Party for Self-Defense. Due to her activism, she was persecuted and framed in the United States.

Two years later, Assata escaped from prison with the help of the Black Liberation Army.

She has been living as a political refugee in Cuba since the mid-80s. American law enforcement officials and right-wing politicians have put a bounty on her head, and continue to lobby for pressure to be put on the Cuban regime to extradite her.

On 2 May 1973, Black Panther Assata Shakur (aka Joanne Chesimard) lay in a hospital, close to death, handcuffed to her bed, while local, state, and federal police attempted to question her about the shootout on the New Jersey Turnpike that had claimed the life of a white state trooper and Zayd Shakur, a Black revolutionary.

Long a target of J. Edgar Hoover's campaign to defame, infiltrate, and criminalize Black nationalist organizations and their leaders, Shakur had already been dogged by police accusations of criminal activities, although the cases against her were always dismissed due to the complete lack of evidence.

More than simply a political chronology, in this book Assata Shakur shares the life experiences that led her to embrace revolutionary politics and the fight for human liberation. She discusses her childhood, life in the Black Panther Party, and what it was like at the time to be faced by government repression, sanctioned by the FBI's lethal Counter-Intelligence Program.

Assata had faced the standard repressive fare of trumped up charges and bogus arrests since shortly after she joined the Black Panther Party. The harassment and vilification continued, forcing her into the underground. On 2 May 1973, she and her comrades Sundiata Acoli and Zayd Shakur were driving on the New Jersey Turnpike when a state trooper pulled them over in a case of Driving While Black.

Shots were exchanged and Zayd and one of the white state troopers were killed. Shot and seriously injured in the incident, Assata Shakur was at the time on the FBI's most wanted list, and orders had been given for her capture dead or alive, because she was supposed to be armed, dangerous, a kidnapper and murderer. Although, Zayd Shakur was the only one on whom a weapon was found, Assata and Sundiata were both tried and convicted of murder in 1977.

Frantz Fanon

Franz Fanon was born in Fort-de-France, Martinique, on 20 July 1925. Psychiatrist, writer, veteran anti-colonialist, Franz Fanon marked the 20th century by his thought and action, despite a short life due to illness.

Franz Fanon did his graduate studies at the Faculty of Medicine of Lyon, France and was appointed in 1953, Surgeon General of the psychiatric hospital in Blida. Algeria. He had already published in 1952, *Black Skin, White Masks*, his phenomenal book.

In 1956, two years after the outbreak of the war of national liberation in Algeria, Fanon took the side of the colonized and oppressed peoples. He resigned from his post at the hospital and joined the National Liberation Front (FLN) in Algeria.

He had important responsibilities in the FLN. Member of the editorial of its central body, 'El Mujahid', he was senior advisor to several states of black Africa and ambassador of the Provisional Government of the Algerian

Republic (GPRA) in Ghana. He escaped several attacks in Morocco and Italy. Until his death, Franz Fanon set no limits to fighting for the cause of oppressed peoples.

He transitioned to the ancestral realm in Washington 6 December 1961 at the age of thirty-six from leukemia and is buried in the cemetery Chouhada, Tunisia.

Another one of his books, *The Wretched of the Earth*, is studied till this day by lovers of justice worldwide.

Haile Selassie

Haile Selassie (1892–1975) was an emperor of Ethiopia whose influence as an African leader far surpassed the confines of his country. Haile Selassie was born on 23 July 1892, the son of Ras Makonnen, a cousin and confidant of Emperor Menilek II. Baptized Lij Tafari, Haile Selassie spent his youth at the imperial court of Addis Ababa, where, surrounded by constant intrigues, he learned much about the exercise of power.

Menilek no doubt recognized Tafari's capacity for hard work, his excellent memory, and his mastery of detail when he rewarded the youth's intellectual and personal capabilities by appointing him, at the age of twenty, dejazmatch (commander) of the extensive province of Sidamo. Upon the death of Menilek in 1913, his grandson, Lij Yasu, succeeded to the throne.

Yasu's apparent conversion to Islam alienated the national Christian church and gave impetus to the opposition movement led by Ras Tafari (as Haile Selassie was now designated), which joined noblemen and high church officials in deposing Yasu in 1916. Zawditu, the daughter of Menilek, then became empress, with Ras Tafari appointed regent and heir to the throne.

Throughout the regency, the Empress, conservative by inclination and more concerned with religion than politics, served to counteract Ras Tafari's rising interest in national modernization; the result was an uneasy coalition of conservative and reforming forces which lasted for nearly a decade.

In 1926, Tafari took control of the army, an action which, when coupled with his previous success in foreign affairs, including admission of Ethiopia to the League of Nations in 1923, made him strong enough to assume the title of negus (king).

When Zawditu died in April 1930, he demanded the title negasa negast (king of kings) and took complete control of the government with the throne name of Haile Selassie I ('Power of the Trinity').

In 1931, the new emperor promulgated a written constitution to symbolize his interest in modernization and intention to increase the power of central authority, which had been waning since the death of Menilek. Haile Selassie's efforts were cut short, however, when Mussolini's Italy invaded the country in 1935.

The Italian military deployed superior weaponry, airplanes, and poison gas to crush the ill-fated resistance led by the emperor; the ensuing Fascist occupation marked the first loss of national independence in recorded Ethiopian history. In 1936, Haile Selassie went into exile in England, where he appealed in vain to the League of Nations for help.

In early 1941, British expeditionary forces, aided by the heroic Ethiopian resistance, liberated the country, enabling Haile Selassie to triumphantly re-enter his capital in May. The centralized Italian colonial administration, backed by force and with a vastly improved road network, meant that the emperor returned to find that a great deal of provincial autonomy had been destroyed, leaving him in certain ways stronger than before he left.

Throughout the next decade, he rebuilt the administration, improved the army, passed legislation to regulate the government, church, and financial system, and further extended his control of the provinces by crushing revolts in Gojjam and Tigre. But in general, the emperor had gradually grown more cautious, and in his reluctance to antagonize conservative elements by any 'hasty' modernization, he allowed pitifully little infusion of new blood into the government.

In the 1950s, Haile Selassie worked for the absorption of the important Red Sea province of Eritrea (accomplished in 1962), founded the University Coelege of Addis Ababa, and welcomed home many Ethiopian college graduates from abroad. His Silver Jubilee of 1955 served as the occasion to present a revised constitution, followed in 1957 by the first general election.

Haile Selassie's continued efforts to hold political balance between several major politicians and the recurrent frustration of many newly returned graduates, who still found few places in government, eventually led dissident elements to attempt a government coup in December 1960. The coup failed, but it gave a short and violent jolt to the heretofore uneventfulness of Ethiopian politics and hinted of future possibilities.

In the 1960s, the emperor was clearly recognized as a major force in the pan-African movement, demonstrating his remarkable capacity for adapting to changing circumstances. It was a great personal triumph for him when, in 1963, the newly founded Organization of African Unity established its headquarters in Addis Ababa.

Unlike other African leaders, Haile Selassie, of course, had not had to struggle once in office to prove his legitimate authority to his people; his control of government for over forty years had given him enough time to identify with it. By 1970, the emperor had slowly withdrawn from many day-to-day administrative concerns and had become increasingly involved with foreign affairs. He probably made more state visits than any other head of state, enjoying such jaunts for their own sake even when they had little practical use.

To him, diplomacy seemed inseparable from prestige. At home, Haile Selassie more than ever evinced a trait of caution in his approach to modernization. Though receptive to Western innovations, he never throughout his long reign advanced faster than the consensus would allow, although by his 40th year in power, he appeared somewhat more concerned with adjustment to, and authorization of, change rather than with the active initiation of changes themselves.

A famine in Wello province in 1973 seriously undermined the credibility and legitimacy of Selassie's regime. With a strain on the nation, Selassie was forced to abdicate on 13 September 1974. The new octogenarian emperor, Selassie spent his final year of life on house arrest. His death was announced by the Dergue on 27 August 1975.

Alexandre Dumas Pere

Alexandre Dumas was born on 24 July 1802 in Villers-Cotterets, forty km NE of Paris. His birth certificate names him Dumas Davy de la Pailleterie. His grandfather was the Marquis Antoine-Alexandre Davy de la Pailleterie and his grandmother was Marie-Cessette Dumas, an enslaved Afrikan from Jeremie, Saint-Domingue (now part of Haiti). She gave birth to Thomas-Alexandre and died when he was young.

When they eventually returned to Paris, his grandfather did not approve of his father enlisting the army under the name of Davy de la Pailleterie, so he enlisted as Thomas-Alexandre Dumas. Thomas-Alexandre worked his way to the title of General under Napoleon Bonaparte.

Alexandre grew up in Villers-Cotterets, and traveled to Paris when he was twenty. By twenty-five, he had his first success as a playwright. Dumas has written many interesting anecdotes about these years in Mes Memoires. Many people do not realize that Dumas became famous not for his novels, but for his plays.

Dumas wrote hundreds of plays, novels and travel diaries. He wrote several children's stories, and a culinary dictionary. He started several magazines and wrote in them weekly. He was one of the most prolific writers ever, and did not shy away from collaborating with others or rewriting older stories.

His most successful novels are not deep, but contain marvelous adventures and actions, and bigger-than-life characters. He wrote many historical novels where he took great liberty with the truth in order to achieve a good story, but never claimed that they were historically accurate.

His son, Alexandre Dumas fils, wrote several important novels *including La Dame aux Camelias*, the basis of Verdi's opera La Traviata. After many years of writing, traveling, and carousing, after he had made and lost several fortunes, Dumas transitioned to the ancestral realm in Puys, near Dieppe, on 5 December 1870.

Although, he was originally buried where he had been born, in 2002 French President, Jacques Chirac, had his body exhumed. During a televised ceremony, his new coffin, draped in a blue velvet cloth and flanked by four Republican Guards (costumed as the Musketeers—Athos, Porthos, Aramis, and D'Artagnan), was transported in a solemn procession to the Pantheon of Paris, the great mausoleum where French luminaries are interred.

In his speech, President Chirac said: "With you, we were D'Artagnan, Monte Cristo, or Balsamo, riding along the roads of France, touring battlefields, visiting palaces and castles—with you, we dream."

Also during that speech, Chirac acknowledged the racism that had existed, saying that a wrong had now been righted, with Alexandre Dumas enshrined alongside fellow authors Victor Hugo and Emile Zola. The honor recognized that although France has produced many great writers, none has been so widely read as Alexandre Dumas. His stories have been translated into almost a hundred languages, and have inspired more than two hundred motion pictures.®

Alexandre Dumas' home outside of Paris, the Chateau de Monte-Cristo, has been restored and is open to the public. The Alexandre Dumas Paris Metro station was named in his honor in 1970.

Some of his great books include *The Three Musketeers, The Count of Monte Cristo, Twenty Years After,* and *The Knight of Sainte Hermine.*

Hatshepsut

Hatshepsut was the daughter of Tehutimose I and his royal wife, Ahmose. She was born on 27 July 1503 B.C.E. After coming of age, Hatshepsut married Tehutimose II. As his chief queen, Hatshepsut bore him one daughter, Neferure, one of three known offspring of Thutmose II.

Thutmose III, son of one of Thutmose II's minor wives, became the Shekhem Ur Shekhem on the death of Tehuitmose II. Tehutimose III was very young (estimated between two and ten years old), and Hatshepsut became regent for her stepson and nephew.

Hatshepsut gradually assumed the titles, powers and even the ceremonial clothing and beard of a male Shekhem Ur Shekhem, claiming legitimacy through a divine birth, even calling herself a 'female Heru'. She was formally crowned as king in about year 7 of her co-reign with Tehutimose III. Senemut, an architect, became a key advisor and powerful official under the reign of Hatshepsut.

He was also her architect and built her several monuments that were at the vanguard of the times. Hatshepsut made a trading expedition to Punt, a legendary land thought by some to be Eritrea and argued by others to be Uganda. Overall, Hatshepsut demonstrated great leadership as ruler and was a pioneer of female empowerment in ancient Africa. She transitioned after a long rule to the ancestral realm.

Queen Mother Moore

Queen Mother Moore was born Audley Moore in New Iberia, Louisiana, on 27 July 1898, and acquired the appellation Queen Mother on her first trip to Ghana, where she attended the funeral of Kwame Nkrumah in 1972. She was in the forefront of the struggle for seventy-seven years.

Her family was scarred by virulent racism. Her great-grandmother was raped by her slave master and her grandfather was lynched. Forced to quit school in the fourth grade, she studied to be a hairdresser to take care of her sisters. In the 1920s, she traveled around the country, only to learn that racism was not confined to the South.

She finally settled in Harlem where she organized, mobilized and demonstrated against racist oppression and imperialism directed toward Africa and people of African descent. She was locked into perpetual struggle against black oppression at all levels, joining numerous groups and founding a number of her own.

Initially inspired by Marcus Garvey's emphasis on African pride and culture, she waged battle on the Black Nationalist, Communist and Pan-Africanist fronts. In keeping with her credo, "There was nothing left to do but struggle," her list of activities defy enumeration.

Impressed by the Communist Party's role as the vanguard in the defense of the Scottsboro Boys, she joined the party. However, she left when she realized that the party could, or would, not translate its ideas about black self-determination into action. In 1955, she joined a small band of activists demanding reparations for slavery and its insidious legacy which has permeated black lives up to this day.

During Black History Month 2002, on 6 February, the Queen Mother Moore Reparations Resolution for Descendants of Enslaved Africans in New York City bill was submitted to the City Council.

Spanning an era from the heyday of Marcus Garvey to the second coming of Nelson Mandela, our Warrior Queen waged war on the hydra of black oppression whenever it raised an ugly head. It can definitely be said, in deference to Mandela, that the struggle was truly her life. She transitioned at the grand old age of ninety-seven.

Nandi of the Zulu

Mother of the great leader Shaka Zulu, Nandi is the everlasting symbol of hard work patience and determination. She withstood and overcame many obstacles to rise to a great position of power in all of Zululand, modern day South Africa.

The year was 1786. The king of Zululand was overjoyed. His wife, Nandi, had given birth to a son, his first son, whom they named Shaka. But the king's other wives, jealous and bitter, pressured him to banish Nandi and the young boy into exile. Stead-fast and proud, she raised her son with the kind of training and guidance a royal heir should have.

For her many sacrifices, Nandi was finally rewarded when her son, Shaka, later returned to become the greatest of all Zulu Kings.

When Nandi's hard work and devotion paid off and Shaka became king, she stood by his side and inspired him for her whole life. So strong was the bond between mother and child that Shaka almost lost his mind when his mother transitioned. He would always hold her in his heart as a perfect example of mothering.

To this day, the Zulu people use her name, 'Nandi', to refer to a woman of high esteem.

Tenkamenin

The ancient Empire of Ghana which includes most of modern day northwestern Africa (Mauritania, Mali and Senegal) reached the height of its greatness during the reign of Tenkamenin. The King of Ghana of the time was given the title of Wagadou.

Tenkamenin was a brave and fair king who according to the great African tradition always remained a servant of his people. His main preoccupations were good governance and justice for all. At the time of his rule, Ghana was the greatest civilization in the world with ample supplies of gold and philosophies grounded in the ancient ways of Africa.

Through his careful management of the gold trade across the Sahara desert into West Africa, Tenkamenin's empire flourished economically. But his greatest strength was in government. Each day he would ride out on horseback and listen to the problems and concerns of his people. He insisted that no one be denied an audience and that they be allowed to remain in his presence until satisfied that justice had been done.

His principles of democratic monarchy and religious tolerance make Tenkamenin's reign one of the great models of African rule.

Even until this day, his memory lives on in the pantheon of great African ancestors who modeled great leadership.

August

Chief Mirambo

Mytela Kasanda, or Mirambo, was a Nyamwezi Chief who gained control of much of east central Africa. He was born into the royal family of the small chiefdom of Uyowa, in modern day Tanzania. He likely became chief after the death of his father around 1860. He went on to become a powerful trader throughout the Great Lakes region, in what is now Tanzania.

Through trade with Europeans, Mirambo gained access to guns which along with his courage and that of his troops were critical in establishing his military supremacy in the region. With the aid of an army comprised mostly of adolescent boys, Mirambo gained control of the kingdom of Urambo, gaining tribute from noble families.

By unifying several Nyamwezi groups, Mirambo also gained control over major Swahili-Arab trade routes, establishing the Nyamwezi kingdom as a major regional economic and military player.

Trading primarily in ivory, Mirambo emerged as the dominant regional power around 1870. By 1875, he signed a treaty with the Sultan of Zanzibar, furthering Nyamwezi political stability. Mirambo continued to expand the kingdom of Urambo between 1876 and 1880, eventually controlling trade routes north to Buganda and as far west as Lake Tanganyika.

As European involvement in the East-African political sphere expanded, Mirambo came into conflict with the Arab allies of Sir Henry Morton Stanley over trade routes. Impressed by the military success of his enemy, Stanley called Mirambo 'the African Bonaparte'. Mirambo shared much of the east central African territory with Kabaka Mutesa, ruler of the Buganda kingdom. The two trader-kings maintained an uneasy peace while vying for control of the region.

Despite his military prowess and the substantial kingdom he established, an expanded Urambo collapsed a few years after Mirambo's transition to the ancestral realm in 1884. His name lived on until today and he is revered as a great national hero in Tanzania.

Edward Blyden

Edward Wilmot Blyden (1832–1912) was a Liberian educator and statesman. More than any other figure, he laid the foundation of West African nationalism and of Pan-Africanism.

Edward Blyden was born in St. Thomas, Virgin Islands, on 3 Aug. 1832, to free, literate parents. He decided at an early age to become a clergyman. He went to the United States in May 1850 and sought to enter a theological college but was turned down because of his race. In January 1851, he emigrated to Liberia, a African-American colony which had become independent as a republic in 1847.

He continued his formal education at Alexander High School, Monrovia, whose principal he was appointed in 1858. In 1862, he was appointed professor of classics at the newly opened Liberia College, a position he held until 1871. Although, Blyden was self-taught beyond high school, he became an able and versatile linguist, classicist, theologian, historian, and sociologist. From 1864 to 1866, in addition to his professorial duties, Blyden acted as secretary of state of Liberia.

From 1871 to 1873, Blyden lived in Freetown, Sierra Leone. There he edited *Negro*, the first explicitly pan-African journal in West Africa. He also led two important expeditions to Fouta Djallon in the interior. Between 1874 and 1885, Blyden was again based in Liberia, holding various high academic and governmental offices. In 1885, he was an unsuccessful candidate for the Liberian presidency.

After 1885, Blyden divided his time between Liberia and the British colonies of Sierra Leone and Lagos. He served Liberia again in the capacities of ambassador to Britain and France and as a professor and later president of Liberia College. In 1891 and 1894, he spent several months in Lagos and worked there in 1896–1897 as government agent for native affairs.

While in Lagos, he wrote regularly for the Lagos Weekly Record, one of the earliest propagators of Nigerian and West African nationalism. In Freetown, Blyden helped to edit the Sierra Leone News, which he had assisted in founding in 1884 "to serve the interest of West Africa…and the race generally."

He also had helped found and edit the Freetown West African Reporter (1874–1882), whose declared aim was to forge a bond of unity among English-speaking West Africans. Between 1901 and 1906, Blyden was director of Moslem education; he taught English and 'Western subjects' to Moslem youths with the object of building a bridge of communication between the Moslem and Christian communities. He transitioned to the ancestral realm in Freetown on 7 Feb. 1912.

Ta-Wsret

Queen Ta-Wsret ruled over Kamit (Ancient Egypt) during the last stretch of its Golden Age. She was the last legitimate female ruler to reign over Kamit. After her rule, Kamit fell into the hands of the Barbarian hordes and would never achieve its greatness of the past.

Ta Wsret was born of royal birth in Kamit and she belonged to the nobility. During her life, she was instructed in the ways of being a queen and she found that these instructions were totally necessary. At the time she lived, Kamit was in a period of tumult and uprisings brewed.

The Shekhem Ur Shekhem (King, Pharaoh) Sitptah of that time was very weak and his actions led to him being deposed by a high government official named Sitptah. Sitptah took over and he could only legitimize his rule by marrying a daughter of royal blood. Hence he courted Queen Ta-Wsret. She complied seeing the seed of greatness within him and they were wed.

During Sitptah's rule, Kamit became a little more stable, but this stability was very precarious. He deposed uprisings and held on to power as well as he could. Sitptah eventually transitioned to the ancestral realm and when this occurred, Ta-Wsret took over the mantle of leadership from him.

Ta-Wsret went on to rule for eight years after her husband's death, but was unable to restore stability to Kamit which was at the end of a cycle. Upon her transition, Kamit's golden age ended and foreigners took over. Nevertheless her name went down in history as the last legitimate and authentic black queen of ancient Kamit.

Jaja of the Opobo

Jaja of Opobo was born in Igboland and sold as enslaved to a Bonny trader at the age of twelve, he was named Jubo Jubogha by his first master. He was later sold to Chief Alali, the head of the Opubo Annie Pepple Royal House. Called Jaja by the British, this gifted and enterprising individual eventually became one of the most powerful men in the eastern Niger Delta.

The Niger Delta, where the Niger empties itself into the Gulf of Guinea in a system of intricate waterways, was the site of unique settlements called city-states.

From the 15th to the 18th century, Bonny, like the other city-states, gained its wealth from the profits of the trade. Here, an individual could attain prestige and power through success in business and, as in the case of Jaja, a slave could work his way up to head of state. The House was a socio-political institution and was the basic unit of the city-state.

In the 19th century—after the abolition of the slave trade in 1807—the trade in slaves was supplanted by the trade in palm oil, which was so vibrant that the region was named the Oil Rivers area.

The Houses in Bonny and other city-states controlled both the internal and external palm oil trade because the producers in the hinterland were forbidden to trade directly with the Europeans on the coast; the Europeans never left the coast for fear of malaria.

Astute in business and politics, Jaja became the head of the Anna Pepple House, extending its activities and influence by absorbing other houses, increasing operations in the hinterland and augmenting the number of European contacts. A power struggle ensued among rival factions in the houses at Bonny, leading to the breakaway of the faction led by Jaja.

He established a new settlement, which he named Opobo. He became King Jaja of Opobo and declared himself independent of Bonny.

Strategically located between Bonny and the production areas of the hinterland, King Jaja controlled trade and politics in the delta. In so doing, he curtailed trade at Bonny and fourteen of the eighteen Bonny houses moved to Opobo.

In a few years, he had become so wealthy that he was shipping palm oil directly to Liverpool. The British consul could not tolerate this situation. Jaja was offered a treaty of 'protection', in return for which the chiefs usually surrendered their sovereignty. After Jaja's initial opposition, he was reassured, in vague terms, that neither his authority nor the sovereignty of Opobo would be threatened.

Jaja continued to regulate trade and levy duties on British traders, to the point where he ordered a cessation of trade on the river until one British firm agreed to pay duties. Jaja refused to comply with the consul's order to terminate these activities, despite British threats to bombard Opobo. Unknown to Jaja, the Scramble for Africa had taken place and Opobo was part of the territories allocated to Great Britain.

This was the era of gunboat diplomacy, where Great Britain used her naval power to negotiate conditions favorable to the British.

Lured into a meeting with the British consul aboard a warship, Jaja was arrested and sent to Accra, where he was summarily tried and found guilty of 'treaty breaking' and 'blocking the highways of trade'.

He was deported to St. Vincent, West Indies, and four years later, he transitioned to the ancestral realm en route to Nigeria after he was permitted to return.

Ironically, Jaja's dogged insistence on African independence and effective resistance exposed British imperialism and made him the first victim of foreign territorial intrusion in West Africa. The fate of Jaja reverberated through the entire Niger Delta. Amazed at this turn of events, the other delta chiefs quickly capitulated.

In addition, the discovery of quinine as the cure for malaria enabled the British traders to bypass the middlemen and deal directly with the palm oil producers, thus precipitating the decline of the city-states.

King Jaja's downfall ensured a victory for British supremacy, paving the way for the eventual imposition of the colonial system in this region by the end of the century. Jaja's heroism and brave struggle is notable till this day.

Menelik, The Great

Born 17 August 1844, Menelik II was one of the most celebrated of Ethiopia's rulers, and led the most successful campaign of African resistance to repel the onslaught of European colonialism. Menelik's reign (1889–1913) coincided with the European Scramble for Africa. After serving as governor of Shoa for twenty-five years, Menelik became emperor in 1889.

During his reign, he doubled the area he inherited, incorporating vast areas of southern Ethiopia into his domain, mainly through conquest.

Always eager to embrace new technology in his quest to modernize ancient Ethiopia, Menelik's innovations were unprecedented in Ethiopian history. Among these were first and foremost the creation of the capital, Addis Ababa, in the mid-1880s; construction of modern bridges and telegraph lines; concession for a railroad; establishment of the bank of Abyssinia, the first hotel, hospitals, and schools; national currency; mint; a postal system and national newspaper.

Italy, with a colony already established in Eritrea, had designs on Ethiopia. In 1889, Ethiopia and Italy negotiated the Treaty of Wuchale. Written in Amharic and Italian, the most significant article of the treaty was viewed differently by both parties. The Amharic text stated that Italy's services were available to the emperor for all communications with foreign powers, while the Italian text made this compulsory.

Italy applied this article to claim a protectorate over Ethiopia, which was duly recognized by the European powers. To affirm their claim, the Italians, aided and abetted by the French and British, advanced into northern Ethiopia and, in January 1890, occupied the town of Adowa.

While the dispute was being debated, Menelik was simultaneously importing large amounts of arms from France and Russia, and continuing to expand his domain. Finally expressing his disapproval of the Treaty of Wuchale and Italy's fallacious claim, he informed the European powers that "Ethiopia has need of no one, she stretches her hand unto God."

Recognizing his country's sovereignty, religion, and way of life was at stake, Menelik mobilized his army. The confrontation occurred at Adowa on 1 March 1896, where Ethiopia decisively defeated the Italian invaders. It was the first major African victory over an European Army since Hannibal's time two thousand years before.

On 16 October 1896, the Italians agreed to The Peace Treaty of Addis Ababa, which nullified the Treaty of Wuchale and recognized the absolute independence of Ethiopia. Menelik maintained his independence and unified his country by defeating the Europeans. Ethiopia's international prestige in the world was enhanced and its victory over the Europeans provided Africans in the Diaspora with a much-needed source of pride, inspiration and hope.

Menelik displayed great foresight in developing his military strength, which proved to be considerably superior to the Italian army he encountered, and also in using European trade and technology without yielding any political ground. In addition, his diplomatic maneuvers exploited the greed of Italy, France, and Britain, and shrewdly played them off against each other.

After a lengthy illness, he transitioned to the ancestral realm in 1913.

Marcus Garvey

Marcus Garvey and the Universal Negro Improvement Association (UNIA) form a critical link in the Pan-Afrikan centuries-long struggle for freedom, justice, and equality. As the leader of the largest organized mass movement in modern black history and progenitor of the modern 'black is beautiful' ideal, Garvey is now best remembered as a champion of the back-to-Africa movement. In his own time, Marcus Garvey was hailed as a redeemer, a 'Black Moses'.

Though Marcus Garvey failed to realize all his objectives, his movement still represents a liberation from the psychological bondage of racial inferiority.

Garvey was born on 17 August 1887 in St. Ann's Bay, Jamaica. Marcus Garvey left school at fourteen, worked as a printer, joined Jamaican nationalist organizations, toured Central America, and spent time in London. Content at first with accommodation, on his return to Jamaica, Marcus Garvey aspired to open a Tuskegee-type industrial training school. In 1916, Marcus Garvey came to America at Booker T. Washington's invitation, but arrived just after Washington died.

Garvey arrived in America at the dawn of the 'New Negro' era. Black discontent, punctuated by East St. Louis's bloody race riots in 1917 and intensified by postwar disillusionment, peaked in 1919s Red Summer. Shortly after arriving, Garvey embarked upon a period of travel and lecturing. When Marcus Garvey settled in New York City, Marcus Garvey organized a chapter of the UNIA, which Marcus Garvey had earlier founded in Jamaica as a fraternal organization.

Drawing on a gift for oratory lecturing, Marcus Garvey melded Jamaican peasant aspirations for economic and cultural independence with the American gospel of success to create a new gospel of racial pride. 'Garveyism' eventually evolved into a religion of success, inspiring millions of black people worldwide who sought relief from racism and colonialism.

To enrich and strengthen his movement, Garvey envisioned a great shipping line to foster black trade, to transport passengers between America, the Caribbean, and Africa, and to serve as a symbol of black grandeur and enterprise. The UNIA incorporated the Black Star Line in 1919. The line's flagship, the S.S. Yarmouth, made its maiden voyage in November and two other ships joined the line in 1920.

The Black Star Line became a powerful recruiting tool for the UNIA, but it was ultimately sunk by expensive repairs, discontented crews, and top-level mismanagement and corruption.

By 1920, the UNIA had hundreds of chapters worldwide; it hosted elaborate international conventions and published the Negro World, a widely disseminated weekly that was soon banned in many parts of Africa and the Caribbean. Over the next few years, however, the movement began to unravel under the strains of internal dissension, opposition from black critics, and government harassment.

In 1922, the federal government indicted Garvey on mail fraud charges stemming from Black Star Line promotional claims and Marcus Garvey suspended all BSL operations (Two years later, the UNIA created another line, the Black Cross Navigation and Trading Co., but it, too, failed). Garvey was sentenced to prison. The government later commuted his sentence, only to deport him back to Jamaica in November 1927.

Marcus Garvey never returned to America. In Jamaica, Garvey reconstituted the UNIA and held conventions there and in Canada, but the heart of his movement stumbled on in America without him. While Marcus Garvey dabbled in local politics, Marcus Garvey remained a keen observer of world events, writing voluminously in his own papers. His final move was to London, in 1935.

He transitioned to the ancestral realm on 10 June 1940 after having given the Afrikans worldwide a legacy of pride and nation building.

Dinah Salifou

Mohammad Salifou Dinah was born in 1858. He was the eldest son of King Makoumba and ruled Nalou from 1887 to 1897 in the region known as the Southern Rivers, modern day Guinea. This area was the subject of an ancient Anglo-French commercial rivalry, intrigue and struggle.

After a period of extremely turbulent and violent succession, Dinah replaced his uncle, Youra Towel, who was the brother and successor of Lamina Towel. Dinah Salifou received the support of the French, who awarded him a certificate demonstrating their acceptance of his capacity as king.

He went on to struggle for the independence of his people and tried to overcome the French who tried to take over his land. After a brave struggle, he was eventually ambushed and arrested by the French, and detained in the military post of Boke.

Later on, he was moved to Goree and St. Louis. He was finally freed but as an act of intimidation and to control his actions the French held his son hostage. Dinah Salifou wished to mark its independence vis-a-vis the French, while seeking their support to rid him of his cousin, Tocba, who had his eye on his throne.

Even though he converted his people to Islam, he himself maintained lots of precepts of his African Traditional Religion.

He was regarded as a very strong ruler, but his trust was abused by the French. Due to his importance, South Dr. Bayol, a French dignitary, invited him to Paris for the Universal Exhibition of 1889 which saw the erection of the Eiffel Tower. For Dinah Salifou, this was a great journey that demonstrated that he was the equal of the French, but he would later regret it. During his absence, unrest flared up in the region, at the instigation of his cousin, Tocba.

Dinah invited the French once again to come to his assistance. On this occasion, however, the French who did not see it in their best interest to support him turned him down. Instead, they placed him under house arrest in St. Louis.

Later on, Dinah Salifou was offered a pension by the French Governor de Lamothe.

The pension was later reduced and the brave warrior of his people transitioned to the ancestral realm in poverty in 1897. His memory remains, however, as a brave strategist who always sought the welfare and pride of his people.

Fred Hampton

Fred Hampton was born in Chicago on 30 August 1948 and grew up in Maywood, a suburb of the city. A bright student, Hampton graduated from Proviso East High School in 1966, before enrolling at Triton Junior College where he studied law. While a student, Hampton became active in the civil rights movement.

He joined the National Association for the Advancement of Colored People (NAACP), and was appointed leader of the Youth Council of the organization's West Suburban branch.

In October 1966, Bobby Seale and Huey Newton formed the Black Panther Party in Oakland, California. Initially formed to protect local communities from police brutality and racism, the Black Panthers eventually developed into a Marxist revolutionary group. The group also ran medical clinics and provided free food to school children. Other important members included Stokely Carmichael, H. Rap Brown, Bobby Hutton and Eldridge Cleaver.

Hampton founded the Chicago chapter of the Black Panther Party in November 1968. He immediately established a community service program. This included the provision of free breakfasts for school children and a medical clinic that did not charge patients for treatment.

Hampton also taught political education classes and instigated a community control of police project. One of Hampton's greatest achievements was to persuade Chicago's most powerful street gangs to stop fighting against each other. In May 1969, Hampton held a press conference where he announced a non-aggression pact between the gangs, and the formation of what he called a 'rainbow coalition' (a multiracial alliance of black, Puerto Rican, and poor youths).

Later that year, Hampton was arrested and charged with stealing $71 worth of sweets, which he then allegedly gave away to local children. Hampton was initially convicted of the crime but the decision was eventually overturned.

The activities of the Black Panthers in Chicago came to the attention of J. Edgar Hoover and the FBI. Hoover described the Panthers as 'the greatest threat to the internal security of the country' and urged the Chicago police to launch an all-out assault on the organization. In 1969, the Panther party headquarters on West Monroe Street was raided three times and over hundred members were arrested.

In the early hours of the 4 December 1969, the Panther headquarters was raided by the police for the fourth time. The police later claimed that the Panthers opened fire and a shoot-out took place. During the next ten minutes, Fred Hampton and Mark Clark were killed. Witnesses claimed that Hampton was wounded in the shoulder and then executed by a shot to the head.

The panthers left alive, including Deborah Johnson, Hampton's girlfriend, who was eight months pregnant at the time, were arrested and charged with attempting to murder the police. Afterward, ballistic evidence revealed that only one bullet had been fired by the Panthers whereas nearly a hundred came from police guns.

This strong and just man transitioned to the ancestral realm having lead a fearless struggle against injustice and imperialistic aggression.

September

Phillis Wheatley

Was the first recorded Afrikan poet in America. Born in Senegambia, she was put in bondage at eight and kidnapped and brought to the U.S. The ship on which she was kidnapped and brutalized was called the Phillis, and the U.S. terrorist kidnappers who purchased her on arrival to the U.S. had the last name of Wheatley. She hence called herself Phillis Wheatley.

She lived in Boston with the Wheatleys and early on in life they noticed her affinity for letters. Since the Wheatleys had her become a domestic servant to their daughter, Mary, she did not have to go through the excess brutality of plantation bondage. The Wheatleys were quite progressive and once they noticed Phillis affinity for letters, they assisted her in studying Latin, science, English, geography and history. She studied the Bible extensively.

By the age of twelve, Phillis was reading Greek and Latin classics and the Bible fluently. She would regularly read during the day and write during the night. Her poetry was so good that she was invited to London where she gave a reading to the mayor of London and was supposed to also give a reading to King George 3rd. However, she had to return prematurely from her visit.

In 1773, Phillis Wheatley was granted freedom due to her popularity and influence as a poet. Her old master went on to die in 1778 and at that time she was married to a black grocer. Due to the complexity of being free black people in those times, her husband went into debt and Phillis Wheatley was unable to publish another one of her poems.

Instead, she was forced to become a domestic laborer when her husband was imprisoned and she was left to care for their sickly daughter. Due to these difficult times, Wheatley transitioned in 1784 at the tender age of thirty-one.

She is honored today by having a statue in her honor in Boston and also by having a building in her name at the University of Massachusetts. Her writing is seen as the foundational writing in Afrikan-American literature. She clearly was one of the greatest poets of American history and her works were second to none.

Lewis Latimer

Was born 4 September 1848. His parents had been in bondage, but had chosen to escape. They went to Trenton, New Jersey, where Lewis Latimer grew up. At the age of fifteen, Lewis Latimer joined the U.S. Navy and stayed with the navy for two years. After this, he was employed as an office boy in a patent law firm.

In the firm, he learned to use an L Square, ruler and other similar tools, and was quickly recognized by his boss for his immaculate sketching of patent drawings. He was, therefore, promoted to the position of head draftsman. In 1874, he co-patented an improved toilet system for railway toilets called the Water Closet for Railroad Cars.

Word spread about Latimer's great skill and expertise and for this reason, Alexander Graham Bell hired Latimer as a draftsman in Bell's patent law firm. In Bell's firm, Latimer patented the necessary drawings required to receive a patent for Bell's telephone.

Once again word spread about his excellence and in 1879, he moved to Bridgeport, Connecticut, with his Afrikan family that included his brother, mother and wife. In Bridgeport, he was employed as an assistant manager and draftsman by the U.S. Electric Lighting Company, a rival of Thomas Edison. Latimer received a patent in January 1881 for the 'Process of Manufacturing Carbons', an improved method for the production of carbon filaments for lightbulbs.

The Edison Electric Light Company in New York City hired Latimer in 1884, as a draftsman and an expert witness in patent litigation on electric lights.

Lewis Latimer lived a long and healthy life and only transitioned to the ancestral realm at eighty. He had a small family consisting of a wife and two daughters. His genius and versatility would go down in history as unsurpassed by many. Without him, innovations such as the telephone and the light bulb might indeed have not been invented and propagated for long years after.

He was inducted into the National Inventors Hall of Fame and his home was turned into a museum in his honor. The community also had a park and a school named after this grandiose and multi-talented man.

J. A. Rogers

Was a Jamaican-American author who was a very important person that contributed to the dissimulation of the true Afrikan story of our past greatness.

Joel Augustus Rogers was born in Negril, Jamaica, on 6 September 1880. He was one of eleven children in his family, and even though his parents were only able to give their children basic education, they stressed the value of learning to them.

Rogers migrated to the U.S. in 1906 and henceforth lived in Harlem for most of his life. He lived during the Harlem Renaissance and was good friends of lots of the artists that stirred on this cultural reconnection.

He worked as a Pullman Porter and was able to satisfy his thirst for learning by traveling across the country and visiting numerous libraries as well as talking to numerous people.

He used lots of the research gathered in his traveling days to write his future books. His first book was entitled *From Superman to Man*, and was a discussion between a racist southerner and a black porter in which the porter points out all the great achievements of blacks and the fallacy behind racist theory.

In the 20s, Rogers worked as a journalist in several major papers and finally found a niche in Marcus Garvey's *Daily Negro Times*. However, this journal was short lived. Rogers continued being a journalist and reported on the coronation of Haile Selassie in Ethiopia. He also interviewed Marcus Garvey when he was in prison.

He served as the only black U.S. correspondent in World War II. Later on his life, he went on to write numerous books on the achievements of blacks that challenged the racist stigma attached to them. He was very well read and his writings till this day are cherished by many. He transitioned to the ancestral realm in 1966, but not without having left a legacy of great literacy that enabled blacks worldwide to appreciate their true greatness.

El Hadj Omar

El Hadj Omar was a West Afrikan political leader, Islamic leader and Toucouleur military commander.

El Hadj Omar was born in modern day Senegal. He attended Koranic School before making a pilgrimage to Mecca to earn his title as El Hadj. On his pilgrimage, he healed the son of Ibrahim, Pasha.

In 1826, after several years of learning, El Hadj returned to Sokoto in West Afrika and after being married, he moved to Futa-Djallon in Guinea to prepare for a jihad (holy war).

With his army, El Hadj went on to conquer several regions in Mali and West Afrika, but was stopped by the French at Median Fort.

El Hadj went on to conquer most of the land of the Bambaras in modern day Mali and Burkina Faso.

He fought the French colonial invaders in several battles and each time showed bravery and tact. On several occasions, he was on the point of wining these battles when unexpected things happened. As a Muslim, he showed great devotion to Allah and was willing to put his life on the line for what he believed in.

He transitioned to the ancestral realm in a glorious fashion while in battle against the imperialist French. In his memory, his descendants fought the French vigorously until they were finally defeated, but they never abandoned the struggle. El Hadj was a major proponent of the self-determination of his people through the vehicle of Islam. He was a man of faith, whose military might and prowess are venerated up until today.

Queen of Sheba

Makeda was the queen of the ancient Kingdom of Sheba which included modern day Ethiopia, Eritrea, Yemen and parts of Somalia. She was a great monarch who ruled her empire with dignity and integrity.

During her reign, the only other ruler in the world who had a comparable empire was Solomon. Solomon was said to possess great wisdom, and therefore Makeda decided that she would visit him in Jerusalem (Heru-Salam).

Makeda's journey to Jerusalem was like no other, with her traveled several carriages of subjects along with gold that was sufficient to fill the Nile River. When she arrived in Jerusalem, Solomon was in awe of her great power and of her beauty. She was the most beautiful woman he had ever seen.

Makeda consulted with Solomon and found that he had wisdom. She also found that he was totally hypnotized by her beauty. Before going to sleep at night, she made him swear not to try to impose himself on her. Solomon agreed, but only if Sheba promised not to take anything valuable from his palace without asking.

The feast which Makeda had partook in to celebrate her arrival consisted of very spicy food, therefore Makeda was thirsty and woke up in the middle of the night to drink some water. The sneaky and smart Solomon caught her in the act and appraised her that she had broken her promise, since water was the most valuable thing he owned. He, therefore, was released of his promise and spent the night with the great queen.

After her journey, Makeda traveled back to her empire and applied some of the wisdom she had acquired from Solomon to make some changes. She also bore a child from her union with Solomon called Menelik the first.

He would later travel to Jerusalem to see his father and return to Sheba with the Arc of the Covenant, which till this day is secured in Ethiopia.

Makeda was the matriarch of the great Ethiopian dynasty that ruled Ethiopia for centuries and was revered worldwide. Her greatness, beauty and wisdom were second to no other ruler.

Amilcar Cabral

Was born on 12 September 1924, and was an Afrikan revolutionary, nationalist, writer and agronomic engineer. He was born in Guinea Bissau and educated in Cape Verde, and then later on in Lisbon. He studied agronomy in Portugal and founded student movements dedicated to Afrikan liberation.

He returned to Afrika in 1950 and spearheaded the creation of several liberation movements all over the Portuguese colonies in Afrika.

Beginning in 1963, Cabral led his liberation movement in a guerrilla movement which evolved into a military conflict against the Portuguese ruling authorities of Portuguese Guinea. The goal of the conflict was to attain independence for both Portuguese Guinea and Cape Verde. Over the course of the conflict, as the group captured territory from the Portuguese, Cabral was made the de facto leader of a large portion of Guinea-Bissau.

Before the struggle, Cabral had trained his revolutionary group in guerrilla warfare in neighboring Ghana with the support of Kwame Nkrumah. As an agronomist, he taught his army to plant crops and enabled them to help local farmers increase their output. In the territories he freed, he also installed a rotating hospital system.

Having struggled and won independence for his people, Amilcar Cabral was summoned by the Portuguese to go to Guinea, Conakry to sign document stating the independence of his country Guinea-Bissau. In a conniving, deceptive and cowardly plot, the Portuguese set up one of his rivals to assassinate him and the great man fell victim to their deception on 20 January 1973.

His half-brother, Luis Cabral, became the first ruler of an independent Guinea-Bissau, benefiting from the great struggle of a great man who always showed, dignity, integrity and love toward his people and the rest of humanity.

In his honor is named the international airport in Cape Verde and also a West Afrikan soccer tournament. His undaunted spirit lives on in the hearts of Afrikan freedom-fighters worldwide.

Queen Tiye

Queen Tiye was the daughter of Yuya and Tjuyu, and went on to become the great royal wife of Amenhotep 3rd. Her father originated in Upper Kamit (southern part of Kamit) in which he was a High Priest and supervisor of oxen.

She married Amenhotep in the 2nd year of his reign and with him went on to have had six children, of which Akenaton went on to become ruler. She was a queen of great beauty and also of great integrity. Her manners were second to none and people in Kamit from far and wide would travel to pay homage to her.

Her husband was so much in awe of her that he had several shrines devoted to her, a temple and even an artificial lake built in her honor.

Tiye wielded a great deal of power during both her husband's and son's reigns. Amenhotep III became a fine sportsman, a lover of outdoor life, and a great statesman. He often had to consider claims for Kamit's gold and requests for his royal daughters in marriage from foreign kings such as Tushratta of Mitanni and Kadashman-Enlil I of Babylon.

The royal lineage was carried by the women of Ancient Egypt and marriage to one would have been a path to the throne for their progeny. Tiye became her husband's trusted adviser and confidant. Being wise, intelligent, strong, and fierce, she was able to gain the respect of foreign dignitaries. Foreign leaders were willing to deal directly through her. She continued to play an active role in foreign relations and was the first Kamitic Queen to have her name recorded on official acts.

She continued to exert great influence when her son became king, and lived a long healthy life in which she saw Kamit grow and blossom. She transitioned into the ancestral realm in the 12th year of her son's reign. She was buried along with her family and this was a memorable occasion for all of those in Kamit who had loved and appreciated their graceful matriarch.

Tiye's beauty was second to none and her effigy came down in history. Until today it is preserved and depicts her fullest beauty, with her braided Afrikan hair, her dark brown skin and her wonderfully Afrikan features. Queen Tiye reminds us that our natural Afrikan beauty is the best way for us to thrive.

Sunny Ali Ber

Was born Ali Kolon in Songhai and went on to become the greatest ruler of ancient Songhai. He was educated under his father in both Koranic School as well as in the traditional ways. His father was Silman Dandi, who himself was a wise and dignified ruler.

When his father transitioned, Sunny Ali took the reins of power in ancient Songhai. He reinforced his infantry and cavalry and gave reverence to Allah and Islam as well as his ancestors. He never repressed traditional Afrikan religions because he knew that all truths needed to be embraced. There was no persecution under the basis of religion in his reign, and his reign was more liberal than many reigns even up until today.

Using the gri-gri of his ancestors and the discipline of Islam, Sunny Ali Ber extended his empire to cover a great portion of the Niger River Delta. His strategies proved to be very fruitful and he was able to gain control of the main trading and educational cities of Timbuktu and Djenne. Sunni expelled lots of scholars of Timbuktu as well as the Tuareg due to their view of Islam being very exclusive and repressive toward traditional Afrikan religions.

By doing this, he consolidated his power. Furthermore during his reign, Songhai went on to exceed the size of ancient Ghana and ancient Mali. Songhai was revered the world over and known to be not only a seat of power but a seat of higher learning and culture.

Sunny Ali Ber ruled with righteousness and was the high judge for his people in cases of litigation. He also listened and honored his council of elders when they advised him. He perfectly balanced the world of Islam with the traditional ways of the ancestors and hence was blessed with great success.

The great king joined the ancestors in 1492, drowned upon making an attempt to cross the Niger River. His transition was testimony to his life as a man of action, a man of diplomacy and a man who was able to merge two visibly alternate worldviews with ease and dexterity.

Jan Matzeliger

Jan Matzeliger was born on 15 September 1852 in Paramaribo, Suriname. He became a sailor early on in life, and then in the early 1870s, he moved to the U.S. He had had an interest in mechanics in his native country, but it is when he came to the U.S. that this interest blossomed.

Jan Matzeliger went on to work in a machinery shop for several years. He eventually grew tired of this and went to work in a shoe factory. The job was made very difficult because at the time there were no machines to attach the upper part of the shoe to its sole. This task had to be done manually by a 'hand laster'.

Due to this, the shoe output was fifty pairs in a ten hour day. This practice was very tiresome and unproductive, therefore Jan Matzeliger decided that he had to do something to help the process.

He, therefore, started to work assiduously to create an innovation to improve this task. After five years of hard work, Jan Matzeliger made an invention that would revolutionize the way shoes were made forever more.

He got a patent for this invention in 1883. His invention was a machine which could produce between 150 and 700 shoes per day, cutting shoe prices across the nation by half. His invention was an automatic method for lasting shoes.

Jan Matzeliger was a true machinery genius who employed himself for the betterment of society. He was deeply concerned with the welfare of his fellow humans and always demonstrated this caring. His invention was very profitable for his estate, but unfortunately he did not live to see this great fortune as he transitioned into the ancestral realm as a victim of one of the great killers of the time, Tuberculosis, in 1889, just six years after his patent.

His memory, however, was treasured by friends, family and strangers, and it is for this reason that a U.S. postage stamp with his likeness was released in 1991. Jan Matzeliger was a true contemporary genius who made our era of shoe production move forward exponentially. Every time you buy or wear a shoe, you should be thankful to this great man.

Agostinho Neto

Agostinho Neto was born on 17 September 1922 in rural Angola. He moved shortly after to Luanda, the capital city where he went to school and his father was a pastor.

After finishing school in Angola, he migrated to Portugal to pursue his studies in medicine. While studying medicine, Neto took part in covert political activity of a revolutionary sort. He was so involved in the movement that he was arrested in Portugal in 1951 for his activism. Seven years later, he was released from prison and went on to finish his studies.

He returned to Angola in 1959 where he became chairman of The Popular Movement for the Freedom of Angola. Due to his activism, he was arrested once again in 1960. His patients marched for his release, but were met with violence and atrocities by the Portuguese authorities, who killed thirty of them and wounded two hundred in the Massacre of Icolo e Bengo.

The Portuguese refused to listen to the people and sent Neto into exile. He first was sent to Cape Verde and then to Portugal. After international protests, Neto was freed and put under house arrest.

Knowing this was unjust, he escaped and traveled to Morocco and then Zaire, from there he went to several countries to seek aid in his war against the ruthless and unjust Portuguese. Cuba was the only country that accepted and hence, Neto became close allies with Che Guevera.

In 1974, Portugal went through a revolution and their dictator was removed. This along with the protracted brave struggle of the Angolans enabled Angola to gain independence. Agostinho Neto was the natural choice for president of an independent Angola. His government maintained its links with its allies from Cuba and the Soviet Union, and were engaged in a Civil War against South Africa and Western cronies.

The great Neto joined the ancestral plane in 1979 after a surgery in Moscow due to cancer. He is remembered in his native land today with statues and a university named after him. Even countries as far as Serbia paid him tribute by naming a street in his memory.

Agostinho Neto will be remembered as a great man of multiple talent, who healed his people both physically and spiritually.

Kwame Nkrumah

Kwame Nkrumah was born on 21 September 1909, and went on to be one of the most pivotal Afrikan leaders of the century. His place of birth was in rural Gold Coast (Ghana). He went to school in Accra and in 1935, left Ghana to pursue university studies in the U.S. He received a bachelor of Sacred Theology not too long after. Nkrumah continued his studies and was awarded a Masters of Philosophy in 1942.

During his studies in the U.S., Nkrumah was politically active in Pan-Afrikan student unions and met with the ideas of the great minds of the time, including Garvey and C. L. R James. He went to London in 1945 after World War II and along with the great Trini, Pan-Afrikan, George Padmore, organized the fifth Pan-Afrikan Congress. The goal of this congress was to abolish colonialism in Afrika.

Even though Nkrumah finished his studies with a Masters of Arts, he was later offered multiple honorary doctorates by several higher learning institutions.

In 1947, Nkrumah was offered to work as Secretary General to the United Gold Coast Convention which would explore paths to independence in the Gold Coast. After popular protests in 1948, Nkrumah was arrested, but soon after released. After his release, he traveled around the country meeting with people in village councils.

During his journeys, he encouraged women to vote and be empowered, and united his country folk together to form a political party called the Convention People's Party. The British colonialists then offered partial independence to the Gold Coast and wanted for only those with enough property or a high enough wage to vote, however Nkrumah rejected this and demanded universal suffrage.

He encouraged civil disobedience and was sentenced to three years in jail. Due in great part to his dedication to freedom, Britain had no choice but to offer Ghana its independence on 6 March 1957. Kwame Nkrumah took on the title of Osageyefo and became Ghana's first free leader, and also first president of the first decolonized country in Sub-Saharan Afrika.

When Nkrumah became prime minister, he changed Ghana to a republic and became its first president. He stirred Ghana in a communalist direction in synch with Afrikan traditional governments, but many referred to his government as socialist and put them in league with the U.S.S.R. Nkrumah went on to help found the Organization for Afrikan Unity and he promoted the idea of Afrikan Unity and one single Afrikan government.

In 1966, during the blossom of his rule, while he traveled to North Vietnam and China, the U.S. armed some soldiers in his army and backed a coup d'tat. The great man was overthrown and replaced by Western lackeys. He never returned to Ghana, but was offered by Sekou Toure to be a co-president of Guinea.

He lived and worked there until 1972 when he transitioned to the ancestral realm. His remains were put into a large memorial tomb in Accra, to which many pan-Afrikans journey today in order to show their respect to the father of the modern Ghanaian nation and one of the greatest black leaders of his time.

Shaka Zulu

Shaka Zulu was born in 1787 in Zululand. He went on to become one of the most powerful Zulu rulers ever. Shaka was the son of a chief and his mother was the daughter of a chief. His early years were spent living with his mother and in her compound where he went through male rites of passage in a fighting unit.

He went on to become a warrior under a king to which the Zulu paid tribute. In his service, he distinguished himself often with displays of bravery and courage.

Upon the death of the king of the Zulu's, the king to which Shaka was a vassal, helped him to take power and become king of Zululand. Together, they perfected some war techniques that would help Shaka defeat many nations in the future. When the king to which he was a vassal was killed, Shaka was convinced to take revenge and that he did severely and sternly.

Shaka then went on to expand his territory using a balanced and strategic mix of diplomacy and warfare. He militarized the Zulu people and made conscription mandatory for all males. Zululand now encompassed a land mass that the Zulu's would have never dreamed possible with Shaka at the helm.

Tragedy struck, however, when Nandi, Shaka's mother, transitioned. Shaka was distraught and being beside himself, enacted illogical laws and restrictions. At this time, his half-brother had become power hungry and one evening when Shaka had sent most of his troops to the northern front to increase his empire's territory, he was lunged upon and killed by his two half-brothers. They took over the reins of king but were unable to live up to Shaka's greatness.

Shaka was one of the main people that gave the Zulu's a warrior mentality which enabled them to defeat the British later on under Cetawayo.

There are several monuments erected in his honor in KwaZulu Natal in South Afrika and he is an integral part of South Afrikan, Afrikan and black history. The Zulu Nation founded by the Godfather of Hip Hop Music Afrika, Bambaataa, draws inspiration from great Zulus like Shaka. He was clearly one of Afrika's and the world's greatest military geniuses.

George Padmore

Malcolm Nurse (later known as George Padmore) was born in Arouca, Trinidad, on 24 September 1902. His grandfather was enslaved Afrikan and his father was a school teacher. As a young man, Padmore met C. L. R. James and the two men became close friends.

Padmore worked as reporter in Trinidad before moving to the United States in 1924 to study sociology in New York. He joined the American Communist Party and provided articles for the *Daily Worker*.

In 1929, Padmore went to the Soviet Union where he became head of the Negro Bureau of the Red International of Labor Unions. The following year, he helped organize the first International Conference of Negro Workers. In 1933, the Soviet Union dissolved the International Trade Union Committee of Negro Workers. When Padmore complained about this action, he was expelled from the Comintern and denounced as a nationalist.

In 1934, Padmore resigned his positions and moved to London, where he collaborated with C. L. R. James and other Caribbean and African intellectuals. In response to the Italian invasion of Ethiopia, James and Padmore organized the International African Services Bureau, of which he was chairman and James editor.®

In his capacity as leader of the IASB, Padmore helped organize the 1945 Manchester Conference, which was attended by Kwame Nkrumah, Jomo Kenyatta, W. E. B. DuBois, Jaja Wachuku. This conference helped set the agenda for decolonization in the post-war period.

When Ghana became independent in 1957, Padmore moved there and served as an advisor to Nkrumah.

After the war, Padmore worked as Kwame Nkrumah's personal representative. George Padmore transitioned to the ancestral realm in 1959. He was one of the fathers of the end of Afrikan colonization.

David Walker

David Walker was an Afrikan-American born on 27 September 1785. He was a very outspoken critic of slavery and his great act of defiance and bravery will never be forgotten.

David Walker was born free in the Cape Fear region of North Carolina. As an adult, he moved to Charleston where he became affiliated with the strong African Methodist Episcopal Church community of activists. During this time, he visited strong settlements of freed blacks in Philadelphia and eventually settled down in Boston.

In Boston, he immediately became active in the black community on Beacon Hill where he operated a used clothing store. During this time, he also became a writer for the influential *Freedom's Journal*, an abolitionist newspaper.

Boston at the time was at the forefront of the abolitionist struggle and therefore, the perfect place for David Walker to be in. He worked with the church and also became a Prince Hall Freemason. His person co-founded The Massachusetts General Colored Association, the first abolitionist organization in Boston committed to freeing blacks from chattel slavery.

In 1829, David Walker published *David Walker's Appeal* which was a piercing indictment of slavery and racism with a passionate call for action by Black men. In his appeal, he argued that Afrikan-American chattel slavery was the worst and most brutal slavery that ever existed and implored that blacks do anything in their capacity to rid the world injurious aberration.

David Walker used a biblical framework to demand that all blacks be freed as this was the only natural Christian thing to do.

David Walker used grassroots channels to distribute his Appeal among blacks, and soon whites and their institutions were up in arms against the distribution of his truth. In his Appeal, Walker wrote whites gave nothing to blacks upon manumission except the right to exercise the liberty they had immorally prevented them from so doing in the past. They were not giving blacks a gift but rather returning what they had stolen from them and God.

To pay respect to whites as the source of freedom was thus to blaspheme God by denying that he was the source of all virtues and the only one with whom one was justified in having a relationship of obligation and debt.

Walker transitioned to the ancestral realm in 1830 under strange circumstances. His memory and defiance lives on. He as a person best exemplifies the principles of the U.S. constitution and Declaration of Independence.

October

Nat Turner

Born on 2 October 1800, Nat Turner became one of the most important Afrikan-American heroes during enslavement.

His birthplace was Southampton County, Virginia, and soon after his birth, he lost contact with his father who had escaped enslavement. Nat Turner, therefore, remained close to his paternal grandmother who raised him. His kidnapper was Samuel Turner and hence, Nat Turner was referred to by the same last name.

His maternal grandmother was a Coromantee who had been kidnapped from West Afrika. Nat Turner grew up in Southampton, Virginia, which at that time was composed mostly of blacks. Young Nat was very bright and intelligent and at a very young age learned to read and write.

He was also deeply religious and often times immersed in the Bible and prayer. From his prayers, he would have visions that he would use to direct his actions.

He eventually became so knowledgeable on the Bible that he was called upon to conduct Baptist services. His congregation would call him 'The Prophet' and were highly inspired by him. He was also noted to have influence on white people because several times he had asked them to cease their wickedness with their enslaved laborers and this had led them to be kinder.

One day while walking in a field, Nat Turner had a vision in which he was told "the first shall be last and the last shall be first." The vision was clear to him and he knew that he would have to slay his enemies. He, therefore, gathered together his four most trusted comrades and planned an uprising, a take-over and emancipation for his people.

In 1831, he started preparing his freedom struggle. On 13 August, there was a solar eclipse and Nat Turner knew this was a sign to start the struggle, which he did. The struggle started with just a few enslaved Afrikans and they went from plantation to plantation freeing the enslaved Afrikans and neutralizing the enslavers. Eventually, they formed a militia about seventy people strong.

His rebellion lasted until October 1831 when he was caught, tortured and hanged. He was very successful in empowering blacks and giving them a desire for freedom. His uprising also created fear among enslavers and helped accelerate the emancipation of blacks. Nat Turner was a visionary who was not willing to be subjugated to any man.

His fight for freedom was no less than the fight for freedom of any other people in the world including the fathers of the American Revolution. He manifested the saying that "I would rather die on my feet than live on my knees." Today in New Jersey, there is a park named in honor of this great warrior.

I. T. A Wallace Johnson

Isaac Theophilus Akunna Wallace Johnson was born into a poor Krio family in the outskirts of Freetown, Sierra Leone, in 1895. From his humble beginnings, he went on to be one of the most inspirational West Afrikans of his generation.

Both of his parents were from the blue collar working class and Wallace-Johnson received his education at The United Methodist Collegiate. He was unable to complete his studies because his family needed an extra income and therefore, he dropped out of school to become a customs officer. As soon as he became a permanent worker with the customs agency, he led a strike for increased pay and better working conditions.

All employees involved in the strike were fired, but then re-hired after due process. During his time out of work, he published articles for a paper called *Aurora*.

Not long after regaining his position with the customs unit, he quit and became enlisted as a clerk in The Carrier Corps during World War I. In the war, he served in the British infantry in Cameroon and the Middle East. After the war, he worked for the Freetown municipal government and exposed a corruption scandal in his article *A Cloud of Doom*. This article led to self-rule entitlements in Freetown to be removed by the British Government.

Wallace-Johnson was fired and took a job on an American ocean liner. There he traveled around the world and visited many English speaking countries. In his travels, he met blacks from around the world and became part of several unions.

At this time in his life, he attended meetings overseas representing workers unions and he also published articles in a paper called the *Negro Worker*. The British empire banned circulation of this paper because it was perceived as a threat to them ruling other people.

Wallace-Johnson, therefore, went to Russia where he studied communism and trade unionism a little more. When he returned to Afrika, he worked in present-day Ghana. He contributed articles to newspapers and agitated with unions. He went on to found the West African Youth League (WAYL) in 1935 and became its first secretary.

That same year, the WAYL used funds to support Ethiopia against the imperialist Italians who had attacked. He created another paper for WAYL called *Dawn*.

Wallace Johnson was arrested for sedition by the British and sent to jail, however he took the case to the highest court of the land The Privy Council in London. He gathered support and was eventually released. Upon being released he returned to Freetown were he revived the WAYL and got them involved in local politics.

The movement was very successful until 1939 when Wallace Johnson was once again arrested under an emergency war act without just cause. He was sentenced without even having a case brought to a jury. He was released in 1944 and reorganized the WAYL. He eventually merged the WAYL into the National Council of the Colony of Sierra Leone, but eventually left that organization to join his new party the United Sierra Leone Progressive party and took part in independence talks.

He later on joined forces with Siaka Stevens and the APP, but unfortunately transitioned to the ancestral realm due to a car crash on 10 May

1965. He is revered and remembered to this day as a great Afrikan hero who spoke truth to power and he has a statue in his honor in Freetown outside of parliament. He will be forever known as a courageous and intellectual man who could not be censored.

King Mutato

In 1440, the empire of Monomotapa was under the leadership of the fierce and awesome King Mutato, or 'Mutato, the Great'. His vast empire had been developed by Vakarang immigrants who were invaders. The Monomotapa Empire covered what is known today as Zimbabwe, the Kalahari Desert, Mozambique, and parts of Transvaal in South Africa.

King Mutato established effective political rule, and promoted economic development and prosperity. The Monomotapa used iron technology and allied crafts, long before the Christian era. With over 4000 active mines, and gold being the leading export commodity, iron work was still highly regarded. The drive for excellence in everything produced was reflected in the artistic work throughout the empire.

The building of the temples and beautiful stone structures, rivaled the construction associated with the great pyramids in Egypt. The Monomotapa were great stonemasons and architects. According to records in stone, a highly developed civilization existed in South Africa, at the same time of the great Egyptian and Ethiopian era, in the North.

King Mutato mastered a plan to unite the blacks throughout the entire Monomotapa Empire. Their enemies knew that if they could keep the blacks fighting among themselves, they would be a divided people, lacking in power, and the enemy would have access to their wealth.

Mutato moved quickly to recruit, develop, and train armies, under the supervision of capable generals. Additional strategic leadership by Matope, Mutato's son, who came into power after Mutato's death, strengthened and unified Monomotapa. However, after Matope's death, Monomotapa swiftly declined, and the empire began to break up.

Fannie Lou Hamer

Fannie Lou Hamer, known as the lady who was 'sick and tired of being sick and tired', was born 6 October 1917, in Montgomery County, Mississippi. She was the granddaughter of enslaved Afrikans. Her family were sharecroppers—a position not that different from enslavement. Hamer had nineteen brothers and sisters. She was the youngest of the children.

In 1962, when Hamer was forty-four years old, SNCC volunteers came to town and held a voter registration meeting. She was surprised to learn that African-Americans actually had a constitutional right to vote. When the SNCC members asked for volunteers to go to the courthouse to register to vote, Hamer was the first to raise her hand.

This was a dangerous decision. She later reflected, "The only thing they could do to me was to kill me, and it seemed like they'd been trying to do that a little bit at a time ever since I could remember." When Hamer and others went to the courthouse, they were jailed and beaten by the police.

Hamer's courageous act got her thrown off the plantation where she was a sharecropper. She also began to receive constant death threats and was even shot at. Still, Hamer would not be discouraged. She became a SNCC Field Secretary and traveled around the country speaking and registering people to vote.

Hamer co-founded the Mississippi Freedom Democratic Party (MFDP). In 1964, the MFDP challenged the all-white Mississippi delegation to the Democratic National Convention. Hamer spoke in front of the Credentials Committee in a televised proceeding that reached millions of viewers.

She told the committee how African-Americans in many states across the country were prevented from voting through illegal tests, taxes and intimidation. As a result of her speech, two delegates of the MFDP were given speaking rights at the convention and the other members were seated as honorable guests.

Hamer was an inspirational figure to many involved in the struggle for civil rights. She transitioned to the ancestral realm on 14 March 1977, at the age of fifty-nine.

Gabriel Prosser

Gabriel Prosser (ca. 1775–1800) was the African-American leader of an unsuccessful revolt in Richmond, Va., during the summer of 1800. Gabriel Prosser was enslaved to Thomas H. Prosser and was about twenty-five years old when he came to the attention of Virginia authorities late in August 1800. Little is known of his childhood or family background.

He had two brothers and a wife, Nanny, all slaves of Prosser. Gabriel Prosser learned to read and was a serious student of the Bible, where he found inspiration in the accounts of Israel's delivery from slavery. Prosser possessed shrewd judgment, and his master gave him much latitude. He was acknowledged as a leader by many enslaved Afrikans around Richmond.

With the help of other enslaved Afrikans, especially Jack Bowler and George Smith, Prosser designed a scheme for a slave revolt. They planned to seize control of Richmond by slaying all whites (except for Methodists, Quakers, and Frenchmen) and then to establish a kingdom of Virginia with

Prosser as king. The recent, successful American Revolution and the revolutions in France and Haiti—with their rhetoric of freedom, equality, and brotherhood—supplied examples and inspiration for Prosser's rebellion.

In the months preceding the attack, Prosser skillfully recruited supporters and organized them into military units. Authorities never discovered how many enslaved Afrikans were involved, but there were undoubtedly several thousand, many armed with swords and pikes made from farm tools by slave blacksmiths.

The plan was to strike on the night of 30 August 1800. Men inside Richmond were to set fire to certain buildings to distract whites, and Prosser's force from the country was to seize the armory and government buildings across town. With the firearms thus gained, the rebels would supposedly easily overcome the surprised whites.

On the day of the attack, the plot was disclosed by two slaves who did not want their masters slain; then Virginia governor, James Monroe, alerted the militia. That night, as the rebels began congregating outside Richmond, the worst rainstorm in memory flooded roads, washed out bridges, and prevented Prosser's army from assembling. Prosser decided to postpone the attack until the next day, but by then the city was too well defended.

The rebels, including Prosser, dispersed. Some enslaved Afrikans, in order to save their own lives, testified against the ringleaders, about thirty-five of whom were executed. Prosser himself managed to escape by hiding aboard a riverboat on its way to Norfolk. In Norfolk, however, he was betrayed by other enslaved Afrikans, who claimed the large reward for his capture on 25 September.

Returned to Richmond, Prosser, like most of the other leaders, refused to confess to the plot or give evidence against other enslaved Afrikans. He was tried and found guilty on 6 Oct. 1800, and executed the next day. He was a great military leader who failed just by a hairpin to change the whole course of history as we know it.

Elijah Muhammad

Elijah Muhammad (1897–1975) was the leader of the Nation of Islam ('Black Muslims') during their period of greatest growth in the mid-20th century. He was a major advocate of independent, black-operated businesses, institutions, and religion. Elijah Muhammad was born Elijah (or Robert) Poole on 7 October 1897, near Sandersville, Georgia.

His parents were ex-enslaved Afrikans, who worked as sharecroppers on a cotton plantation; his father was also a Baptist preacher. As a youngster, Elijah worked in the fields and on the railroad, but he left home at age sixteen to travel and work at odd jobs. He settled in Detroit in 1923, working on a Chevrolet assembly line.

Poole and his two brothers became early disciples of W. D. Fard, the founder of the Nation of Islam. Fard, of mysterious background, appeared in Detroit in 1930, selling silk goods and telling his customers in Detroit's Afrikan-American ghetto of their ancestral 'homeland' across the seas. Soon

Fard began holding meetings in homes, and then in rented halls, telling his listeners tales purporting to describe their non-white kin in other lands and urging them to emulate these brothers and sisters in such matters as dress and diet.

Fard proclaimed Islam the one correct religion for African-Americans, denouncing Christianity as the religion of their enslavement kidnappers. His meetings became dominated by his denunciations of the injustices done to blacks by whites. Soon, Fard announced the opening of the Temple of Islam. It featured much anti-white invective and embodied an unorthodox form of Islam, but the movement also emphasized African-American self-help and education.

Fard disappeared, as mysteriously as he had arrived, in the summer of 1934. The movement he had founded quickly developed several factions, the most important of which was led by Poole, who had become a top lieutenant to Fard and whose name along the way had been changed to Elijah Muhammad. The movement had long had a policy of requiring members to drop their 'slave' names.

Settling in Chicago, away from hostile Muslim factions in Detroit, Muhammad built what quickly became the most important center of the movement. Chicago soon featured not only a Temple of Islam, but a newspaper called *Muhammad Speaks*, a University of Islam (actually a private elementary and high school), and several movement-owned apartment houses, grocery stores, and restaurants. Temples were opened in other cities, and farms were purchased so that ritually pure food could be made available to members.

The movement was a sharply disciplined one. Members had strict rules to follow regarding eating (various foods, such as pork, were forbidden), smoking and drinking (both banned), dress and appearance (conservative, neat clothing and good grooming were required), and all kinds of personal behavior (drugs, the use of profanity, gambling, listening to music, and dancing were all outlawed).

Muhammad also revised the theology of the movement. Under his system, Fard was proclaimed the earthly incarnation of Allah, the Muslim name for God; (Elijah) Muhammad was his divinely-appointed prophet. Muhammad also taught that blacks constituted the original human beings, and would soon reclaim leadership in the world. It was understood that violent war might be likely before the transition could be completed. In the meantime, Muhammad advocated an independent nation for African-Americans.

In 1942, Muhammad was one of a group of militant African-American leaders arrested on charges of sedition, conspiracy, and violation of the draft laws. He was accused of sympathizing with the Japanese during World War II and of encouraging his members to resist the military draft. He had, indeed, argued that all nonwhites are oppressed by whites, and that it made no sense for African-Americans to fight those who were victims of white racism as much as they themselves were.

Muhammad was certainly no pacifist, but he argued that the only war in which African-Americans should participate would be the coming 'Battle of Armageddon', in which blacks would reassert their rightful superiority. For his words and actions, Muhammad spent four years, from 1942 to 1946, in federal prison at Milan, Michigan.

Factions occasionally withdrew from Muhammad's movement. In the early 1960s, Muhammad came to be overshadowed by the charismatic Malcolm X, leader of the New York Temple. Tensions between Malcolm X and Muhammad's leadership grew; finally, after Malcolm X commented that John F. Kennedy's assassination was a case of 'the chickens coming home to roost', Muhammad suspended him.

Shortly thereafter, in 1964, Malcolm X founded his own movement, which moved toward a more orthodox form of Islam. However, Malcolm X was assassinated on 21 February 1965.

Elijah Muhammad transitioned to the ancestral realm on 25 February 1975.

Some of his followers retained the old name of the Nation of Islam, and were led by Louis Farrakhan (born Louis Eugene Walcott of British West Indian parents in 1934). Farrakhan generally retained Elijah Muhammad's ideas and practices, including the strict behavioral rules. He achieved prominence when he became a major adviser to Jesse Jackson during the latter's presidential campaign in 1984.

Mary Ann Shadd

Born to free parents in Wilmington, Delaware, Mary Ann Shadd was the eldest of thirteen children. She was educated by Quakers and later taught throughout the northeastern states. Following in the footsteps of her activist parents, who were part of the Underground Railroad, Shadd pursued the path taken by those heading north to freedom in Canada.

Settling in Windsor, she wrote educational booklets outlining the advantages of Canada for settlers willing to work and the need for living within one's means. She set up an integrated school in Windsor that was open to all who could afford to attend (education was not publicly provided at that time). She moved to St. Catharines and then Toronto, where she met and married widower Thomas Cary.

To promote information about the successes of Black people living in freedom in Canada, she began the Provincial Freeman newspaper, becoming the first woman in North America to publish a newspaper, although at first she had to have a man stand in for her as the apparent publisher.

Prior to returning to the U.S., Shadd obtained Canadian citizenship. In 1851, she was the only woman to attend the First Convention of Colored Freemen held outside of the U.S. Then she worked as a recruitment agent to support the Union side during the American Civil War.

Shadd moved to Washington, D.C., where she taught, then pursued law studies and became the first black woman to complete this degree at Howard University. She joined efforts to gain women's suffrage (the vote) and was herself the first Black woman to vote in a national election.

She transitioned to the ancestral realm in Washington, D.C. on 5 June 1893. Shadd's former residence in the U Street Corridor was declared a National Historic Landmark in 1976.

Ken Saro-Wiwa

Ken Saro-Wiwa was born in 10 October 1941, the eldest son of a prominent family in Ogoni, which is today in Rivers State, Nigeria. After leaving university, he initially pursued an academic career. During the Biafran war (1967–1970), he was a Civilian Administrator for the Port of Bonny, near Ogoni in the Niger Delta. He went on to be a businessman, novelist and television producer.

His long-running satirical TV series *Basi & Co* was purported to be the most watched soap opera in Africa. Two of his best known works were drawn from his observations and experiences of the Biafran war. His most famous work, *Sozaboy: a Novel in Rotten English*, is a harrowing tale of a naive village boy recruited into the army. *On a Darkling Plain*, is a diary of his experiences during the war.

Ken Saro-Wiwa was consistently concerned about the treatment of Ogoni within the Nigerian Federation and in 1973 was dismissed from his post as

Regional Commissioner for Education in the Rivers State cabinet, for advocating greater Ogoni autonomy. During the 1970s, he built up his businesses in real estate and retail and in the 1980s, concentrated on his writing, journalism and television production.

Throughout his work, he often made references to the exploitation he saw around him as the oil and gas industry took riches from the beneath the feet of the poor Ogoni farmers, and in return left them polluted and disenfranchised.

In his book of short stories, *Forest of Flowers* (1986), the following passage from the story *Night Ride*, reflects Saro-Wiwa's anger at seeing multinational oil companies, like Shell, appropriating land from local people:

"An old woman had hobbled up to him. My son, they arrived this morning and dug up my entire farm, my only farm. They mowed down the toil of my brows, the pride of the waiting months. They say they will pay me compensation. Can they compensate me for my labors? The joy I receive when I see the vegetables sprouting, God's revelation to me in my old age? Oh my son, what can I do?"

"What answer now could he give her? I'll look into it later, he had replied tamely. Look into it later. He could almost hate himself for telling that lie. He cursed the earth for spouting oil, black gold, they called it. And he cursed the gods for not drying the oil wells. What did it matter that millions of barrels of oil were mined and exported daily, so long as this poor woman wept those tears of despair? What could he look into later?"

"Could he make alternate land available? And would the lawmakers revise the laws just to bring a bit more happiness to these unhappy wretches whom the search for oil had reduced to an animal existence? They ought to send the oil royalties to the men whose farms and land were despoiled and ruined. But the lawyers were in the pay of the oil companies and the government people in the pay of the lawyers and the companies. So how could he look into it later?"

In 1990, Saro-Wiwa started to dedicate himself to the amelioration of the problems of the oil producing regions of the Niger Delta. Focusing on his homeland, Ogoni launched a non-violent movement for social and ecological justice. In this role, he attacked the oil companies and the Nigerian government accusing them of waging an ecological war against the Ogoni and precipitating the genocide of the Ogoni people. He was so effective, that by 1993 the oil companies had to pull out of Ogoni. This cost him his life.

Sundiata Keita

Sundiata Keita (ca. 1210–ca. 1260) was the founder of the Mali empire in West Africa. He is now regarded as a great magician-king and the national hero of the Malinke-speaking people.

Sundiata, or Sun Djata, was also known in the Tarikhs (Moslem chronicles) as Mari Djata. Keita is a widely used family name. He is to West African history what King Arthur is to English history. Sundiata was the son of Maghan Kon Fatta, ruler of the small Malinke kingdom of Kangaba, situated on the Niger River a short distance to the southwest of Bamako, the capital of modern Mali.

Sundiata was handicapped from birth, and his life story follows the universal theme of a culture hero's overcoming of extreme adversity to attain greatness. When his father died, he miraculously recovered from his handicap and was a man with unparalleled strength. He was known to be able to uproot a tree with his bare hands.

About 1224, the Susu people to the north conquered Kangaba in a wave of expansion under their magician-king, Sumanguru Kante. Sundiata and his mother went into voluntary exile from Kangaba about 1220 to avoid the risk of assassination by his jealous half-brother, Kankaran Tuman, who had become king about 1218.

Kankaran then meekly submitted to Susu rule, and later Sundiata was recalled by his people to free them from this foreign tyranny.

In about 1230, Sundiata put together a rabble force in the far north and slowly advanced to the south, increasing his troop strength with successive victories over Susu provinces. By 1234, he was ready to take on the main Susu army, which he met and defeated in the epic battle of Kirina northeast of Kangaba. This victory is clearly the major event in his life, and it marks the beginning of the Mali empire.

Before he retired from active leadership of his armies about 1240, Sundiata and his generals expanded the new empire in all directions, even incorporating the formerly great Ghana empire and the previously unconquered gold fields of the Senegal River valley.

We know that Sundiata ruled for about twenty-five years, but little is known about his later life. He transitioned to the ancestral realm in about 1260, apparently the victim of an accident in his capital.

Fela Kuti

Fela Anikulapo Kuti, born in Abeokuta, Nigeria on 15 October 1938. He was a singer-composer, trumpet, sax and keyboard player, bandleader, and politician. Kuti was one of Afrika's most controversial musicians and throughout his life he continued to fight for the rights of the common man (and woman), despite vilification, harassment, and even imprisonment by the government of Nigeria.

Born to Yoruban parents, Kuti was strongly influenced by both parents, his mother being Funmilayo, a leading figure in the nationalist struggle. Practically all of his records are dominated by political events and discussions from the approach of Pan-Africanism.

In 1954, Kuti joined the Cool Cats as a singer in that highlife band (highlife being the rage of the Lagos music scene at the time). During this period, Kuti developed his own unusual sound which he described as highlife-jazz. In 1968, Kuti announced the arrival of Afro-beat, within the year was promoting his sound all over the U.S.A. on a ten-month tour where he became influenced by American jazz.

When he returned to his homeland, he opened a nightclub, 'the Shrine', and changed the name of his band to 'Africa 70' (and later to Egypt 80).

His bands traditionally included the typical huge line-up consisting of many singers and dancers, numerous saxophonists, trumpeters, drummers, percussionists, and of course, many guitarists blending African rhythms and jazz horn lines with politicized song lyrics. His music was intricate, rather than calling it Afro-beat, you might more arguably consider it Afro-jazz.

Entire recordings often consisted of just a few songs and this propensity for jamming set up a roadblock for Fela to attain commercial acceptance in the United States. He also abhorred performing a song after recording it, and this led to audience disinterest in the U.S. where the people wanted their music to be recognizable hits.

Kuti continued his outspoken attacks on the Nigerian government. When the people returned to power in 1979, Kuti began his own political party, MOP (Movement of the People). The military returned to power in 1983 and within the year Kuti was sentenced to five years in prison on a spurious currency smuggling charge. He was released in 1986 after yet another change of government.

Fela Anikulapo Kuti transitioned to the ancestral realm on Saturday, 2 August 1997, at 4pm (local time) in Lagos, Nigeria. It had been rumored for some time that Fela had a serious illness he was refusing treatment for.

Halle Dillon Johnson

Dr. Halle Tanner Dillon Johnson was the first female physician to pass the Alabama state medical examination and was the first woman physician at Tuskegee Institute. She was the eldest of nine children born to African Methodist Episcopal bishop Benjamin Tucker Tanner and Sarah Elizabeth Miller in Pittsburgh, Pennsylvania, in 1864. Her brother, Henry Ossawa Tanner, became a noted artist. Shortly after Halle was born, the Tanners moved to Philadelphia where the children were educated.

In the middle 1880s, Halle Tanner worked with her father on the AME Church Review. In 1886, she married Charles E. Dillon and the two moved to Trenton, New Jersey, where they had a daughter, Sadie. Charles Dillon died of an unknown cause and Halle Tanner Dillon moved back to Philadelphia to live with her parents.

Tanner decided to become a physician and enrolled at the Woman's Medical College of Pennsylvania. The only African-American woman in her class, Tanner graduated with an M.D. and high honors after three years of study in 1891. While at the college, she learned of a job opportunity as resident physician at Tuskegee Institute. She contacted Booker T. Washington, the Principal of Tuskegee. Washington appointed her and helped her prepare for the Alabama state medical examination.

Dr. Tanner Dillon sat for the ten day examination and passed. She served at Tuskegee University as a physician, pharmacist, teacher, and ran a private practice for three years. While at Tuskegee, she founded a training school for nurses and a dispensary (pharmacy). In 1894, she married her second husband, Reverend John Quincy Johnson, an aspiring theologian and mathematics professor at Tuskegee Institute.

The couple moved to Nashville where Reverend Johnson pursued a graduate degree in divinity while serving as pastor of Saint Paul's AME Church. Dr. Tanner Dillon Johnson meanwhile resumed her medical practice.

The couple had three more children but in 1901, Dr. Halle Tanner Dillon Johnson transitioned to the ancestral realm of complications resulting from childbirth.

Jean Jacques Dessalines

Born at the Cormiers Plantation north of Haiti in 1758, Dessalines was enslaved on the plantation of Duclos. He ran away to freedom at the age of thirty-three. He was a very diligent soldier and worked his way into the army of Toussaint Louverture, a Haitain freedom fighter, to become a principal lieutenant.

He went on to become the general-in-chief of the Revolution of St. Domingue after the deportation of Toussaint Louverture. He was a gifted soldier and distinguished himself during several combats, especially at the Battle of Crete-a-Pierrot. There, he launched a splendid call to his soldiers and boosted their courage by leading them to blow up the fortress rather than give it up to the French. He led the indigenous army into victory over the French army of Napoleon Bonaparte in the Battle of Vertieres on 18 November 1803.

On 1 January 1804, after Toussaint was captured and imprisoned by the French, he proclaimed the independence of the colony, which he renamed

Haiti, after its native Arawak people. The same day, he was acclaimed Governor-General-for-Life of Haiti, and on 2 September 1804, he was crowned emperor under the name of Jacques I.

Dessalines was assassinated in a revolt on 17 October 1806 at Pont-Rouge. He is remembered as the Father of the Haitian Nation and the Founder of the Independence of Haiti.

Nefertari

Nefertari whose name means 'The most beautiful' was born around 1279 B.C.E. in ancient Kamit (Egypt). She was of royal lineage and went on to marry Ramses, The Great before he ascended to the throne of Kamit.

She was a strong supporter of Ramses and a great queen in her own right. She gave birth to four sons and two daughters from her husband, and he so highly regarded her that when he built monuments he depicted her as his equal in every aspect. Her likeness was depicted in both Luxor and Karnak which were both sites of great Kamitic temples.

A monster colossus was also erected of her in Abu Simbel Upper Kamit which till this day stands in memory of her greatness. Her husband, Ramses, was the second longest ruler of Kamit ruling for over eighty years. His longevity was due in main part to Nefertari's healthy food and healthy routines that she helped him acquire.

Nefertari transitioned during the reign of her husband but became the archetype of what a strong, beautiful and powerful queen would be.

Dedan Kimathi

Dedan Kimathi Waciuri (31 October 1920–18 February 1957) was a Kenyan rebel leader who fought against British colonization in Kenya in the 1950s. He was convicted and executed by the British colonial government. The British colonial government that ruled Kenya at the time considered him a terrorist, but many Kikuyu and other Kenyans viewed him as a freedom fighter of the Mau Uprising.

Kimathi was born in Thenge Village Tetu division, Nyeri District. At the age of fifteen, he joined the local primary school, Karuna-ini, where he perfected his English skills. He would later use those language skills to write extensively before and during the uprising. He was a Debate Club member in his school.

He was deeply religious and carried a Bible regularly. He worked for the forest department, collecting tree seeds to help him foot his school bill. He later joined Tumutumu CSM School for his secondary learning, but dropped out for lack of funds.

He dabbled with several jobs but never felt fully settled. Notable was his enlisting with the army to fight in the World War II in 1941. However, in 1944, he was expelled for misconduct. In 1946, he became a member of the Kenya African Union. In 1949, he started teaching at his old school, Tumutumu, but left the job within two years.

Nevertheless, he managed to be very influential to whomever he met through the string of jobs he was able to obtain. He became radically political in 1950. He involved himself with the Mau Mau, and later that year administered the oath of the Mau Mau, making him a marked man. He joined Forty Group, the militant wing of the defunct Kikuyu Central Association in 1951.

He was elected as a local branch secretary of KAU in Ol' Kalou and Thomson's Falls area in 1952. He was briefly arrested in that same year, but escaped with the help of local police. This marked the beginning of his violent uprising. He formed Kenya Defense Council to co-ordinate all forest fighters in 1953.

In 1956, he was finally arrested with one of his wives, Wambui. He was sentenced to death by a court presided by Chief Justice Sir Kenneth O'Connor, while he was in a hospital bed at the General Hospital Nyeri. In the early morning of 18 February 1957, he was executed by the colonial government. The hanging took place at the Kamiti Maximum Security Prison.

Kimathi was buried in a mass grave, but later reburied by Kenya as a national hero. Many towns in Kenya have a building or street named after him, including popular t-shirts designed to immortalize his image by brands like Jamhuri wear. The play 'Trial of Dedan Kimathi' was written by Ngugi wa Thiong'o (the brother of a Mau member) and provides a detailed account of Kimathi.

A statue of Kimathi is being built on Kimathi Street in Nairobi. Its foundation stone was laid in 11 December 2006. Kimathi was married to Mukami Kimathi. Among their children are sons, Wachiuri and Maina, and daughters, Nyawira and Wanjugu.

Bobby Seale

Robert George Seale (born 1936) was a militant activist who, with Huey P. Newton and Bobby Hutton, founded the Black Panther Party for Self Defense in 1966.

Born to a poor African-American carpenter and his wife in Dallas, Texas, on 22 October 1936, Robert George (Bobby) Seale and his family moved to Port Arthur, Texas, and then to San Antonio, Texas, before finally settling in Oakland, California, during World War II. Attributing his failure to make the basketball and football teams to racial prejudice, Seale quit Oakland High School and joined the U.S. Air Force.

After three years in the Air Force, Seale was court-martialed and given a bad conduct discharge for disobeying a colonel at Ellsworth Air Force Base in South Dakota.

Seale returned to Oakland and, while working as a sheet metal mechanic in various aerospace plants, earned his high school diploma through night school. In 1962, he began attending Oakland City College (Merritt College). Seale became aware of the African-American struggle for civil rights when he joined the Afro-American Association (AAA), a campus organization that stressed black separatism and self-improvement.

Through the AAA, he met activist Huey P. Newton in September 1962. Seale and Newton soon became disenchanted with the AAA, however, believing that the organization offered little more than ineffectual cultural nationalism. In their view, this cultural nationalism would not help lessen the economic and political oppression felt in the African-American community, especially in the ghetto.

Both greatly admired Malcolm X and were particularly impressed with his teachings. They were especially drawn to the idea that black people had to defend themselves against white brutality and inaccurate education. The assassination of Malcolm X in 1965 pushed them to adopt Malcolm's slogan, "Freedom by any means necessary," and they founded the Black Panther Party for Self-Defense in October 1966.

Beginning as an armed patrol dedicated to the defense of Oakland Blacks against the brutality of the city police, the Black Panthers gained local notoriety for their fearlessness and militant demand for Black rights. In 1967, the Black Panther Party (BPP) garnered national attention when it sent an armed contingent to the state capitol in Sacramento to protest a proposed gun-control law and to assert the constitutional right of blacks to bear arms against their white oppressors.

Coupling food programs for needy families and 'liberation schools' for political education with defiant calls for black control of community institutions and for 'power to the people', the BPP opened recruitment centers across the nation in 1968. According to J. Edgar Hoover, the head of the Federal Bureau of Investigation (FBI), the BPP had become "the No. 1 threat to the internal security of the nation."

Fearful of the growing popularity of the BPP and their insistence that Black Power grows out of the barrel of a gun, Hoover ordered the FBI to employ "hard-hitting counterintelligence measures to cripple the Black Panthers" in November 1968.

For their participation in the demonstrations at the Democratic National Convention in Chicago in 1968, Seale was brought to trial with seven white radicals, including Youth International Party founders Jerry Rubin and Abbie

Hoffman, and the founders of Students for a Democratic Society, Tom Hayden and Rennie Davis, on 24 September 1969. The eight were indicted in a federal court in Chicago under the new anti-riot provision of the 1968 Civil Rights Act, which made it illegal to cross state lines to incite a riot or instruct in the use of riot weapons.

Because his attorney, Charles Garry, had just undergone surgery and could not be present, Seale asked for a delay two weeks before his trial. Judge Julius Hoffman refused. Seale then retained William Kunstler, who was representing the other seven defendants. Upon Garry's advice, fired Kunstler and asked to represent himself, which would have given him the opportunity to cross-examine witnesses and present evidence during the trial.

However, Judge Hoffman insisted that Kunstler was sufficient representation and proceeded with the trial.

When Seale continued to protest, with repeated outbursts and by refusing to follow courtroom procedure and decorum, Hoffman had him bound and gagged during the trial. On 5 November 1969, the judge sentenced Seale to four years in jail for sixteen counts of contempt of court, each of which contributed three months to his sentence. During his prison term, Seale was also indicted for ordering the torture and execution of Alex Rackley, former Black Panther suspected of being a government informer.

On 25 May 1971, the conspiracy trial ended in a hung jury and the judge ordered all charges dropped against Seale and the other defendants. The following year the federal government suspended the contempt charges and released Seale from prison.

Seale returned to Oakland to find the BPP decimated by police infiltration, killings, and arrests. At least two dozen Black Panthers had died in gun fights with the police and dozens more had been imprisoned. The BPP had also been rendered impotent by internal disputes in which Black nationalist advocates warred against the program of revolutionary socialism called for by Newton and Seale.

In 1973, Seale ran for mayor of Oakland, finishing second out of nine candidates with 43,710 votes to the incumbent's 77,476.

Claiming combat weariness, Seale left Oakland and the Panthers in 1974. In 1978, he published his autobiography, *A Lonely Rage*, which described the emotional and psychological changes he had undergone as a black activist. His

1970 book, *Seize the Time*, portrayed the story of the Black Panthers and the political views of Huey Newton.

In retrospect, Seale found consolation in Newton's belief that, to move a single grain of sand is to change a world. "We moved a grain of sand and several hills beside," Seale affirmed. "I swear I'm surprised we lived through it."

Throughout the 1980s, Seale continued to develop and support organizations dedicated to combating social and political injustices. He still lectures about his past and current experiences struggling for civil rights for African-Americans. In 1987, he published *Barbeque'n with Bobby*, the proceeds from which go to various non-profit social organizations.

Paul Bogle

Paul Bogle, a Baptist Deacon is remembered for his role in the Morant Bay rebellion. His date of birth has been estimated between 1815 and 1822. He lived in Stony Gut in St. Thomas, just north of Morant Bay; while many people in the area were small farmers and laborers, he was successful, well-educated and owned about five hundred acres of land. He was also eligible to vote at a time when there were only 104 voters in the parish of St. Thomas, due in part to the large voting fee, in order to participate.

He became a supporter of landowner and politician and fellow Baptist, George William Gordon. In 1864, Gordon made Bogle a deacon in the Baptist church. As social injustices and peoples grievances grew, Bogle led a group of small farmers forty-five miles to discuss their grievances with Governor Eyre in Spanish Town, but they were denied an audience. This left the people of Stony Gut with a lack of confidence, and distrust for the government, and Bogle's supporters grew in number.

The beginnings of the Morant Bay Rebellion first started on 7 October 1865 when Bogle and his supporters, attended a trial for two men from Stony Gut, a black man was put on trial and imprisoned for trespassing on a long abandoned plantation. One member of Bogle's group protested in the court, over the unjust arrest and was immediately arrested, angering the crowd further.

He was rescued moments later, when Bogle and his men took to the market square, and retaliated. The police were severely beaten and forced to retreat that day.

On Monday, the 9, warrants were issued against Bogle and a number of others for riot and assault. The police arrived in Stony Gut to arrest Bogle but met with stiff resistance from the residents. They fought the police, again forcing them to retreat to Morant Bay.

A few days later, on 11 October 1865, there was a vestry meeting in the Court House. Bogle and his followers armed with sticks and machetes went to the Court House. The authorities were shaken, and a few people in the crowd threw stones at the volunteer militia who fired into the crowd killing seven people.

The crowd retaliated, and set fire to the Court House and nearby buildings. When the officials tried to leave the burning building, they were killed by the irate crowd outside.

The reprisals came quickly, the troops destroyed Stony Gut, and Paul Bogle's chapel, Bogle was captured by the Maroon militia, and taken to Morant Bay where he was put on trial and hung at the burned-out courthouse. Gordon was taken by boat to Morant Bay where he was tried for conspiracy and hung on 23 October. In total, over four hundred black residents were killed and many more flogged.

Back in Britain, there was public outcry, there was increased opposition from liberals against Eyre's handling of the situation, and by the end of 1865, the 'Governor Eyre Case' had become the subject of national debate. In January 1866, a Royal Commission was sent to investigate the events. Governor Eyre was suspended and recalled to England and eventually dismissed. Jamaica became a Crown Colony, being governed directly from England.

The 'Eyre Controversy' turned into a long and increasingly public concern, dividing well known figures of the day, and possibly contributing to the fall of the government of Lord John Russell in 1866.

The Morant Bay rebellion turned out to be one of the defining points in Jamaica's struggle for both political and economic enhancement. Bogle's demonstration ultimately achieved its objectives and paved the way for the new attitudes.

In 1969, the Right Excellent Paul Bogle was named a National Hero of Jamaica because of his great stand to free his people from the rule of tyranny.

November

Lokman

Lokman is the most celebrated sage of the East. So great is his fame, there that there is still a saying, "To teach wisdom to Lokman," which is the equivalent of "Carrying coals to Newcastle." In Islam, his fame equals that of Solomon in the Christian-Jewish world. Mohammed quoted him as an authority and named the thirty-first chapter of the Koran after him.

Much that is said about him is legendary. The Arabs say that he lived about 1100 B.C., was a coal-black Ethiopian with woolly hair, and was the son of Baura, who was a son or a grandson of a sister of Job. Lokman is often confused with Aesop, who was also an African. Aesop lived about five hundred years later than Lokman.

Of Lokman's intimate life, all we know are what may be deduced from his proverbs and from the anecdotes about him. The following are some of them: Some choice fruit was missing from the master's garden and Lokman was accused by his fellow slaves of being the thief. To prove his innocence, Lokman took an emetic and threw up his food. At his request, the master forced his accusers to do likewise, whereupon it was proved that they were the guilty ones.

On another occasion, the caravan with which he was traveling was held up by brigands. Unmoved by the tears and lamentations of the merchants and their wives, the robbers were taking everything when one of the victims, as a last resort, told Lokman that he ought to give the thieves lessons in good conduct and wisdom.

He felt sure, he said, that Lokman by Iris eloquence could make them return at least a part of their goods, to which Lokman replied, "It would be a greater pity to prostitute lessons of wisdom to rascals incapable of understanding and appreciating them; there is no file that can clean iron of its rust after the rust has eaten through."

When asked how he came to possess such great wisdom, Lokman replied, "It is in seeing the actions of vicious and wicked people and comparing them with what my conscience tells me regarding such actions that I have learned what I ought to avoid and what I ought to do. The wise and prudent man will draw a useful lesson even from poison itself, while the precepts of the wisest man mean nothing to the thoughtless."

Given a bitter melon by his owner, Lokman ate it with apparent relish. Astonished at his act of obedience, the master asked him how he had been able to eat such a distasteful fruit. Lokman replied, "I have received so often of your kindness that it is not astonishing I have eaten the single bitter fruit that you have given me in my life." His master, touched by this reply, set him free.

One of the most beautiful of Lokman's fables is the following: A drop of water escaping from a cloud was falling into the sea. Ashamed and confused in seeing itself about to be lost in that vast immensity it said, "What am I in comparison with this vast ocean. Certainly my existence is less than nothing in this abyss without limit."

But as it dropped into the ocean, it was swallowed by an oyster and in time it became a magnificent pearl. The oyster was caught and the pearl was found and sold to a great king who wore it in the center of his crown, where, on state occasions, its beauty held the attention of the noblest in the land.

Among his best-known fables are the following: A hare meeting a lioness one day said reproachfully, "I have always a great number of children while you have but one or two now and then."

The lioness replied, "It is true but my one child is a lion."

A fly buzzing around full of its own importance finally lit on the horns of the bull and said, "Let me know if I am too heavy for you and I will take myself off."

The bull replied, "Who are you? I did not know when you came, nor shall I know when you leave."

To illustrate that some persons are deaf to all appeals save those involving their own interests. Lokman related the following fable:

A blacksmith had a dog that slept soundly while he was hammering on the forge, but as soon as he began eating, the dog awoke. The master said, "O wicked dog, why does the sound of the hammer whose noise shakes the earth not trouble your sleep while the little noise I make in eating does?"

The prestige of this African who lived 3000 years ago is still great in the East. His influence on the philosophy and morality of the West is hardly less potent. That Lokman served as a model for all the storytellers who came after him is incontestable.

Felix Moumie

Felix Moumie was a Cameroonian Freedom Fighter and medical doctor of the prestigious William Ponti School of Dakar, Felix Roland Moumie was born on 1 November 1925, near Foumban in west Cameroon. He met UM NYOBE, the leader of the struggle for independence of Cameroon in Senegal when he was a student. On his return to Cameroon, UM NYOBE decided to make this brilliant student president of UPC (Union of the People of Cameroon) in 1952 during the Eseka Congress.

Moumie clearly showed his adherence to fair play ideas and was appointed director of the party school. The colonial administration was opposed to UM NYOBE, considering him too strong. The information service considered him an extremist full of communist ideas. Being a militant, he was transferred many times from one town to another.

He met his wife, Marthe Akamayong, in Ebolowa with whom he had a daughter, who went on voluntary exile in Portugal.

On December 1954, the new governor, Roland Pre, decided to take all UPC leaders to Douala in order to better control them. On 31 December 1954, Felix Moumie presented him a new year's card with wishes written manually in the name of UPC, on which he declared that nothing will be given to him. He said that Cameroon, the country for which they are fighting for its independence, they are ready to go up to extreme sacrifices.

Moumie later traveled to Senegal. During his stay in Senegal, he made some solid relations with some Afrikan and international progressives. On his return to Cameroon, he used these relations to become the adviser of many African heads of state a few of them being Ahmed Sekou Toure, Kwame Nkrumah, Patrice Lumumba and Ben Bella. In May 1955, the UPC was dissolved by Roland Pre and its members were forced to go into hiding.

Felix Moumie found himself in Kumba with his companions: Ernest Ouandie Abel Kingue, Ndeh Ntumazah. He was obliged to make several journeys between Acrra and Conakry. He made his base in Cairo (Egypt), where Abdel Gamal Nasser President of Egypt supported and helped him by financing his activities and offering scholarships to progressives Cameroonian students.

Since he loved people of the mass media, he allowed naively a fake journalist to approach him (this journalist was an agent of the French secret services in the name of William Betchel.) This journalist gained his confidence and became his communication adviser. During one of his journeys in Geneva, the journalist invites him to a restaurant on 15 October 1960. He is accompanied to this invitation by Jean Martin Tchaptchet.

As soon as he entered the restaurant, he was surprised to receive a phone call knowing that nobody knew where he was. He went on to answer the phone call. With Felix Moumie distracted, the fake journalist takes this opportunity to introduce thallium in Moumie's glass. When Moumie comes back, he complains that there was nobody on line. He keeps on talking and does not drink.

The journalist repeats this trick for the second time. When Moumie goes to answer the phone call, he introduces thallium in his second glass. Moumie finally drinks these glasses, he faints and he is taken to the hospital where he transitioned to the ancestral realm on 3 November 1960 of poisoning. This great man, even though assassinated, lives on in the minds of Afrikans as a hero who struggled for our freedom.

Benjamin Banneker

Benjamin Banneker was born in Maryland on 9 November 1731. His father and grandfather were formerly enslaved.

A farmer of modest means, Banneker nevertheless lived a life of unusual achievement. In 1753, the young man borrowed a pocket watch from a well-to-do neighbor; he took it apart and made a drawing of each component, then reassembled the watch and returned it, fully functioning, to its owner.

From his drawings, Banneker then proceeded to carve, out of wood, enlarged replicas of each part. Calculating the proper number of teeth for each gear and the necessary relationships between the gears, he constructed a working wooden clock that kept accurate time and struck the hours for over fifty years.

At age fifty-eight, Banneker began the study of astronomy and was soon predicting future solar and lunar eclipses. He compiled the ephemeris, or information table, for annual almanacs that were published for the years 1792 through 1797. *Benjamin Banneker's Almanac* was a top seller from Pennsylvania to Virginia and even into Kentucky.

In 1791, Banneker was one of the architects that designed Washington D.C.

The 'Sable Astronomer' was often pointed to as proof that African-Americans were not intellectually inferior to European Americans. Thomas Jefferson himself noted this in a letter to Banneker.

Banneker transitioned to the ancestral realm on Sunday, 9 October 1806, at the age of seventy-four. A few small memorial traces still exist in the Ellicott City/Oella region of Maryland, where Banneker spent his entire life, except for the Federal survey. It was not until the 1990s that the actual site of Banneker's home, which burned on the day of his burial, was determined.

In 1980, the U.S. Postal Service issued a postage stamp in his honor.

Ibn Saud

(1879–1953) King of Hijaz and Najd 1927–32, king of Saudi Arabia 1932–53.

Ibn Sa'ud was both an effective warlord and a charismatic religious leader. Originally, he was the leader of his family, the Sa'uds, as well as the leader of the dominant religious movement of Arabia, Wahhabism. His political strategies included using his religious authority to wage jihad, as well as intermarrying with families from which he sought support.

The latter strategy resulted in seventeen wives, forty-five sons and 215 daughters. Eventually, his secular support grew strong enough for him to break with his Wahhabi troops.

Ibn Sa'ud founded the kingdom of Saudi Arabia, after successfully waging war against his main opponent, the Rashids. For the first period of his reign as king, he did not establish any state structures. But beginning in 1950, petroleum revenues grew to a level through which the reality of Saudi politics changed dramatically, as well as did the Saudi society.

Little was done during his reign to develop Saudi Arabia. One of the few reforms of Ibn Sa'ud was to declare it a duty for nomads to settle at desert wells, which made it easier for the ensuing state to control its inhabitants. Throughout his reign, he had no regular civil service or administrators. This changed shortly before his death.

Being a devout Muslim and a conservative traditionalist, Ibn Sa'ud had not anticipated the dramatic changes brought by the increase of petroleum revenues. At the time of his transition, he was deeply frustrated by all the changes in his lifetime.

Bai Bureh

Bai Bureh was the great ruler and military strategist who led the Temne uprising against the British in 1898.

His father was an important Loko war-chief, and his mother, probably a Temne woman, from the region around modern Makeni. He was sent as a young man to Gbendembu, a training school for warriors where he earned the nickname 'Kebalai', meaning 'one whose basket is never full' or 'one who never tires of war'.

Kebalai became a famous war leader in the 1860s and 1870s, serving under a Soso ruler in a long Jihad to establish correct Islamic practices. In 1886, Kebalai was crowned ruler of Kasseh, a small kingdom near Port Loko, and given the royal title of Bai Bureh.

The new ruler soon gained a reputation for stubborn independence that annoyed the British administration in Freetown. On one occasion, Bai Bureh refused to recognize a peace treaty the British had negotiated with the Limba without his participation, and on another occasion, he led warriors on a raid across the border into French Guinea.

When the British declared their Protectorate in 1896, they quickly issued a warrant for Bai Bureh's arrest, fearing that he would foment resistance to the new 'hut tax'. But the British could not capture him, and so began a long war of aggression to which Bai Bureh valiantly responded by organizing a large-scale guerilla revolt that lasted for ten months.

He brought warriors from several Temne states under his command, as well as some Loko, Soso, and Limba fighters, and he held the initiative over the vastly more powerful British for the first four months. Bai Bureh's forces surprised the British troops time and again, subjecting them to punishing fire from behind concealed war fences, before slipping away unseen into the bush.

Bai Bureh acquired a reputation for supernatural power, and was believed to be bullet-proof and to have the ability to become invisible or stay for long periods under water. The British offered a reward of £100 for information leading to Bai Bureh's capture, but no one would come forward. A colonial official wrote that Bai Bureh's men "loved their chief, and remained loyal to him to the very last."

Bai Bureh was finally captured on 11 November 1898 and taken under guard to Freetown, where crowds gathered around his quarters day and night to gain a glimpse of the great man. The British sent Bai Bureh in exile to the Gold Coast (Ghana), but brought him back in 1905, reinstating him as a Chief of Kasseh. Sierra Leone's greatest hero transitioned to the ancestral realm in 1908.

St. Augustine

Accepted by most scholars to be the most important figure in the ancient Western church, St. Augustine was born in Tagaste, Numidia in North Africa. His mother was a Christian, but his father remained a pagan until late in life. After a rather unremarkable childhood, marred only by a case of stealing pears, Augustine drifted through several philosophical systems before converting to Christianity at the age of thirty-one.

At the age of nineteen, Augustine read Cicero's Hortensius, an experience that led him into the fascination with philosophical questions and methods that would remain with him throughout his life. After a few years as a Manichean, he became attracted to the more skeptical positions of the Academic philosophers.

Although, tempted in the direction of Christianity upon his arrival at Milan in 383, he turned first to neoplatonism. During this time, Augustine fathered a child by a mistress. This period of exploration, including its youthful excesses (perhaps somewhat exaggerated) are recorded in Augustine's most widely read work, *the Confessions*.

During his youth, Augustine had studied rhetoric at Carthage, a discipline that he used to gain employment teaching in Carthage and then in Rome and Milan, where he met Ambrose, who is credited with effecting Augustine's conversion and who baptized Augustine in 387. Returning to his homeland soon after his conversion, he was ordained a presbyter in 391, taking the position as bishop of Hippo in 396, a position which he held until his death.

Besides *the Confessions*, Augustine's most *celebrated work is his De Civitate Dei (On the City of God)*, a study of the relationship between Christianity and secular society, which was inspired by the fall of Rome to the Visigoths in 410. Among his other works, many are polemical attacks on various heresies: *Against Faustus, the Manichean; On Baptism; Against the Donatists;* and many attacks on Pelagianism and Semi-Pelagianism.

Other works include treatises *On the Trinity; On Faith, Hope, and Love; On Christian Doctrine*; and some early dialogues.

St. Augustine stands as a powerful advocate for orthodoxy and of the episcopacy as the sole means for the dispensing of saving grace. In the light of later scholarship, Augustine can be seen to serve as a bridge between the ancient and medieval worlds. A review of his life and work, however, shows him as an active mind engaging the practical concerns of the churches he served.

Nnamdi Azikiwe

(Born 16 November 1904, Zungeru, Nigeria—died 11 May 1996, Enugu) first president of independent Nigeria (1963–66).

Azikiwe attended various grammar and high schools in Onitsha, Calabar, and Lagos. He spent almost ten years (1925–34) studying in the United States, where he attended several schools, including Howard University in Washington D.C. In 1934, he went to the Gold Coast (now Ghana), where he founded a newspaper and was a mentor to Kwame Nkrumah (first president of Ghana) before returning to Nigeria in 1937.

There he founded and edited newspapers and also became directly involved in politics, first with the Nigerian Youth Movement and later (1944) as a founder of the National Council of Nigeria and the Cameroons (NCNC), which became increasingly identified with the Igbo people of southern Nigeria after 1951. In 1948, with the backing of the NCNC, Azikiwe was elected to the Nigerian Legislative Council, and he later served as premier of the Eastern region (1954–59).

Azikiwe led the NCNC into the important 1959 federal elections, which preceded Nigerian independence. He was able to form a temporary government with the powerful Northern People's Congress, but its leader, Abubakar Tafawa Balewa, took the key post of prime minister. Azikiwe received the largely honorary posts of president of the Senate, governor-general, and finally, president.

In the conflict over Biafra (1967–70), Azikiwe first backed his fellow Igbo, traveling extensively in 1968 to win recognition of Biafra and help from other African countries. In 1969, however, realizing the hopelessness of the war, he threw his support to the federal government. When Olusegun Obasanjo turned the government over to civilian elections in 1979, Azikiwe ran unsuccessfully for president as a candidate of a newly formed Nigerian People's Party and retired from politics.

Azikiwe was often at odds with Obafemi Awolowo, a political rival who did not agree with his attempts to form coalition alliances with other ethnic groups, particularly those from the north. An important figure in the history of politics in Nigeria, Azikiwe had broad interests outside that realm. He served as chancellor of the University of Nigeria at Nsukka from 1961 to 1966, and he was the president of several sports organizations for football, boxing, and table tennis. Among his writings is an autobiography, *My Odyssey: An Autobiography* (1970).

Sarraounia

Sarraounia was ruler of a traditionalist group of Eastern Hausas. Queen Sarraounia of the Aznas in Africa fought French colonists in 1899. While some kingdoms readily collaborated with the French, she never debased herself to such a level. The French made alliances with neighboring groups in the hope of finally subduing her and her kingdom.

Lots of other kingdoms capitulated without a fight. Sarraounia mobilized her people and resources, military as well as magical, to confront the French force which launched a fierce attack on her fortress capital of Lougou. Overwhelmed by the superior firepower of the French, she and her fighters retreated tactically from the fortress, and engaged the attackers in a protracted guerrilla battle which eventually forced the French to abandon their project of subduing her.

Sarraounia means queen or chiefess, and among the Azna people of Lougou and surrounding Hausa towns and villages, the term refers to a lineage of female rulers who exercised both political and religious power. The 1986 film *Sarraounia* is based on her life.

Zumbi of Palmares

Zumbi was born free in Palmares in 1655, believed to be descended from the Imbangala warriors of Angola. He was captured by the Portuguese and given to a missionary, Father Antonio Melo, when he was approximately six years old. Baptized Francisco, Zumbi was taught the sacraments, learned Portuguese and Latin, and helped with daily mass.

Despite attempts to pacify him, Zumbi escaped in 1670 and, at the age of fifteen, returned to his birthplace. Zumbi became known for his physical prowess and cunning in battle, and was a respected military strategist by the time he was in his early twenties.

By 1678, the governor of the captaincy of Pernambuco, Pedro Almeida, weary of the longstanding conflict with Palmares, approached its leader Ganga Zumba with an olive branch. Almeida offered freedom for all runaway enslaved Afrikans if Palmares would submit to Portuguese authority, a proposal which Ganga Zumba favored. But Zumbi was distrustful of the Portuguese.

Further, he refused to accept freedom for the people of Palmares while other Afrikans remained enslaved. He rejected Almeida's overture and challenged Ganga Zumba's leadership. Vowing to continue the resistance to Portuguese oppression, Zumbi became the new leader of Palmares.

Fifteen years after Zumbi assumed leadership of Palmares, Portuguese military commanders, Domingos Jorge Velho and Bernardo Vieira de Melo, mounted an artillery assault on the Quilombo. 6 February 1694, after sixty-seven years of ceaseless conflict with the cafuzos, or Maroons, of Palmares, the Portuguese succeeded in destroying Cerca do Macaco, the republic's central settlement.

Before the king Ganga Zumba was dead, Zumbi had taken it upon himself to fight for Palmares' independence. In doing so, he became known as the commander-in-chief in 1675. Due to his heroic efforts, it increased his prestige. Palmares' warriors were no match for the Portuguese artillery; the republic fell, and Zumbi was wounded in one leg.

Though he survived and managed to elude the Portuguese and continue the rebellion for almost two years, he was betrayed by a mulatto who belonged to the Quilombo and had been captured by the Paulistas, and, in return for his life, led them to Zumbi's hideout. Zumbi was captured and beheaded on the spot 20 November 1695.

The Portuguese transported Zumbi's head to Recife, where it was displayed in the central praea as proof that, contrary to popular legend among enslaved Afrikans, Zumbi was not immortal. This was also done as a warning of what would happen to others if they tried to be as brave as him. Remnants of Quilombo dwellers continued to reside in the region for another hundred years.

20 November is celebrated, chiefly in Brazil, as a day of black consciousness. The day has special meaning for those Brazilians of Afrikan descent who honor Zumbi as a hero, freedom fighter, and symbol of freedom. Zumbi has become a hero of the 20th century Afro-Brazilian political movement. And he is a national hero in Brazil as well.

Dinknesh

Born: c. 3.2 million years ago.

The fossil known as Dinknesh/Lucy is one of the oldest and best-preserved skeletons of a hominid (two-footed, humanlike primate). Lucy was of the species Australopithecus afarensis. Her remains were found in Hadar, Ethiopia, in 1974 by American anthropologist, Donald Johanson, and his student, Tom Gray.

She was named for the Beatles song *Lucy in the Sky with Diamonds*, which was being played at a party that celebrated her discovery.

During her life, Dinknesh stood about 3.5 feet tall and weighed close to 65 pounds. The shape of her leg bones, pelvis, and spine indicate that she walked upright. She is estimated to have been between twenty-five and thirty years old when she died of an unknown cause. Compared with humans, Lucy had a small skull, long arms, and short legs.

Dinknesh skeleton, which is about forty percent complete, is stored in a safe in Ethiopia, though casts of it have been exhibited worldwide. It is nearly 3.2 million years old.

Sojourner Truth

The woman we know as Sojourner Truth was born into slavery in New York as Isabella Baumfree (after her father's owner, Baumfree). She was sold several times, and while owned by the John Dumont family in Ulster County, married Thomas, another of Dumont's captives. She had five children with Thomas.

In 1827, New York law emancipated all slaves, but Isabella had already left her husband and run away with her youngest child. She went to work for the family of Isaac Van Wagenen.

While working for the Van Wagenen's—whose name she used briefly—she discovered that a member of the Dumont family had sold one of her children to slavery in Alabama. Since this son had been emancipated under New York law, Isabella sued in court and won his return.

Isabella experienced a religious conversion, moved to New York City and to a Methodist perfectionist commune, and there came under the influence of a religious prophet named Mathias. The commune fell apart a few years later, with allegations of sexual improprieties and even murder. Isabella herself was accused of poisoning, and sued successfully for libel. She continued as well during that time to work as a household servant.

In 1843, she took the name Sojourner Truth, believing this to be on the instructions of the Holy Spirit and became a traveling preacher (the meaning of her new name). In the late 1840s, she connected with the abolitionist movement, becoming a popular speaker. In 1850, she also began speaking on woman suffrage. Her most famous speech, "Ain't I a Woman?", was given in 1851 at a women's rights convention in Ohio.

Sojourner Truth met Harriet Beecher Stowe, who wrote about her for the *Atlantic Monthly* and wrote a new introduction to Truth's autobiography, *The Narrative of Sojourner Truth.*

Sojourner Truth moved to Michigan and joined yet another religious commune, this one associated with the Friends. She was at one point friendly with Millerites, a religious movement that grew out of Methodism and later became the Seventh Day Adventists.

During the Civil War, Sojourner Truth raised food and clothing contributions for black regiments, and met Abraham Lincoln at the White House in 1864. While there, she tried to challenge the discrimination that segregated street cars by race. After the War ended, Sojourner Truth again spoke widely, advocating for some time a 'Negro State' in the west.

She spoke mainly to white audiences, and mostly on religion, 'Negro' and women's rights, and on temperance, though immediately after the Civil War she tried to organize efforts to provide jobs for black refugees from the war.

Active until 1875, when her grandson and companion fell ill and transitioned to the ancestral realm, Sojourner Truth returned to Michigan where her health deteriorated, and she herself transitioned to the ancestral realm in 1883 in a Battle Creek sanatorium of infected ulcers on her legs. She was buried in Battle Creek, Michigan, after a very well-attended funeral. Her life of struggle and success remains a strong testimony of the resilience of the human spirit.

December

Usman Dan Fodio

Shaihu Usman Dan Fodio (also referred to as Shaikh Usman Ibn Fodio; alternative spelling, Shehu), 1754–1817, was a writer and Islamic reformer. Dan Fodio was one of a class of urbanized ethnic Fulani living in the Hausa city-states in what is today northern Nigeria. He lived in the city-state of Gobir.

Dan Fodio was well-educated in classical Islamic science, philosophy and theology and became a revered religious thinker. His teacher, Jibril ibn 'Umar, argued that it was the duty and within the power of religious movements to establish the ideal society, free from oppression and vice. Dan Fodio used his influence to secure approval to create a religious community in his hometown of Degel that would, he hoped, be a model town.

However, in 1802, the ruler of Gobir and one of Dan Fodio's students, Yunfa turned against him, revoking Degel's autonomy and attempting to assassinate Dan Fodio. Dan Fodio and his followers fled into the western grasslands where they turned to help from the local Fulani nomads. Yunfa turned for aid to the other leaders of the Hausa states, warning them that Dan Fodio could trigger a widespread Jihad.

Yunfa proved right and Dan Fodio was declared Amirul Momineen or Leader of the Faithful. This, in effect made him political as well as religious leader, giving him the authority to declare and pursue a Jihad, raising an army and becoming its commander. A widespread uprising began in Hausaland. This uprising was largely composed of the Fulani, who held a powerful military advantage with their cavalry. It was also widely supported by the Hausa peasantry who felt over-taxed and oppressed by their rulers.

After only a few short years of the Fulani War, Dan Fodio found himself in command of the largest state in Africa, the Fulani empire. Dan Fodio worked to establish an efficient government, one grounded in Islamic law. Already aged at the beginning of the war, Dan Fodio retired in 1815 passing the title of Sultan of Sokoto to his son, Muhammed Bello.

Osei Tutu

Osei Tutu was the fourth ruler in Asante royal history, succeeding his uncle, Obiri Yeoba. The Asante comprise the largest contingent of the Akan or Twi-speaking peoples. Akan societies are matrilineal, with a person belonging to the clan of his mother. Inheritance, succession and status are lineally determined. Osei Tutu belonged to the Oyoko Clan.

By the middle of the 16th century, previous migrations of clan groups resulted in the development of a number of Akan states within a thirty mile radius of modern-day Kumasi, Ghana. The dense concentration of states in this limited area was primarily due to the region being a known source of gold and kola; two important trade routes—one from Jenne and Timbuktu in the western Sudan and the other from Hausaland—entered the area.

These states were all dominated by the Denkyira. In the middle of the 17th century, the last of the clan groups, the Oyoko Clan, arrived.

Exploiting the clans' mutual hatred for their oppressor, Osei Tutu, and his priest-counselor, Okomfo Anokye, succeeded in merging these states into the

Asante Union. This was a carefully orchestrated political and cultural process, which was implemented in different stages.

First, the union was spiritually brought into being through the Golden Stool, invoked by Okomfo Anokye, and explained as the embodiment of the soul of the Asante Union. The ruler—in essence the religious and political leader—and the occupant of the stool was to be known as the Asantehene and to be subsequently selected from the lineage of Osei Tutu and Obiri Yeoba.

Second, Kumasi was chosen as the capital of the Asante Union, and Osei Tutu was now both the Kumasihene and the Asantehene. The Odwira Festival was inaugurated. Established as an annual and common celebration, and attended by all member states, this served as a unifying force for the nation.

Third, Osei Tutu, assisted by Okomfo Anokye, developed a new constitution for the Union. The Asantahene, who was also the Kumasihene, was at its head, with the kings of the states of the union forming the Confederacy or Union Council.

Fourth, as one of the key objectives for forming the Asante Union was to overthrow the Denkyira, Osei Tutu placed strong emphasis on the military organization of the Union. Supposedly borrowing the military organization from the Akwamu, Osei Tutu honed the Union army into an effective and efficient fighting unit.

With the Asante Union firmly established and its military organization in place, Osei Tutu entered wars for expansion.

After avenging his uncle's death at the hands of the Dormaa and bringing some recalcitrant states into line, Osei Tutu focused on the Denkyira. In 1701, the absolute defeat of the Denkyira and their abettors, the people of Akyem, brought the Asante to the attention of the Europeans on the coast for the first time. The victory broke the Denkyira hold on the trade path to the coast and cleared the way for the Asante to increase trade with the Europeans.

In 1717, Osei Tutu was killed in a war against the Akyem.

Osei Tutu and his adviser, Okomfo Anokye, forged the Asante Union from a number of different clan groups who submerged their old rivalries and hatred for the common good—the overthrow of their common oppressor, the Denkyira. Skillfully utilizing a combination of spiritual dogma and political skill, and ably supported by military prowess, Osei Tutu tripled the size of the small kingdom of Kumasi which he had inherited from his uncle, Obiri Yeoba, and laid the foundation for the Asante Empire in the process.

Eslanda Robeson

Eslanda Goode was born in Brooklyn, New York, on 15 December 1896. She married Paul Robeson in 1921 but continued her studies and, after graduating from the University of Columbia in 1923, became the first African-American analytical chemist at Columbia Medical Center. Soon after she attended the London School of Economics and later earned a doctorate in Anthropology from Hartford Seminary.

Like her husband, Eslanda Robeson was committed to fighting for social justice for black people. In 1951, she was one of three protesters who disrupted the United Nations post-war conference on genocide. In 1958, as one of the few women delegates, she attended the All-African Peoples Conference in the newly independent Ghana.

She appeared in two films alongside her husband, *The Experimental Borderline* (d. Kenneth Macpherson, 1930) and *Big Fella* (d. J. Elder Wills,

1937), and also published two books: *The Biography Paul Robeson, Negro* (1930) and *African Journey* (1945).

With the development of the cold war, the life of the Robesons changed dramatically. The couple had first visited the Soviet Union in 1934 and were impressed by the apparent absence of racism, and agreed with the stance of communism against racism, colonization, and imperialism. While aware of the Great Purge by or before 1938, they accepted this (as Robeson explained to his son, "Sometimes...great injustices may be inflicted on the minority when the majority is in a pursuit of a great and just course") and did not speak out against it.

By 1938, however, they helped Eslanda's brother, Francis, to escape, her brother John had already departed the year prior, and Paul Jr. did not continue with his education at a Moscow 'model school'. With their pro-Soviet views, both became targets during the McCarthy days. Robeson's career came to a standstill, their income dropped dramatically, and the Connecticut estate had to be sold.

On 17 July 1953 Eslanda, like her husband, was called to testify before the US Senate; asked if she was a communist she took the Fifth Amendment and challenged the legitimacy of the proceedings. Her passport was revoked until the decision was overturned in 1958. Fighting for the decolonization of Africa and Asia she continued to work for the Council on African Affairs and to write as the UN correspondent for the *New World Review*, a pro-Soviet magazine.

Once the passports had been returned to the Robesons, they flew to London and the Soviet Union. Eslanda made her third and final trip to Africa attending the first postcolonial All-African Peoples' Conference in Ghana in 1958. In 1963, she was diagnosed with breast cancer. She returned from Russia to the U.S. and transitioned to the ancestral realm in New York in 1965, having lived a life at the service of uplifting blacks worldwide.

Queen Nzingha

Queen Nzingha of Ndongo belonged to the Mbundu, a large and ancient ethnic group that lived in modern-day Angola. The Mbundu were divided into tribes, including the Songo, Lenge, Libolo, Hungu, Pende, Ndongo, and Imbangala. Every group was made up of clans descended from their mother's side of the family.

Every clan was identified with their mother's clan and all the marriages were marriages between clans related maternally. Nzingha's family ruled the Ndongo people.

She was a great athlete and highly intelligent. She was skilled in diplomacy and was cunning. The only problem is that she was a female. Nzingha was followed by two more daughters, Mukambu (born in 1584) and Kifunji (born in 1587). Although, Kangela had failed her duty to bear male heirs, Kiluanji still deeply loved his wife.

Nzingha grew up in a world normally suited for males. She was educated in the fields of hunting and archery and in diplomacy and trade. Mbandi also received this training, although his training was more vigorous. He was awful. He never ceased from whining and complaining and eating. The only person who sympathized with him was his mother.

Nzingha's relationship with Mbandi was rooted in hatred. She could not stand her half-brother and often picked fights with him (normally winning unless his mother interfered and went crying to Kiluanji). However, Nzingha often could not control herself off the training fields and was even reputed to be banished from attending court when she insulted Mbandi at a meeting in front of all the concubines, children, and government officials. But the people adored Nzingha and she was brought back.

Nzingha's relationship with her sisters was different. They all loved one another and got along well, often joining Nzingha on her hunts and during training. One of Nzingha's childhood friends was a man named Njali, a prisoner from another tribe that became one of Kiluanji's closest confidants. He taught Nzingha the ways of war and hunting, from picking the best poison to put on the tip of her spear to how to sneak up on grazing animals.

During Nzingha's teenage years, a man named Giovanni Gavazzi, a Portuguese priest, recorded most of what went on in Kabasa and among the Mbundu people. He was captured as a slave before Nzingha's birth and lived at Kiluanji's court for many years. While most Europeans found the tribes appallingly primitive, Gavazzi embraced the culture and set out to educate the people in European ways while educating the Europeans in the Mbundu ways.

However, while one Portuguese man befriended the Mbundu people, the Portuguese slave traders tried their best to destroy the Mbundu culture. Starting in the 1400s, Portuguese traders had set up ports and cities along the African coast, such as Luanda. Their job was simply to capture Mbundu people to sell. The fate of the slaves was horrible.

Most died on the three-month voyage from Luanda to the West Indies, or threw themselves overboard while still chained to drown. Those who made it spent their lives toiling under Portuguese slave drivers. Kiluanji's reign was plagued by weak relations with the Portuguese to keep the Mbundu safe. He kept peace, but the Portuguese set out to capture and enslave the innocent and betrayed Mbundu people.

Other Mbundu tribes had made deals and alliances with the Portuguese, but Kiluanji refused to give in. Because the other tribes made alliances, the Portuguese advanced closer and closer to Ndongo territory. Thousands of the Ndongo people were captured, and Kiluanji led his people into war with the foreigners.

Nzingha married a fellow royal Mbundu, a prince named Azeze, who had come to Kabasa in 1595 when Nzingha was thirteen to make an alliance between his tribe and the Ndongo. Azeze and Nzingha were both deeply in love, and Azeze admired Nzingha's strength and her abilities on the field. They had a son in the early 1600s, but unfortunately Azeze died in battle a few years afterwards.

Although, she was a widow, Nzingha still refused to lay down her bow and arrow and often went on hunting escapes, her sisters trailing behind her, who also both lost their husbands in battle.

In 1617, Kiluanji died, and the powerless and pathetic Mbandi was given the seat of power over the Ndongo. With his uncles controlling him, Mbandi ordered the deaths of all those who opposed him. Nzingha's son was murdered, as was her mother. Nzingha herself would have been murdered, but the people loved her and an outcry would arise if she were killed.

Nzingha had promised her father before his death that she would do whatever was possible to keep the Portuguese out of the Ndongo territory. When she was called to go to the Portuguese city of Luanda, Nzingha reluctantly led a party to make an alliance with the Portuguese. When she met with the governor of Luanda, she was refused a seat. To show the governor her power and that she would not be below him, she sat on the back of one of her male servants and made him a human bench.

There, she made a peace agreement. Also while she was in Luanda, she came into contact with Father Giovanni, the priest who had lived among the Ndongo. She had him baptize her and took the name Ana de Sousa, in honor of the new Luanda governor, Joao Carreida de Sousa. It was rumored that Nzingha was only baptized to achieve respect from the Portuguese and establish herself as a leader.

Nzingha returned to Kabasa in 1617, and not too long after her arrival, Mbandi died. Without a leader, the Portuguese attacked Kabasa and burned it to the ground. Nzingha fled to the mountains with her people and over the next few years, organized an army to fight back.

Seven years later, in 1624, forty-two year old Nzingha rallied her people and led them to take control of their territory. Nzingha was declared Ngola Kiluanji of the Mbundu of Ndongo, a prediction made when she was born. Her closest aides were her sisters, Mukambu and Kifunji. Never had the Mbundu seen a female government, but it proved capable. Nzingha's childhood friend, Njali, helped her make an alliance with the Imbangala tribes.

For the next forty years, Nzingha led her people into battle against the Portuguese from the rocky slopes of Matamba. Her sisters were captured during a battle, but with the help of slaves in Luanda, they escaped from slavery. Later, Kifunji died from battle wounds.

Nzingha led many battles and peace treaties, some with the Portuguese, some with the Dutch, but she never resisted against slavery and the ill treatment of her people. She never returned to the ruins of Kabasa, and many remember her as the Queen of Matamba, because she ruled from the Matamba mountains and countryside, never from the Ndongo territory, despite her titles.

When she transitioned to the ancestral realm in 1663 at age eighty-two, her sister, Mukambu, took over the seat of power as head of the Mbundu people. Mukambu had Nzingha laid to rest in her leopard skins and with her bow over her shoulder and arrows in her hand. She died as she had lived, a warrior that would not compromise the integrity of her people at any stake.

Steve Biko

Bantu Steven Biko was born on 18 December 1946 in Ginsberg, a township outside King William's Town. Biko, best known of the leaders of the Black Consciousness Movement, is regarded as one of the greatest martyrs of the anti-apartheid struggle.

Biko's philosophy was that political freedom would only be achieved if blacks stopped feeling inferior to whites. This formed the heart of the Black Consciousness Movement. He believed that black people should lead the fight against apartheid.

Biko, who became more and more outspoken, gave up medical school to devote himself to the struggle. Frustrated by the multiracial Nusas, he and his colleagues founded the South African Student's Organization (SASO) in 1969. SASO was involved in providing legal aid and medical clinics, as well as social upliftment programs in black communities.

But the black students, under his leadership, argued that they were black before they were students and that a black political movement should be formed. Finally, in July 1972, the Black People's Convention (BPC) was founded. The BPC effectively brought together about seventy different black consciousness groups and associations.

His movement came into its own in the mid-1970s when the liberation movement appeared to be faltering, with many ANC leaders in jail or exile. In 1973, he was banned by the apartheid government. Under the ban, Biko was restricted to his hometown of King William's Town and he was prevented from writing or saying anything about black consciousness.

On 18 August 1977, Biko was arrested while traveling home from a political meeting with his friend, Peter Jones. He was detained in Port Elizabeth for twenty-six days under the Terrorism Act.

According to testimony given at the Truth and Reconciliation Commission in 1997, "Biko sustained a head injury during interrogation on 7 September 1977, after which he acted strangely and was uncooperative. The doctors who examined him (naked, lying on a mat and manacled to a metal grille) initially disregarded overt signs of neurological injury."

By 11 September 1997, Biko had slipped into a semi-conscious state. The police doctor recommended that he be transferred to hospital. Biko was, however, transported 1,200km to Pretoria in the back of a Land Rover.

A few hours after arriving at Pretoria Central Prison, Biko transitioned to the ancestral realm from brain damage, alone and naked in his cell. He was thirty years old. His only crime had been to struggle for justice for black people under a wicked system.

The police first claimed he had starved himself to death while on a hunger strike. They later changed their story to say Biko had hit his head against a wall in a scuffle. Finally, twenty years later, the police admitted before the Truth and Reconciliation Commission that they had killed Biko.

Biko was buried in the Ginsberg cemetery just outside King William's Town on 25 September 1977.

Carter Woodson

Dr. Carter G. Woodson was born of 19 December 1875 in New Canton, Virginia. Mainly self-taught, he mastered the fundamentals of common school subjects by the time he was seventeen. At age twenty, he entered Douglas High School in Huntington, West Virginia, where he earned his teaching diploma after two years (he later returned as principal).

He subsequently obtained his B.A. and M.A. from the University of Chicago and his Ph.D. in History from Harvard, becoming the second African-American to receive this degree.

In his career as an educator, Dr. Woodson became convinced that the role of his people in history was either ignored or misinterpreted. As a result of this conviction, Dr. Woodson founded the Association for the Study of Negro Life and History to conduct research into the history of African people throughout the world. It is worth noting that he did not believe in 'Negro history' as a separate discipline but instead viewed so-called 'Negro history' as a missing segment of world history, and he devoted his life to reconstructing this segment.

One year later, in 1916, he published the influential *Journal of Negro History*, which has not missed an issue to this day. In 1921, he established Associated Publishers to provide a forum for publication of valuable books on African history not then acceptable to most publishers. In addition, he authored numerous scholarly works and publications.

In 1926, Dr. Woodson inaugurated Negro History Week. The chosen week included 12 February (Abraham Lincoln's birthday) and 14 February (Frederick Douglass's birthday). In cases where only one of these days fell within the week, Frederick Douglass's birthday had priority. It is worth noting that Dr. Woodson realized that Negro History Week would be no longer necessary once this segment of World history was integrated into the curriculum and taught with respect and sensitivity.

He transitioned to the ancestral realm on 3 April 1950 at age seventy-four.

In the 1960s, the name was changed to Black History Week to reflect the increasing racial awareness of African-Americans. In 1976, the celebrations were broadened to include the entire month of February.

Msiri

(Born near Tabora, Tanganyika—died 20 December 1891, Katanga, Congo Free State) African ruler, one of the most successful of the 19 century immigrant adventurers and state builders in Central Africa. About 1856, Msiri settled in southern Katanga in modern day Congo with a few Nyamwezi followers, and by about 1870, he had succeeded in taking over most of this valuable copper region from its previous Lunda rulers.

During the height of his power in the mid-1880s, Msiri not only ruled directly a very large kingdom but also received tribute from neighboring areas. His prosperity was largely based on the copper trade, though he dealt in ivory as well; thus his basic policy was to keep trade routes open toward both the east and west coasts.

In the 1870s, he began to trade with the Arab trader and state builder, Tippu Tib. Msiri was especially interested in buying rifles, which he saw as absolutely necessary to his military strength. Missionaries first entered Msiri's kingdom in 1886. Of greater consequence, however, was the realization by other Europeans that Katanga was rich in minerals.

Msiri refused to negotiate with the British South Africa Company, but in 1891, more importunate expeditions arrived from the Belgian king Leopold II's Congo Free State. One tried to encourage rebellion against Msiri, who was fatally shot while negotiating with another expedition. Though Msiri adopted older patterns of indigenous Lunda state building, he also introduced new political titles and ceremonies and made some changes in customary law.

Of at least equal importance was the introduction by the Nyamwezi into Katanga of the sweet potato, smallpox vaccination, and a technique for making copper wire. He transitioned to the ancestral realm on 20 December 1891 while trying to defend his honor against a Canadian colonialist sent to take over his land.

Thomas Sankara

Thomas Sankara was born on 21 December 1949, in Upper Volta, formerly Burkina Faso; died 15 October 1987 in Ouagadougou, Burkina Faso.

Captain Thomas Sankara was the leader of the Burkinabe Revolution. In the former Upper Volta, known today as Burkina Faso, a group of men decided to launch a revolution that would enable the country 'to accept the responsibility of its reality and its destiny with human dignity'. Thomas Sankara belongs to the group of African leaders who wanted to give the continent in general, and their countries in particular, a new socio-political dimension.

He was the hope of the African youth before being coldly murdered by his best friend, Blaise Compaore.

Born in Yako, Upper Volta, now Burkina Faso, on 21 December 1949, Thomas Sankara was a charismatic left-leaning leader in West Africa. He was sometimes nicknamed 'Tom Sank'. He was considered by some to be an 'African Che Guevara'.

A captain in the Upper Volta Air Force, he was trained as a pilot. He was a very popular figure in the capital of Ouagadougou. The fact that was he was a decent guitarist and liked motorbikes may have contributed to his charisma. Sankara was appointed Secretary of State for Information in 1981 and became prime minister in 1983. He was jailed the same year after a visit by Jean-Christophe Mitterrand; this caused a popular uprising.

A coup d'état organized by Blaise Compaore made Sankara president on 4 August 1983, at the age of thirty-three. The coup d'état was supported by Libya which was, at the time, on the verge of war with France in Chad. Sankara saw himself as a revolutionary and was inspired by Cuba and Ghana's military leader, Flight Lt. Jerry Rawlings.

As president, he promoted the 'Democratic and Popular Revolution' (RDP Revolution Democratique et Populaire).

His government included large number of women. His policy was oriented toward fighting corruption, reforestation, averting famine, and making education and health real priorities. During his rule, he reduced the president's and government officials salaries, and instead of riding in a luxury vehicle, he rode in a poor man's car. He was very frugal and set an example of humbleness which not many, if any, leaders worldwide have ever conformed to after him.

Improving women's status was one of Sankara's explicit goals, that was unprecedented in West Africa. His government banned female circumcision, condemned polygamy, and promoted contraception.

In 1984, on the first anniversary of his accession, he renamed the country Burkina Faso, meaning 'the land of upright people' in Mossi and Dyula, the two major languages of the country. He also gave it a new flag and wrote a new national anthem. On 15 October 1987, Sankara was killed in a coup d'état organized by his former colleague, Blaise Compaore.

A week prior to his transition Sankara addressed people and said that "while revolutionaries as individuals can be murdered, you cannot kill ideas."

Cheikh Anta Diop

Cheikh Anta Diop, a modern champion of Afrikan identity, was born in Diourbel, Senegal, on 29 December 1923. At the age of twenty-three, he journeyed to Paris, France, to continue advanced studies in physics. Within a very short time, however, he was drawn deeper and deeper into studies relating to the Afrikan origins of humanity and civilization.

Becoming more and more active in the Afrikan student movements, then demanding the independence of French colonial possessions, he became convinced that only by re-examining and restoring Africa's distorted, maligned and obscured place in world history could the physical and psychological shackles of colonialism be lifted from our Motherland and from Afrikan people dispersed globally.

His initial doctoral dissertation submitted at the University of Paris, Sorbonne, in 1951, based on the premise that Egypt of the pharaohs was an Afrikan civilization, was rejected. Regardless, this dissertation was published by Presence Africaine under the title *Nations Negres et Culture* in 1955 and won him international acclaim. Two additional attempts to have his doctorate granted were turned back, until 1960 when he entered his defense session with an array of sociologists, anthropologists and historians and successfully carried his argument.

After nearly a decade of titanic and herculean effort, Diop had finally won his Docteur es Lettres! In that same year, 1960, were published two of his other works—*the Cultural Unity of Black Africa* and *Precolonial Black Africa.*

During his student days, Cheikh Anta Diop was an avid political activist. From 1950 to 1953, he was the secretary-general of the Rassemblement Democratique Africain (RDA) and helped establish the first Pan-African Student Congress in Paris in 1951. He also participated in the First World Congress of Black Writers and Artists held in Paris in 1956, and the second such Congress held in Rome in 1959.

Upon returning to Senegal in 1960, Dr. Diop continued his research and established a radiocarbon laboratory in Dakar. In 1966, the First World Black Festival of Arts and Culture held in Dakar, Senegal honored Dr. Diop and Dr. W. E. B. DuBois as the scholars who exerted the greatest influence on Afrikan thought in 20th century. In 1974, a milestone occurred in the English-speaking world when the *African Origin of Civilization: Myth or Reality* was finally published.

It was also in 1974 that Diop and Theophile Obenga collectively and soundly reaffirmed the African origin of pharaonic Egyptian civilization at a UNESCO sponsored symposium in Cairo, Egypt. In 1981, Diop's last major work, *Civilization or Barbarism: An Authentic Anthropology* was published.

Dr. Diop was the director of Radiocarbon Laboratory at the Fundamental Institute of Black Africa (IFAN) at the University of Dakar. He sat on numerous international scientific committees and achieved recognition as one of the leading historians, Egyptologists, linguists and anthropologists in the world. He traveled widely, lectured incessantly and was cited and quoted voluminously.

He was regarded by many as the modern 'pharaoh' of African studies. Cheikh Anta Diop transitioned to the ancestral realm quietly in sleep, after having revived the truth of ancient Egypt being a black African civilization.

Water
Education
Food
Land
Justice
Security
Economy
Peace
VICTORY

Appendix A

After having read through the poems for all twelve months of the year, please try and locate all the great Afrikans on the images for each relative month. This is a good game to play and a good way to test your knowledge of these ancestors. When these tests are done, follow to appendix B where you will find the answer key for the images.

Please note that not all the ancestors and legends summarized are depicted in the images.

Also find enclosed an eternal Gregorian calendar valid until 2050.

Appendix B

January

1. John Henrik Clarke
2. C. L. R James
3. Sekou Toure
4. Mohammed Ali
5. Bessie Coleman
6. Frederick Douglass

February

1. Langston Hughes
2. Rosa Parks
3. Queen Ahmose
4. Bob Marley
5. Cetawayo
6. Empress Taitu
7. Lat Dior
8. Mogho Naba Wobgho
9. Nina Simone
10. W. E. B DuBois
11. W. Farad Mohammed

March

1. Massinissa
2. Queen Candace of Meroe
3. Queen Nicotris
4. Harriet Tubman
5. Garett Morgan
6. Moshoeshoe
7. Mansa Kankan Musa
8. Amina of Zaria
9. Yakub Al-Mansur
10. Walter Rodney
11. Empress Menen

April

1. Queen Neith Hotep
2. Ptahhotep
3. Billie Holiday
4. Paul Robeson
5. Julius Nyerere
6. Marie Joseph Angelique

7. Mumia Abu Jamal
8. Hannibal Barca

May

1. Tehutimes, the Third
2. Elijah McCoy
3. Abraha
4. Martin Delany
5. King Narmer
6. Queen Ahhotep
7. William Grant Still
8. Isnofret
9. Mary Seacole
10. Senmut
11. Hampate Ba
12. Bambaataa
13. Malcolm X
14. Toussaint de Louverture
15. Eugene Chen
16. Samuel Sharpe
17. King Njoya
18. Imhotep

June

1. Shamba Bolongongo
2. Samory Toure
3. Charles Drew
4. John Carlos
5. Alexander Pushkin
6. Al-Jahiz
7. Taharqa
8. Nehanda of MaShona

July

1. Khama, the Good
2. Patrice Lumumba
3. Mary McLeod Bethune
4. Ramses, the Great
5. Ausar
6. General Ahmose
7. Assata Shakur
8. Auset
9. Neb-Het
10. Frantz Fanon
11. Haile Selassie
12. Hatshepsut
13. Nandi
14. Tenkamenin
15. Ida B. Wells

August

1. Chief Mirambo
2. Edward Blyden
3. Queen Ta-Wsret
4. Jaja of Opobo
5. Menelik, the Great
6. Marcus Garvey
7. Nut

September

1. Phillis Wheatley
2. Lewis Latimer
3. J. A Rogers
4. El Hadj Omar
5. Makeda "Queen of Sheeba"
6. Queen Tiye

7. Sunny Ali Ber
8. Jan Matzeliger
9. Kwame N'Krumah
10. Shaka Zulu
11. Winnie Mandela

October

1. Nat Turner
2. I. T. A Wallace-Johnson
3. Fani-Lou Hamer
4. Elijah Mohammed
5. Gabriel Prosser
6. Mary Ann Shadd
7. Ken Saro Wiwa
8. Fela Kuti
9. Jean Jacques Dessalines
10. Nefertari
11. Bobby Seale
12. Paul Bogle

November

1. Benjamin Banneker
2. Ibn Saud
3. Bai Bureh
4. Saint Augustine
5. Zumbi of Palmares
6. DiNiknesh
7. Sojourner Truth

December

1. Usman Dan Fodio
2. Osei Tutu
3. Eslanda Robeson

4. Queen Nzingha
5. Stephen Biko
6. Carter Woodson
7. Thomas Sankara
8. Heru
9. Cheikh Anta Diop

A	B	C	D	E	F	G	H	I	J	K	L	M	N
18 82		18 83			18 84			18 85		18 86		18 87	
	18 88			18 89		18 90		18 91			18 92		
18 93		18 94		18 95			18 96			18 97		18 98	
18 99		19 00		19 01		19 02		19 03			19 04		
19 05		19 06		19 07			19 08			19 09		19 10	
19 11			19 12			19 13		19 14		19 15			19 16
		19 17		19 18		19 19			19 20			19 21	
19 22		19 23			19 24			19 25		19 26		19 27	
	19 28			19 29		19 30		19 31			19 32		

1933		1934		1935			1936			1937		1938	
1939			1940			1941		1942		1943			1944
		1945		1946		1947			1948			1949	
1950		1951			1952			1953		1954		1955	
	1956			1957		1958		1959			1960		
1961		1962		1963			1964			1965		1966	
1967			1968			1969		1970		1971			1972
		1973		1974		1975			1976			1977	
1978		1979			1980			1981		1982		1983	
	1984			1985		1986		1987			1988		
1989		1990		1991			1992			1993		1994	
1995			1996			1997		1998		1999			2000
		2001		2002		2003			2004			2005	
2006		2007			2008			2009		2010		2011	
	2012			2013		2014		2015			2016		
2017		2018		2019			2020			2021		2022	
2023			2024			2025		2026		2027			2028
		2029		2030		2031			2032			2033	
2034		2035			2036			2037		2038		2039	
	2040			2041		2042		2043			2044		
2045		2046		2047			2048			2049		2050	

A

January

S	M	T	W	T	F	S
1	2	3	4	5	6	7
8	9	10	11	12	13	14
15	16	17	18	19	20	21
22	23	24	25	26	27	28
29	30	31				

February

S	M	T	W	T	F	S
			1	2	3	4
5	6	7	8	9	10	11
12	13	14	15	16	17	18
19	20	21	22	23	24	25
26	27	28				

March

S	M	T	W	T	F	S
			1	2	3	4
5	6	7	8	9	10	11
12	13	14	15	16	17	18
19	20	21	22	23	24	25
26	27	28	29	30	31	

April

S	M	T	W	T	F	S
						1
2	3	4	5	6	7	8
9	10	11	12	13	14	15
16	17	18	19	20	21	22
23	24	25	26	27	28	29
30						

May

S	M	T	W	T	F	S
	1	2	3	4	5	6
7	8	9	10	11	12	13
14	15	16	17	18	19	20
21	22	23	24	25	26	27
28	29	30	31			

June

S	M	T	W	T	F	S
				1	2	3
4	5	6	7	8	9	10
11	12	13	14	15	16	17
18	19	20	21	22	23	24
25	26	27	28	29	30	

July

S	M	T	W	T	F	S
						1
2	3	4	5	6	7	8
9	10	11	12	13	14	15
16	17	18	19	20	21	22
23	24	25	26	27	28	29
30	31					

August

S	M	T	W	T	F	S
		1	2	3	4	5
6	7	8	9	10	11	12
13	14	15	16	17	18	19
20	21	22	23	24	25	26
27	28	29	30	31		

September

S	M	T	W	T	F	S
					1	2
3	4	5	6	7	8	9
10	11	12	13	14	15	16
17	18	19	20	21	22	23
24	25	26	27	28	29	30

October

S	M	T	W	T	F	S
1	2	3	4	5	6	7
8	9	10	11	12	13	14
15	16	17	18	19	20	21
22	23	24	25	26	27	28
29	30	31				

November

S	M	T	W	T	F	S
			1	2	3	4
5	6	7	8	9	10	11
12	13	14	15	16	17	18
19	20	21	22	23	24	25
26	27	28	29	30		

December

S	M	T	W	T	F	S
					1	2
3	4	5	6	7	8	9
10	11	12	13	14	15	16
17	18	19	20	21	22	23
24	25	26	27	28	29	30
31						

B

January

S	M	T	W	T	F	S
1	2	3	4	5	6	7
8	9	10	11	12	13	14
15	16	17	18	19	20	21
22	23	24	25	26	27	28
29	30	31				

February

S	M	T	W	T	F	S
			1	2	3	4
5	6	7	8	9	10	11
12	13	14	15	16	17	18
19	20	21	22	23	24	25
26	27	28	29			

March

S	M	T	W	T	F	S
				1	2	3
4	5	6	7	8	9	10
11	12	13	14	15	16	17
18	19	20	21	22	23	24
25	26	27	28	29	30	31

April

S	M	T	W	T	F	S
1	2	3	4	5	6	7
8	9	10	11	12	13	14
15	16	17	18	19	20	21
22	23	24	25	26	27	28
29	30					

May

S	M	T	W	T	F	S
		1	2	3	4	5
6	7	8	9	10	11	12
13	14	15	16	17	18	19
20	21	22	23	24	25	26
27	28	29	30	31		

June

S	M	T	W	T	F	S
					1	2
3	4	5	6	7	8	9
10	11	12	13	14	15	16
17	18	19	20	21	22	23
24	25	26	27	28	29	30

July

S	M	T	W	T	F	S
1	2	3	4	5	6	7
8	9	10	11	12	13	14
15	16	17	18	19	20	21
22	23	24	25	26	27	28
29	30	31				

August

S	M	T	W	T	F	S
			1	2	3	4
5	6	7	8	9	10	11
12	13	14	15	16	17	18
19	20	21	22	23	24	25
26	27	28	29	30	31	

September

S	M	T	W	T	F	S
						1
2	3	4	5	6	7	8
9	10	11	12	13	14	15
16	17	18	19	20	21	22
23	24	25	26	27	28	29
30						

October

S	M	T	W	T	F	S
	1	2	3	4	5	6
7	8	9	10	11	12	13
14	15	16	17	18	19	20
21	22	23	24	25	26	27
28	29	30	31			

November

S	M	T	W	T	F	S
				1	2	3
4	5	6	7	8	9	10
11	12	13	14	15	16	17
18	19	20	21	22	23	24
25	26	27	28	29	30	

December

S	M	T	W	T	F	S
						1
2	3	4	5	6	7	8
9	10	11	12	13	14	15
16	17	18	19	20	21	22
23	24	25	26	27	28	29
30	31					

C

January

S	M	T	W	T	F	S
	1	2	3	4	5	6
7	8	9	10	11	12	13
14	15	16	17	18	19	20
21	22	23	24	25	26	27
28	29	30	31			

February

S	M	T	W	T	F	S
				1	2	3
4	5	6	7	8	9	10
11	12	13	14	15	16	17
18	19	20	21	22	23	24
25	26	27	28			

March

S	M	T	W	T	F	S
				1	2	3
4	5	6	7	8	9	10
11	12	13	14	15	16	17
18	19	20	21	22	23	24
25	26	27	28	29	30	31

April

S	M	T	W	T	F	S
1	2	3	4	5	6	7
8	9	10	11	12	13	14
15	16	17	18	19	20	21
22	23	24	25	26	27	28
29	30					

May

S	M	T	W	T	F	S
		1	2	3	4	5
6	7	8	9	10	11	12
13	14	15	16	17	18	19
20	21	22	23	24	25	26
27	28	29	30	31		

June

S	M	T	W	T	F	S
					1	2
3	4	5	6	7	8	9
10	11	12	13	14	15	16
17	18	19	20	21	22	23
24	25	26	27	28	29	30

July

S	M	T	W	T	F	S
1	2	3	4	5	6	7
8	9	10	11	12	13	14
15	16	17	18	19	20	21
22	23	24	25	26	27	28
29	30	31				

August

S	M	T	W	T	F	S
			1	2	3	4
5	6	7	8	9	10	11
12	13	14	15	16	17	18
19	20	21	22	23	24	25
26	27	28	29	30	31	

September

S	M	T	W	T	F	S
						1
2	3	4	5	6	7	8
9	10	11	12	13	14	15
16	17	18	19	20	21	22
23	24	25	26	27	28	29
30						

October

S	M	T	W	T	F	S
	1	2	3	4	5	6
7	8	9	10	11	12	13
14	15	16	17	18	19	20
21	22	23	24	25	26	27
28	29	30	31			

November

S	M	T	W	T	F	S
				1	2	3
4	5	6	7	8	9	10
11	12	13	14	15	16	17
18	19	20	21	22	23	24
25	26	27	28	29	30	

December

S	M	T	W	T	F	S
						1
2	3	4	5	6	7	8
9	10	11	12	13	14	15
16	17	18	19	20	21	22
23	24	25	26	27	28	29
30	31					

D

January

S	M	T	W	T	F	S
	1	2	3	4	5	6
7	8	9	10	11	12	13
14	15	16	17	18	19	20
21	22	23	24	25	26	27
28	29	30	31			

February

S	M	T	W	T	F	S
				1	2	3
4	5	6	7	8	9	10
11	12	13	14	15	16	17
18	19	20	21	22	23	24
25	26	27	28	29		

March

S	M	T	W	T	F	S
					1	2
3	4	5	6	7	8	9
10	11	12	13	14	15	16
17	18	19	20	21	22	23
24	25	26	27	28	29	30
31						

April

S	M	T	W	T	F	S
	1	2	3	4	5	6
7	8	9	10	11	12	13
14	15	16	17	18	19	20
21	22	23	24	25	26	27
28	29	30				

May

S	M	T	W	T	F	S
			1	2	3	4
5	6	7	8	9	10	11
12	13	14	15	16	17	18
19	20	21	22	23	24	25
26	27	28	29	30	31	

June

S	M	T	W	T	F	S
						1
2	3	4	5	6	7	8
9	10	11	12	13	14	15
16	17	18	19	20	21	22
23	24	25	26	27	28	29
30						

July

S	M	T	W	T	F	S
	1	2	3	4	5	6
7	8	9	10	11	12	13
14	15	16	17	18	19	20
21	22	23	24	25	26	27
28	29	30	31			

August

S	M	T	W	T	F	S
				1	2	3
4	5	6	7	8	9	10
11	12	13	14	15	16	17
18	19	20	21	22	23	24
25	26	27	28	29	30	31

September

S	M	T	W	T	F	S
1	2	3	4	5	6	7
8	9	10	11	12	13	14
15	16	17	18	19	20	21
22	23	24	25	26	27	28
29	30					

October

S	M	T	W	T	F	S
		1	2	3	4	5
6	7	8	9	10	11	12
13	14	15	16	17	18	19
20	21	22	23	24	25	26
27	28	29	30	31		

November

S	M	T	W	T	F	S
					1	2
3	4	5	6	7	8	9
10	11	12	13	14	15	16
17	18	19	20	21	22	23
24	25	26	27	28	29	30

December

S	M	T	W	T	F	S
1	2	3	4	5	6	7
8	9	10	11	12	13	14
15	16	17	18	19	20	21
22	23	24	25	26	27	28
29	30	31				

E

January

S	M	T	W	T	F	S
		1	2	3	4	5
6	7	8	9	10	11	12
13	14	15	16	17	18	19
20	21	22	23	24	25	26
27	28	29	30	31		

February

S	M	T	W	T	F	S
					1	2
3	4	5	6	7	8	9
10	11	12	13	14	15	16
17	18	19	20	21	22	23
24	25	26	27	28		

March

S	M	T	W	T	F	S
					1	2
3	4	5	6	7	8	9
10	11	12	13	14	15	16
17	18	19	20	21	22	23
24	25	26	27	28	29	30
31						

April

S	M	T	W	T	F	S
	1	2	3	4	5	6
7	8	9	10	11	12	13
14	15	16	17	18	19	20
21	22	23	24	25	26	27
28	29	30				

May

S	M	T	W	T	F	S
			1	2	3	4
5	6	7	8	9	10	11
12	13	14	15	16	17	18
19	20	21	22	23	24	25
26	27	28	29	30	31	

June

S	M	T	W	T	F	S
						1
2	3	4	5	6	7	8
9	10	11	12	13	14	15
16	17	18	19	20	21	22
23	24	25	26	27	28	29
30						

July

S	M	T	W	T	F	S
	1	2	3	4	5	6
7	8	9	10	11	12	13
14	15	16	17	18	19	20
21	22	23	24	25	26	27
28	29	30	31			

August

S	M	T	W	T	F	S
				1	2	3
4	5	6	7	8	9	10
11	12	13	14	15	16	17
18	19	20	21	22	23	24
25	26	27	28	29	30	31

September

S	M	T	W	T	F	S
1	2	3	4	5	6	7
8	9	10	11	12	13	14
15	16	17	18	19	20	21
22	23	24	25	26	27	28
29	30					

October

S	M	T	W	T	F	S
		1	2	3	4	5
6	7	8	9	10	11	12
13	14	15	16	17	18	19
20	21	22	23	24	25	26
27	28	29	30	31		

November

S	M	T	W	T	F	S
					1	2
3	4	5	6	7	8	9
10	11	12	13	14	15	16
17	18	19	20	21	22	23
24	25	26	27	28	29	30

December

S	M	T	W	T	F	S
1	2	3	4	5	6	7
8	9	10	11	12	13	14
15	16	17	18	19	20	21
22	23	24	25	26	27	28
29	30	31				

F

January

S	M	T	W	T	F	S
		1	2	3	4	5
6	7	8	9	10	11	12
13	14	15	16	17	18	19
20	21	22	23	24	25	26
27	28	29	30	31		

February

S	M	T	W	T	F	S
					1	2
3	4	5	6	7	8	9
10	11	12	13	14	15	16
17	18	19	20	21	22	23
24	25	26	27	28	29	

March

S	M	T	W	T	F	S
						1
2	3	4	5	6	7	8
9	10	11	12	13	14	15
16	17	18	19	20	21	22
23	24	25	26	27	28	29
30	31					

April

S	M	T	W	T	F	S
		1	2	3	4	5
6	7	8	9	10	11	12
13	14	15	16	17	18	19
20	21	22	23	24	25	26
27	28	29	30			

May

S	M	T	W	T	F	S
				1	2	3
4	5	6	7	8	9	10
11	12	13	14	15	16	17
18	19	20	21	22	23	24
25	26	27	28	29	30	31

June

S	M	T	W	T	F	S
1	2	3	4	5	6	7
8	9	10	11	12	13	14
15	16	17	18	19	20	21
22	23	24	25	26	27	28
29	30					

July

S	M	T	W	T	F	S
		1	2	3	4	5
6	7	8	9	10	11	12
13	14	15	16	17	18	19
20	21	22	23	24	25	26
27	28	29	30	31		

August

S	M	T	W	T	F	S
					1	2
3	4	5	6	7	8	9
10	11	12	13	14	15	16
17	18	19	20	21	22	23
24	25	26	27	28	29	30
31						

September

S	M	T	W	T	F	S
	1	2	3	4	5	6
7	8	9	10	11	12	13
14	15	16	17	18	19	20
21	22	23	24	25	26	27
28	29	30				

October

S	M	T	W	T	F	S
			1	2	3	4
5	6	7	8	9	10	11
12	13	14	15	16	17	18
19	20	21	22	23	24	25
26	27	28	29	30	31	

November

S	M	T	W	T	F	S
						1
2	3	4	5	6	7	8
9	10	11	12	13	14	15
16	17	18	19	20	21	22
23	24	25	26	27	28	29

December

S	M	T	W	T	F	S
	1	2	3	4	5	6
7	8	9	10	11	12	13
14	15	16	17	18	19	20
21	22	23	24	25	26	27
28	29	30	31			

G

January

S	M	T	W	T	F	S
			1	2	3	4
5	6	7	8	9	10	11
12	13	14	15	16	17	18
19	20	21	22	23	24	25
26	27	28	29	30	31	

February

S	M	T	W	T	F	S
						1
2	3	4	5	6	7	8
9	10	11	12	13	14	15
16	17	18	19	20	21	22
23	24	25	26	27	28	

March

S	M	T	W	T	F	S
						1
2	3	4	5	6	7	8
9	10	11	12	13	14	15
16	17	18	19	20	21	22
23	24	25	26	27	28	29
30	31					

April

S	M	T	W	T	F	S
		1	2	3	4	5
6	7	8	9	10	11	12
13	14	15	16	17	18	19
20	21	22	23	24	25	26
27	28	29	30			

May

S	M	T	W	T	F	S
				1	2	3
4	5	6	7	8	9	10
11	12	13	14	15	16	17
18	19	20	21	22	23	24
25	26	27	28	29	30	31

June

S	M	T	W	T	F	S
1	2	3	4	5	6	7
8	9	10	11	12	13	14
15	16	17	18	19	20	21
22	23	24	25	26	27	28
29	30					

July

S	M	T	W	T	F	S
		1	2	3	4	5
6	7	8	9	10	11	12
13	14	15	16	17	18	19
20	21	22	23	24	25	26
27	28	29	30	31		

August

S	M	T	W	T	F	S
					1	2
3	4	5	6	7	8	9
10	11	12	13	14	15	16
17	18	19	20	21	22	23
24	25	26	27	28	29	30
31						

September

S	M	T	W	T	F	S
	1	2	3	4	5	6
7	8	9	10	11	12	13
14	15	16	17	18	19	20
21	22	23	24	25	26	27
28	29	30				

October

S	M	T	W	T	F	S
			1	2	3	4
5	6	7	8	9	10	11
12	13	14	15	16	17	18
19	20	21	22	23	24	25
26	27	28	29	30	31	

November

S	M	T	W	T	F	S
						1
2	3	4	5	6	7	8
9	10	11	12	13	14	15
16	17	18	19	20	21	22
23	24	25	26	27	28	29

December

S	M	T	W	T	F	S
	1	2	3	4	5	6
7	8	9	10	11	12	13
14	15	16	17	18	19	20
21	22	23	24	25	26	27
28	29	30	31			

H

January

S	M	T	W	T	F	S
			1	2	3	4
5	6	7	8	9	10	11
12	13	14	15	16	17	18
19	20	21	22	23	24	25
26	27	28	29	30	31	

February

S	M	T	W	T	F	S
						1
2	3	4	5	6	7	8
9	10	11	12	13	14	15
16	17	18	19	20	21	22
23	24	25	26	27	28	29

March

S	M	T	W	T	F	S
1	2	3	4	5	6	7
8	9	10	11	12	13	14
15	16	17	18	19	20	21
22	23	24	25	26	27	28
29	30	31				

April

S	M	T	W	T	F	S
			1	2	3	4
5	6	7	8	9	10	11
12	13	14	15	16	17	18
19	20	21	22	23	24	25
26	27	28	29	30		

May

S	M	T	W	T	F	S
					1	2
3	4	5	6	7	8	9
10	11	12	13	14	15	16
17	18	19	20	21	22	23
24	25	26	27	28	29	30
31						

June

S	M	T	W	T	F	S
	1	2	3	4	5	6
7	8	9	10	11	12	13
14	15	16	17	18	19	20
21	22	23	24	25	26	27
28	29	30				

July

S	M	T	W	T	F	S
			1	2	3	4
5	6	7	8	9	10	11
12	13	14	15	16	17	18
19	20	21	22	23	24	25
26	27	28	29	30	31	

August

S	M	T	W	T	F	S
						1
2	3	4	5	6	7	8
9	10	11	12	13	14	15
16	17	18	19	20	21	22
23	24	25	26	27	28	29
30	31					

September

S	M	T	W	T	F	S
		1	2	3	4	5
6	7	8	9	10	11	12
13	14	15	16	17	18	19
20	21	22	23	24	25	26
27	28	29	30			

October

S	M	T	W	T	F	S
				1	2	3
4	5	6	7	8	9	10
11	12	13	14	15	16	17
18	19	20	21	22	23	24
25	26	27	28	29	30	31

November

S	M	T	W	T	F	S
1	2	3	4	5	6	7
8	9	10	11	12	13	14
15	16	17	18	19	20	21
22	23	24	25	26	27	28
29	30					

December

S	M	T	W	T	F	S
		1	2	3	4	5
6	7	8	9	10	11	12
13	14	15	16	17	18	19
20	21	22	23	24	25	26
27	28	29	30	31		

I

January

S	M	T	W	T	F	S
				1	2	3
4	5	6	7	8	9	10
11	12	13	14	15	16	17
18	19	20	21	22	23	24
25	26	27	28	29	30	31

February

S	M	T	W	T	F	S
1	2	3	4	5	6	7
8	9	10	11	12	13	14
15	16	17	18	19	20	21
22	23	24	25	26	27	28

March

S	M	T	W	T	F	S
1	2	3	4	5	6	7
8	9	10	11	12	13	14
15	16	17	18	19	20	21
22	23	24	25	26	27	28
29	30	31				

April

S	M	T	W	T	F	S
			1	2	3	4
5	6	7	8	9	10	11
12	13	14	15	16	17	18
19	20	21	22	23	24	25
26	27	28	29	30		

May

S	M	T	W	T	F	S
					1	2
3	4	5	6	7	8	9
10	11	12	13	14	15	16
17	18	19	20	21	22	23
24	25	26	27	28	29	30
31						

June

S	M	T	W	T	F	S
	1	2	3	4	5	6
7	8	9	10	11	12	13
14	15	16	17	18	19	20
21	22	23	24	25	26	27
28	29	30				

July

S	M	T	W	T	F	S
			1	2	3	4
5	6	7	8	9	10	11
12	13	14	15	16	17	18
19	20	21	22	23	24	25
26	27	28	29	30	31	

August

S	M	T	W	T	F	S
						1
2	3	4	5	6	7	8
9	10	11	12	13	14	15
16	17	18	19	20	21	22
23	24	25	26	27	28	29
30	31					

September

S	M	T	W	T	F	S
		1	2	3	4	5
6	7	8	9	10	11	12
13	14	15	16	17	18	19
20	21	22	23	24	25	26
27	28	29	30			

October

S	M	T	W	T	F	S
				1	2	3
4	5	6	7	8	9	10
11	12	13	14	15	16	17
18	19	20	21	22	23	24
25	26	27	28	29	30	31

November

S	M	T	W	T	F	S
1	2	3	4	5	6	7
8	9	10	11	12	13	14
15	16	17	18	19	20	21
22	23	24	25	26	27	28
29	30					

December

S	M	T	W	T	F	S
		1	2	3	4	5
6	7	8	9	10	11	12
13	14	15	16	17	18	19
20	21	22	23	24	25	26
27	28	29	30	31		

J

January

S	M	T	W	T	F	S
				1	2	3
4	5	6	7	8	9	10
11	12	13	14	15	16	17
18	19	20	21	22	23	24
25	26	27	28	29	30	31

February

S	M	T	W	T	F	S
1	2	3	4	5	6	7
8	9	10	11	12	13	14
15	16	17	18	19	20	21
22	23	24	25	26	27	28
29						

March

S	M	T	W	T	F	S
	1	2	3	4	5	6
7	8	9	10	11	12	13
14	15	16	17	18	19	20
21	22	23	24	25	26	27
28	29	30	31			

April

S	M	T	W	T	F	S
				1	2	3
4	5	6	7	8	9	10
11	12	13	14	15	16	17
18	19	20	21	22	23	24
25	26	27	28	29	30	

May

S	M	T	W	T	F	S
						1
2	3	4	5	6	7	8
9	10	11	12	13	14	15
16	17	18	19	20	21	22
23	24	25	26	27	28	29
30	31					

June

S	M	T	W	T	F	S
		1	2	3	4	5
6	7	8	9	10	11	12
13	14	15	16	17	18	19
20	21	22	23	24	25	26
27	28	29	30			

July

S	M	T	W	T	F	S
				1	2	3
4	5	6	7	8	9	10
11	12	13	14	15	16	17
18	19	20	21	22	23	24
25	26	27	28	29	30	31

August

S	M	T	W	T	F	S
1	2	3	4	5	6	7
8	9	10	11	12	13	14
15	16	17	18	19	20	21
22	23	24	25	26	27	28
29	30	31				

September

S	M	T	W	T	F	S
			1	2	3	4
5	6	7	8	9	10	11
12	13	14	15	16	17	18
19	20	21	22	23	24	25
26	27	28	29	30		

October

S	M	T	W	T	F	S
					1	2
3	4	5	6	7	8	9
10	11	12	13	14	15	16
17	18	19	20	21	22	23
24	25	26	27	28	29	30

November

S	M	T	W	T	F	S
	1	2	3	4	5	6
7	8	9	10	11	12	13
14	15	16	17	18	19	20
21	22	23	24	25	26	27
28	29	30				

December

S	M	T	W	T	F	S
			1	2	3	4
5	6	7	8	9	10	11
12	13	14	15	16	17	18
19	20	21	22	23	24	25
26	27	28	29	30	31	

K

January

S	M	T	W	T	F	S
					1	2
3	4	5	6	7	8	9
10	11	12	13	14	15	16
17	18	19	20	21	22	23
24	25	26	27	28	29	30
31						

February

S	M	T	W	T	F	S
	1	2	3	4	5	6
7	8	9	10	11	12	13
14	15	16	17	18	19	20
21	22	23	24	25	26	27
28						

March

S	M	T	W	T	F	S
	1	2	3	4	5	6
7	8	9	10	11	12	13
14	15	16	17	18	19	20
21	22	23	24	25	26	27
28	29	30	31			

April

S	M	T	W	T	F	S
				1	2	3
4	5	6	7	8	9	10
11	12	13	14	15	16	17
18	19	20	21	22	23	24
25	26	27	28	29	30	

May

S	M	T	W	T	F	S
						1
2	3	4	5	6	7	8
9	10	11	12	13	14	15
16	17	18	19	20	21	22
23	24	25	26	27	28	29
30	31					

June

S	M	T	W	T	F	S
		1	2	3	4	5
6	7	8	9	10	11	12
13	14	15	16	17	18	19
20	21	22	23	24	25	26
27	28	29	30			

July

S	M	T	W	T	F	S
				1	2	3
4	5	6	7	8	9	10
11	12	13	14	15	16	17
18	19	20	21	22	23	24
25	26	27	28	29	30	31

August

S	M	T	W	T	F	S
1	2	3	4	5	6	7
8	9	10	11	12	13	14
15	16	17	18	19	20	21
22	23	24	25	26	27	28
29	30	31				

September

S	M	T	W	T	F	S
			1	2	3	4
5	6	7	8	9	10	11
12	13	14	15	16	17	18
19	20	21	22	23	24	25
26	27	28	29	30		

October

S	M	T	W	T	F	S
					1	2
3	4	5	6	7	8	9
10	11	12	13	14	15	16
17	18	19	20	21	22	23
24	25	26	27	28	29	30
31						

November

S	M	T	W	T	F	S
	1	2	3	4	5	6
7	8	9	10	11	12	13
14	15	16	17	18	19	20
21	22	23	24	25	26	27
28	29	30				

December

S	M	T	W	T	F	S
			1	2	3	4
5	6	7	8	9	10	11
12	13	14	15	16	17	18
19	20	21	22	23	24	25
26	27	28	29	30	31	

L

January

S	M	T	W	T	F	S
					1	2
3	4	5	6	7	8	9
10	11	12	13	14	15	16
17	18	19	20	21	22	23
24	25	26	27	28	29	30
31						

February

S	M	T	W	T	F	S
	1	2	3	4	5	6
7	8	9	10	11	12	13
14	15	16	17	18	19	20
21	22	23	24	25	26	27
28	29					

March

S	M	T	W	T	F	S
		1	2	3	4	5
6	7	8	9	10	11	12
13	14	15	16	17	18	19
20	21	22	23	24	25	26
27	28	29	30	31		

April

S	M	T	W	T	F	S
					1	2
3	4	5	6	7	8	9
10	11	12	13	14	15	16
17	18	19	20	21	22	23
24	25	26	27	28	29	30

May

S	M	T	W	T	F	S
1	2	3	4	5	6	7
8	9	10	11	12	13	14
15	16	17	18	19	20	21
22	23	24	25	26	27	28
29	30	31				

June

S	M	T	W	T	F	S
			1	2	3	4
5	6	7	8	9	10	11
12	13	14	15	16	17	18
19	20	21	22	23	24	25
26	27	28	29	30		

July

S	M	T	W	T	F	S
					1	2
3	4	5	6	7	8	9
10	11	12	13	14	15	16
17	18	19	20	21	22	23
24	25	26	27	28	29	30
31						

August

S	M	T	W	T	F	S
	1	2	3	4	5	6
7	8	9	10	11	12	13
14	15	16	17	18	19	20
21	22	23	24	25	26	27
28	29	30	31			

September

S	M	T	W	T	F	S
				1	2	3
4	5	6	7	8	9	10
11	12	13	14	15	16	17
18	19	20	21	22	23	24
25	26	27	28	29	30	

October

S	M	T	W	T	F	S
						1
2	3	4	5	6	7	8
9	10	11	12	13	14	15
16	17	18	19	20	21	22
23	24	25	26	27	28	29
30	31					

November

S	M	T	W	T	F	S
		1	2	3	4	5
6	7	8	9	10	11	12
13	14	15	16	17	18	19
20	21	22	23	24	25	26
27	28	29	30			

December

S	M	T	W	T	F	S
				1	2	3
4	5	6	7	8	9	10
11	12	13	14	15	16	17
18	19	20	21	22	23	24
25	26	27	28	29	30	31

M

January

S	M	T	W	T	F	S
						1
2	3	4	5	6	7	8
9	10	11	12	13	14	15
16	17	18	19	20	21	22
23	24	25	26	27	28	29
30	31					

February

S	M	T	W	T	F	S
		1	2	3	4	5
6	7	8	9	10	11	12
13	14	15	16	17	18	19
20	21	22	23	24	25	26
27	28					

March

S	M	T	W	T	F	S
		1	2	3	4	5
6	7	8	9	10	11	12
13	14	15	16	17	18	19
20	21	22	23	24	25	26
27	28	29	30	31		

April

S	M	T	W	T	F	S
					1	2
3	4	5	6	7	8	9
10	11	12	13	14	15	16
17	18	19	20	21	22	23
24	25	26	27	28	29	30

May

S	M	T	W	T	F	S
1	2	3	4	5	6	7
8	9	10	11	12	13	14
15	16	17	18	19	20	21
22	23	24	25	26	27	28
29	30	31				

June

S	M	T	W	T	F	S
			1	2	3	4
5	6	7	8	9	10	11
12	13	14	15	16	17	18
19	20	21	22	23	24	25
26	27	28	29	30		

July

S	M	T	W	T	F	S
					1	2
3	4	5	6	7	8	9
10	11	12	13	14	15	16
17	18	19	20	21	22	23
24	25	26	27	28	29	30
31						

August

S	M	T	W	T	F	S
	1	2	3	4	5	6
7	8	9	10	11	12	13
14	15	16	17	18	19	20
21	22	23	24	25	26	27
28	29	30	31			

September

S	M	T	W	T	F	S
				1	2	3
4	5	6	7	8	9	10
11	12	13	14	15	16	17
18	19	20	21	22	23	24
25	26	27	28	29	30	

October

S	M	T	W	T	F	S
						1
2	3	4	5	6	7	8
9	10	11	12	13	14	15
16	17	18	19	20	21	22
23	24	25	26	27	28	29
30	31					

November

S	M	T	W	T	F	S
		1	2	3	4	5
6	7	8	9	10	11	12
13	14	15	16	17	18	19
20	21	22	23	24	25	26
27	28	29	30			

December

S	M	T	W	T	F	S
				1	2	3
4	5	6	7	8	9	10
11	12	13	14	15	16	17
18	19	20	21	22	23	24
25	26	27	28	29	30	31

N

January

S	M	T	W	T	F	S
						1
2	3	4	5	6	7	8
9	10	11	12	13	14	15
16	17	18	19	20	21	22
23	24	25	26	27	28	29
30	31					

February

S	M	T	W	T	F	S
		1	2	3	4	5
6	7	8	9	10	11	12
13	14	15	16	17	18	19
20	21	22	23	24	25	26
27	28	29				

March

S	M	T	W	T	F	S
			1	2	3	4
5	6	7	8	9	10	11
12	13	14	15	16	17	18
19	20	21	22	23	24	25
26	27	28	29	30	31	

April

S	M	T	W	T	F	S
						1
2	3	4	5	6	7	8
9	10	11	12	13	14	15
16	17	18	19	20	21	22
23	24	25	26	27	28	29
30						

May

S	M	T	W	T	F	S
	1	2	3	4	5	6
7	8	9	10	11	12	13
14	15	16	17	18	19	20
21	22	23	24	25	26	27
28	29	30	31			

June

S	M	T	W	T	F	S
				1	2	3
4	5	6	7	8	9	10
11	12	13	14	15	16	17
18	19	20	21	22	23	24
25	26	27	28	29	30	

July

S	M	T	W	T	F	S
						1
2	3	4	5	6	7	8
9	10	11	12	13	14	15
16	17	18	19	20	21	22
23	24	25	26	27	28	29
30	31					

August

S	M	T	W	T	F	S
		1	2	3	4	5
6	7	8	9	10	11	12
13	14	15	16	17	18	19
20	21	22	23	24	25	26
27	28	29	30	31		

September

S	M	T	W	T	F	S
					1	2
3	4	5	6	7	8	9
10	11	12	13	14	15	16
17	18	19	20	21	22	23
24	25	26	27	28	29	30

October

S	M	T	W	T	F	S
1	2	3	4	5	6	7
8	9	10	11	12	13	14
15	16	17	18	19	20	21
22	23	24	25	26	27	28
29	30	31				

November

S	M	T	W	T	F	S
			1	2	3	4
5	6	7	8	9	10	11
12	13	14	15	16	17	18
19	20	21	22	23	24	25
26	27	28	29	30		

December

S	M	T	W	T	F	S
					1	2
3	4	5	6	7	8	9
10	11	12	13	14	15	16
17	18	19	20	21	22	23
24	25	26	27	28	29	30
31						

Bibliography

Appiah, K. A., Gates, H. L. (1999) *Africana: The Encyclopedia of the African and African-American Experience*, Basic Civitas Books.

Editorial Committee (1988) *Sierra Leonean Heroes: Men and Women who Helped Build Our Nation*, Commonwealth Printers.

Maasi, S. M., Salim, H. M., *Kupigana Ngumi: Roots of The Ntchru and Ancient Kmt*, Volume 1, Pan Afrakan Kupigana Ngumi Press and Black Gold Press.

Rogers, J. A. (1974) *World's Great Men of Color,* Volume 1 and 2, Macmillan Publishing.

UNESCO International Scientific Committee for the Drafting of the General History of Africa (1981–1990) *General History of Africa,* Volumes 1 to 8, UNESCO.

Sertima, I. V. (1988) *Black Women in Antiquity*, Transaction Publishers.

Sertima, I. V. (1993) *Great Black Leaders: Ancient and Modern*, Journal of African Civilizations Ltd.

Wikipedia: The Free Encyclopedia. Wikimedia Foundation Inc.

www.ingramcontent.com/pod-product-compliance
Lightning Source LLC
Chambersburg PA
CBHW070647250726
48662CB00001B/7

* 9 7 8 1 6 8 5 6 2 8 6 0 4 *